THE COMING GOOD BOOM

THE COMING GOOD BOOM

CREATING PROSPERITY FOR ALL AND SAVING THE ENVIRONMENT THROUGH COMPACT LIVING

DOUGLAS E. BOOTH

To Carol, Edward, and Jeremy, my wonderful family. May they enjoy the fruits of compact living.

Contents

Forward

Economists like to say that there is no such thing as a 'free lunch' whenever we move our social arrangements in a new direction. According to this kind of thinking, a price will inevitably be paid for addressing big, society-wide problems such as global warming. This book, as you will soon see, takes a contrary view—resolving the problem of global warming and moving to a more spatially compact form of human settlement will generate a durable and widespread prosperity and improvements in the quality of life. In short, fixing global warming will be a 'free lunch'. We will all end up being better off independently of any gains to the climate or the natural environment. The turn to clean energy and spatial compactness will set off an unprecedented economic boom driven by innovation in energy conservation, production, and distribution and by increased high density urban living and the private and public construction that will go with it. Unlike the economic expansions of recent decades, growth induced by a shift to clean energy and compact living will truly lift all economic boats. Turning to compact green living and freeing ourselves from the environmental tyranny of fossil fuels will set off an investment boom of a new kind—a good boom that will help cure some of our most intractable social and environmental ills.

If moving toward stabilizing climate becomes a reality—and in all likelihood it will despite the convoluted political path we are currently taking toward limiting greenhouse gas emissions—we will soon start unhooking ourselves from fossil fuels. Not to do so would be an exercise in mindless naivety of historical proportions. The idea of 'peak oil' predicts that we will have to unhook ourselves from fossil fuels anyway by the end of this century, so why not do it sooner rather than later? If we have the insight and fortitude to pursue clean energy today rather than fifty years from now, we will save trillions of dollars that would otherwise drain away into the bank accounts of Arab oil aristocrats and petroleum dictators. These funds instead could be diverted to our own economy through the creation of a clean energy industry and a high-density, compact form of urban life. Because the nuclear energy option is so costly and publicly viewed as too dangerous, the sensible path is to replace fossil fuels with solar and wind energy and pursue the abundant opportunities available to us for energy conservation, the cleanest and greenest energy of all. Given 'peak oil,' the pursuit of fossil fuel carbon capture technology that injects carbon back into the earth from whence it came would seem to be a huge waste of money. Why try to fix something we are running out of anyway? The kinds of economic incentives and public spending that will push us toward clean energy will simultaneously move us in the direction of compact living. Greater spatial compactness will not only reduce the pace of climatic warming, but it will help contain the human footprint on the earth's surface and leave more space for nonhuman nature. This, along with less global warming, will in turn help forestall the mass species extinction event that appears to be in the making. The inevitable trend toward compact living can either be embraced because it is both good for the global environment and a decent way to live, or it can be resisted in a quest to preserve the traditional low density suburban way of life. The choice is ours individually and politically. If we choose to embrace compact living, I believe we will be rewarded with an economic boom and unprecedented prosperity. Saving the planet for ourselves as well as nature will in the end be both an economic and an ethical 'free lunch.' Aristotle's notion that doing good in the world is perfectly compatible with living well will be proven true.

Chapter 1
The Economy and Ecology of Space

Thomas Jefferson and Rural and Urban Ideals

Thomas Jefferson served as the U.S. minister to France from 1784 to 1789 and lived in Paris just off the Champs-Élysées at rue de Berri. Jefferson, like many other of his fellow Americans since, fell head over heals for Paris. Jefferson energetically took to the Parisian life where his diverse interests—diplomat, philosopher, writer, musician, architect, horticulturalist, and connoisseur of fine wines and good food—could find satisfactions impossible to achieve in full at his isolated Monticello estate, much less anywhere else in Virginia or the rest of the colonies. Despite France's recent defeat in the Seven Years War at the hands of the British and undercurrents of political unrest, Paris of the 1780s was the center of the European cultural universe. At the time of Jefferson's arrival, a building boom was underway made evident by construction cranes punctuating the cityscape. After living a year in relatively cramped quarters, Jefferson moved to the more spacious, newly finished Hôtel de Langeac with its eye-catching neoclassical facade on rue de Berri where he could entertain with Virginia graciousness, accumulate furnishings, works of art, and books for his voluminous library, and design and cultivate a large garden to his liking including vegetables from home.[1] Jefferson took time to explore the gardens of Paris, looking for ideas and plants he could bring to his new plot and eventually his beloved Monticello. He traveled to southern France a number of times where he collected the best wines for his Paris table and root stocks for later experimentation in growing grapes back in Virginia. On these trips he enthusiastically explored Roman ruins and other architectural treasures in the French countryside. Of course Paris itself was filled with architectural gems that influenced Jefferson's thinking later on the design of the new capitol at Washington D.C.

Jefferson quickly integrated himself into the cultural, intellectual, and political life of Paris. He attended concerts, operas, and art exhibitions, became a part of Paris's salon culture, and partook of the cafe and street life, especially in the infamous Palais Royale where all of Paris's social classes mixed, licentious behavior ran rampant, and revolutionary sentiments fermented. Jefferson found appalling the condition of the lower classes in France and clearly sympathized with their plight and agreed with their desires for more democracy. His own family values conflicted with the unbridled promiscuity he observed in Parisian society, especially within the aristocratic class (I leave it to others to judge Jefferson's own behavior in his apparent affair with one his slaves, Sally Hemings). He invited the best scientific, artistic, and political minds of the day to his own home for intimate dinners at a well appointed table with the best wines money could buy. He especially enjoyed the company of the mathematical genius, marquis de Condorcet, who shared a love of the classics and the ideals of

Republicanism and human equality with Jefferson. Later Condorcet, a leader in the revolution, apparently took his own life when political forces turned against him and he was declared a traitor.[2]

As the American minister to the court of France, Jefferson pursued the vocation of diplomacy with special skill despite his low rank in the core of diplomats who pressed for the attention of the King, Louis the XVI. Jefferson believed in his heart that democracy in his own country would be solidified by a prosperous agricultural economy composed of individual farm proprietors who owned their own land and possessed a commitment to democracy and republican government as a matter of self interest. Rather than pushing for the development of a manufacturing economy through protective measures, Jefferson pressed for open trade that would expand markets for his country's exports, especially tobacco, rice, and whale oil. In these efforts he met with mixed success. The French crown depended for its finances upon the taxing of all commodities entering the gates of Paris which were collected by private tax collectors known as the farmers-general. This group had given a monopoly in the tobacco trade to American financier, Robert Morris. Jefferson succeeded in weakening, but could not entirely break, Morris's hold on the tobacco trade, but Jefferson did persuade the crown to exclude British whale oil from the lucrative French market where demand for the oil grew in proportion to the popularity of public lighting installed to reduce Parisian street crime.[3]

With political unrest in Paris intensifying daily, Jefferson left in the fall of 1789 for a six month leave back in Virginia to settle his daughters, check on Monticello, and negotiate with his creditors over his ever-accumulating debts further expanded by five years of lavish spending in Paris. He intended to return to his post in the city, but never did. The thirty-eight pieces of luggage and crates he shipped back to Virginia, along with a carriage and a phaeton, contained paintings, busts, clocks, a harpsichord, and books for Jefferson's ballooning library. On top of this was an assortment of plants, including a white fig and two cork oak trees, as well as food stuffs unavailable in Virginia such as macaroni, Parmesan cheese, dates, olive oil, and tea as well as a selection of French wines. Jefferson never shied away from spending on those things he loved and took advantage of the extensive opportunities for doing so in the well-stocked Parisian markets.

Jefferson left Paris in an optimistic frame of mind about the ability of the French to carry out a peaceful revolution and institute a republic form of government with guarantees for basic human rights. About this he couldn't have been more wrong. Many of his closest friends in France ultimately lost there lives in the tumult that soon followed. Jefferson was certainly aware of the deep fissures in French society between rulers and ruled, but he seemed to have little inkling of the deep desire for bloody revenge by the rural an urban poor. He sympathized deeply with the poverty of the peasantry he saw on his travels outside of Paris, but not so much with the degraded condition of the urban proletariat he observed daily in Paris. To Jefferson, the later were a violent and uncouth rabble prone to destructive rebellions that upset the civility of his Parisian routines.[4] Despite his obvious relish for the life of a Parisian bourgeois, he never consciously changed his mind about cities. For Jefferson, "The mobs of great cities add just so much to the support of pure government, as sores do to the strength of the human body."[5] Jefferson loved his own life in the city, but found highly distasteful and threatening what the city did to the lower classes.

Jefferson's political vision for his own country took for it's inspiration the property rights theory of John Locke.[6] Whoever improves the land and embodies labor in it has a natural right to its ownership, according to Locke. Jefferson eagerly agreed with Locke that landowning yeoman farmers will have an abiding interest in a government whose essential purpose is to protect individual rights. Accordingly, Jefferson tells us that "Cultivators of the earth are the most valuable citizens...the most vigorous, the most independent, the most virtuous, and they are tied to their country and wedded to its liberty and interests by the most lasting bands."[7] In short, rural land owners have a deeper stake in a well functioning government than would an urban industrial proletariat. For this reason, Jefferson discouraged the development of city-based industry in the U.S. and emphasized rural expansion and settlement by independent farmers.

Jefferson perfectly embodies the contradictory attitudes about the comparative virtue of city and rural life that we Americans hold to this very day. We love wide open country spaces and the privacy that goes with them, yet we enjoy immediate proximity to like-minded others and to cultural and economic institutions that thrive in a compact, populace environment. Cities that we find to be exciting and energizing, we also see as repulsive for their congestion, poverty, corruption, violence, and dirt. We enjoy the quiet of the country and the beauty of its natural setting, but living in it risks boredom. Jefferson himself relished Monticello and busied himself with a multitude of construction projects and experimentations in cultivation, but his diverse cultural interests yearned for Parisian cosmopolitanism and consumer riches. Yet in the end he came down philosophically on the side of the rural life.

The single most consequential legislative manifestation of Jefferson's philosophy did not come until the presidency of Abraham Lincoln with the passage of the Homestead Act in 1862. The Act granted to anyone who had never taken up arms against the United States 160 acres of undeveloped land outside the original thirteen colonies. To obtain full ownership, an applicant needed to first file a claim on a specific parcel with the local land office, live on the land and undertake improvements, and file for a deed of title. Advocates for the Act anticipated that it would vastly expand the class of "Jeffersonian" smallholders in this country who could serve as the backbone of its democratic institutions. Escaping European political oppression and economic exploitation, most immigrants came to this country with the special hope of obtaining free land. For some states, such as Wisconsin, Minnesota, Nebraska, and Kansas where 160 acres proved to be a sufficient amount of land for prosperous farming, the Act turned out to be a boon to immigrant settlement. For western dry landscapes beyond the 100th meridian, 160 acres was just not enough to provide the most basic sustenance to an immigrant family. Many attempted to eke out a living on their homesteads across the Great Plains and succeeded for a time in wet years, but droughts endemic to the region eventually hit, and many settlers had to move on. Legendary abuses of the Homestead Act in great swaths of the West put land in the hands of large cattle barons who used fraudulent acquisitions to enclose important water resources. Similar abuses in the forested northwest caused much land to end up in the hands of large timber companies.[8] In short, most immigrants failed in their quest for landownership and ended up in the burgeoning, densely packed industrial cities of the Eastern and Midwestern U.S. By the end of the Nineteenth Century, 66 percent of the foreign born lived in cities in comparison to 36 percent of the native population.[9] Many, if not most, immigrants were precluded from realizing dreams they might have had of becoming rural landholders.

Industrialization caused a substantial majority of immigrants to find their material mode of life in the city, not the country. At the end of the Nineteenth Century, factories with their puffing smoke stacks—a mark of civic pride judging from old posters—crowded around ports and rail lines to cheapen shipping costs and to have ready access to large pools of labor who settled in densely packed neighborhoods nearby. Transportation costs on ships and trains between cities were comparatively cheap, but to move goods around within cities by wagon was quite expensive—hence the reason for crowding industrial operations around railheads and docks. Economic reality trumped the Jeffersonian ideal for immigrants and natives alike, although the rural dream in itself remained alive. The upper and middle classes in cities like Boston aspired to the life of the English country aristocrat who owned a house in London from which to enjoy urban culture and conduct business and political affairs (as Jefferson had in Paris) but also possessed a rural estate to retreat to for rest, reflection, and enjoyment of the great outdoors. In response to such aspirations, members of the Boston elite often bought country cottages to which they could escape on the weekends. Many immigrants looked with nostalgia back to their own rural heritage, remembering the beauty of the green hills and woods they left behind, but forgetting about the poverty and oppression that drove them away.[10] An idealized vision of rural life cut across class lines despite its differing origins.

Before the arrival of the streetcar, except for the very rich who owned carriages, everyone lived compactly in cities because of the need to walk everywhere. This limited the extent of human interaction roughly to a radius of what one could walk in an hour, about three miles. The old pedestrian city of Boston extended outward to a maximum of two and one half miles from city hall. Despite the availability of vacant land, little development could be found beyond this boundary. At first only the wealthy could totally escape the unpleasant conditions of the industrialization-induced factory districts and tenements by taking advantage of the costly but convenient new steam railroad lines that would take them to spacious dwellings in nearby country towns where what Sam Bass Warner calls the "rural ideal" could be realized.

In such locales, one could enjoy the pleasures of family life, the security of a small community, and the presence natural surroundings nearby.[11]

Space was essential to the pleasures of rural life sought by Boston's urban elite as it is today in our own quest for the suburban dream. The "rural ideal" historically and for us today includes the values of family, community, and beautiful landscapes, all of which require space. The enjoyment of family interactions relies on ample private, shared space in and around the home; the security of a small community implies a protective barrier of space from threatening others and a shared space with those one trusts; and access to rural and natural landscapes infers the presence of undeveloped land nearby. Most of all space is wanted for its own sake. When given the opportunity we willingly acquire larger domiciles on more spacious lots with a greater margin of distance from our neighbors. Space counts as a part of our vision of the good life today as it did more than a hundred years ago.

The requirement for compactness in mid-nineteenth Century urban life for all but the wealthiest was fundamentally economic. Industrial enterprises needed to be near ports and railheads to keep the cost of moving goods around low, and working class tenements needed to be near the industrial districts so workers could get to them on foot. Because business communication was either face-to-face or by hand-delivered documents, managerial and office functions and other commercial activities had to abut the industrial districts, and to be close to their customers, retail enterprises located nearby. Compactness was a matter of economic necessity, but it added to life's unpleasantness—smoke from factories, noise, smells from waste and sewage, congestion on crowded streets. No wonder that Boston's elite wanted to escape to the country.

The coming of the horse-pulled streetcar and later the much faster electric trolley removed constraints on space inherent in the early industrial city. On the electric trolley, one could cover six or more miles in an hour's time. This meant that the distance between work and home could now be stretched out. With trolley lines running outward beyond the old city limits, houses could from this moment on be constructed beyond the old city boundaries and successfully marketed to middle class families who could afford the trolley. By the end of the Century, the limits of development around Boston pushed outward from a two-plus mile radius to ten miles from the center. Roughly half of Boston's population, including wealthy merchants and professionals at the high end of the income distribution on down to well paid artisans and skilled craftworkers could now move further out into more spacious dwellings. Soon a spatial class hierarchy emerged with the wealthiest living furthest from the center, middle income households closer in, and the poorest paid occupying the old housing nearest the urban center. The later couldn't afford trolley fare and walked to work while the rest took advantage of the trolley for getting around the city. Those who moved outward increased the spaciousness and quality of their dwellings, and those who arrived first on the urban edge enjoyed all elements of the rural idea including undisturbed open space before the rest of the city caught up to them.   The wealthiest furthest out came closest to a permanent realization of a quasi-rural style of life through a mix of careful landscaping and proximity to the countryside beyond the urban edge.   Those who moved outward but failed in their quest for access to natural landscapes on the urban edge nonetheless gained in space, quietness, cleanliness, and the security of neighborhood social homogeneity. [12]

From the turn of the center on, the quality of life in cities improved regardless of the middle class's outward flight.   Progressives pushed for more parks, improvements in water supply and sewage disposal, better sanitation, street paving, greater attention to public health, smoke controls, building codes and zoning, and, perhaps most important of all, more green space and parks.   Cities throughout the country put in place expansive park systems, many of which were designed by Frederick Law Olmstead, the architect of New York City's famous Central Park.[13]   In the early twentieth century American city, to shop in the best department stores, use a major library, attend an opera, visit a museum, see the latest musical, or get a great restaurant meal, one needed to travel downtown.   Such experiences were largely unavailable in the suburbs.   The virtues of compactness Jefferson found in eighteenth century Paris began to surface in the American city.

Despite improving cities, Americans at the midpoint of the Twentieth Century held in their hearts a version of the Jeffersonian rural ideal— detached spacious homes on large plots of land, local community control of municipal government, neighbors like oneself, and expansive green landscapes. The subsequent suburban boom proves this point, but before we tackle this issue, we need to recognize that lurking deeper in the American and European culture is another vision of space, one that Jefferson discovered in his Parisian experience. This could be described as an "urban ideal"—access to society's defining public institutions and spaces and proximity to cultural, social, and economic opportunities available only where populations achieve a minimum scale.

Jane Jacobs elaborates this "urban ideal" in her classic work, *The Death and Life of Great American Cities*. Here she postulates the following: (1) populations in successful city neighborhoods should be dense enough to support a diversity of activities and functions such as residences, shops, restaurants, offices, and theaters; (2) blocks should be short so one can take varied routes from one point to another; and (3) buildings should be varied in age and size to support a diversity of functions and provide visual interest.[14] Jacobs' notion of an urban ideal takes a neighborhood focus and boils down to the following: high population densities, diversity of economic and cultural functions, and a pedestrian-friendly scale in streets, buildings, and public spaces.   Where this ideal is realized, streets will be busy all day with varied and interesting traffic.   With people going out for shopping in the morning or coming to work in local offices, heading to a cafe for lunch at noon, and enjoying a night out at a local theater, streets will be busy from dawn to bedtime. All this human presence means that streets will feel secure and safe—someone will no doubt always be watching the local comings and goings.

The one element of urban life given short shrift by Jacobs, but certainly noticed in Paris by Jefferson, who especially enjoyed wandering through the city's gardens and nearby wooded landscapes, is access to green open spaces. While Jacobs advocates powerfully for socially attractive cities, we need to turn to the work of landscape architect Ian McHarg to find the idea of access to nature as an essential part of urban life. McHarg recognizes that urban settings are fundamentally cultural artifacts, but points to numerous cities able to take advantage of their natural landscapes, such as their watersheds, marshes, steep slopes, and woodlands, to retain elements of nature within urban boundaries. For McHarg, "The problem of man and nature is not one of providing decorative background for human play, or even ameliorating the grim city: it is the necessity of sustaining nature as a source of life, milieu, teacher, sanctum, challenge, and most of all, of rediscovery of nature's corollary of the unknown in the self, the source of meaning."[15]   Add McHarg's vision of nature in the city to the urban visions of Jefferson and Jacobs, and we have a complete "urban ideal"—high population density; multiple economic, social, and cultural functions; significant public spaces and institutions; pedestrian friendly scale; and green and natural landscapes within city boundaries. Americans at the mid-twentieth century could have chosen to pursuit an "urban ideal" in their cities, but chose instead to vacate those cities in favor of the rural lands beyond.

Spatially Expansive Living: The Suburban Experience

Brookfield, Wisconsin, with a population of just over 39,000, spreads out over 75 square kilometers (29 square miles—let's get used to the metric system) 24 kilometers (15 miles) west of the area's largest city, Milwaukee, on both sides of Interstate 94, a major route connecting the eastern and western U.S. Brookfield is a busy suburb with a large regional shopping mall called Brookfield Square (Milwaukee residents know it as a consumer's paradise), numerous office and industrial parks, and numerous single family homes on relatively large lots. During the day the population swells to as much as 75,000 as residents in the surrounding area come into the city to work and shop. One could easily live and work in Brookfield without darkening the door of Milwaukee, the region's central city.[16] Because of low population density, the presence of numerous disconnected cul-de-sacs, and lack of very much public transit, to get around Brookfield one needs to own a motor vehicle. The cul-de-sac approach to suburban street design means to get from a subdivision to the one next door, which could just a few steps away, you need to drive out of the first one onto a local highway, and drive through the entrance to the second one. To its credit, Brookfield is planning a recreation path along existing undeveloped "environmental" corridors called the "Emerald Way" that will connect many of its subdivisions with one another and its shopping malls and natural areas. Walking or biking in some cases between two points will be quicker on the path than driving. Dominated by low density single family housing, the city also plans to construct denser, more urban-like multifamily dwellings near the current business center that will attract to older residents who want to downsize.

The City of Brookfield is a recent creation. At the close of World War II, the only population concentration of any kind in the area was at the junction of two railroad lines near a small depot. Otherwise, the area was largely open, agricultural land—a place where one could go to realize the rural ideal and many did exactly that from the 1950s onward. A spreading out of the Milwaukee urban area, expansion of automobile ownership, the construction of a freeway to Milwaukee, and the ready availability of government backed mortgage financing brought the suburban boom to Brookfield. The city incorporated in 1954 with a population of 7,900 and soon became a bedroom community for commuters to the Milwaukee. Once freeway construction was completed in the 1960s, population expanded rapidly, and by the 1990s the city had become a local hub of retailing, office, and manufacturing employment. Today with a median family income of $76,000, Brookfield is among the most affluent and racially homogeneous of Milwaukee's suburbs and still attempts to retain its rural flavor in its residential areas, although the city is close to being fully built and suffers from growing traffic congestion. Driving its main thoroughfares at rush hour or on a Saturday morning when the shoppers are out can be a tedious exercise. Yet in Brookfield today, it is still possible to own a home on half-acre lot, to send one's children to quality schools under local control, enjoy fairly close access to rural landscapes, and travel in the comfort of one's own car to shopping and work.

Brookfield is important not because it stands out, but because in its ordinariness as a fairly affluent suburb it represents modern aspirations. After World War II, Americans took a pass on the possibilities of an urban ideal and chose the rural instead. In place of urban compactness, Americans opted for suburban spatial expansiveness. Many of Milwaukee's central city residents pushed outward onto the surrounding rural landscape from the 1950s on. Between 1950 and 1990, Milwaukee's urban area population increased by 68 percent, but the amount of developed land expanded by more than 500 percent.[17] A majority of the area's residents sought the rural ideal in newly constructed single family dwellings beyond the city's boundaries in formerly rural open spaces.

At the mid-Twentieth Century, middle-class Americans everywhere (not just in Milwaukee) turned their backs on the old, established central cities as places to live, and they did this for good reasons. Streets were traffic-clogged, city governments were often corrupt (but not in Milwaukee with its tradition of municipal socialism), crime was fearsome, the quality of schools was in decline, the air was often polluted, the streets were noisy, housing was densely packed and overcrowded, and low-income immigrants of a different race were arriving daily. By contrast the suburbs looked like a dream—open green spaces, new, detached single family houses that one could own, local control of government, social and racial homogeneity, and the ability to commute to work in the privacy of one's car. What could be better? Before the war, cities retained the hub-and-spoke shape and relatively high density given them by the electric trolley. People either walked to work or they rode the trolley, and many lived compactly in apartments or other kinds of multifamily housing. Outward spreading of the relatively well off to new "streetcar suburbs" for single-family housing occurred in all the large cities, but population densities stayed relatively high. The economic and cultural heart and soul of the city remained at its center, but all this was about to change.

Americans could have followed the prewar approach of basing the shape of urban space on public mass transit, but they chose a distinctly different path—the creation of an urban transportation system rooted in a love affair with the automobile. Doing so set off an economic boom lasting for upwards of twenty years driven by the new industries of the day—motor vehicles, petroleum, highway construction, and the large scale fabrication of suburban housing. By the end of the Twentieth Century, a majority of urban Americans lived in suburbs instead of central cities. Today the typical American lives in a locally governed, low-density suburb and commutes from a detached single family home to an office park, low rise industrial facility, regional shopping center, or big box retailer, and in the process avoids setting foot at in a high-density central city. The movement of goods within and between cities takes place mainly by trucks on freeways and urban highways instead of by railway. The original advantages of railheads and ports in central cities have been lost to the flexibility of the truck and its ease of moving within and between suburbs. Not only did people move to the suburbs, but along with them so have businesses. The multistory central city factory located on a rail line found itself replaced by the low-rise suburban plant with its truck bays and close access to freeways. The densely packed department stores and high-rise offices in the central city business district now had to compete with low-rise suburban shopping malls and office parks with their convenient parking. This movement to the suburbs is unsurprising in the larger context of American values. Americans retain their deeply rooted, pre-industrial desire to live in rural landscapes. Psychologically we are a nation of want-to-be yeoman farmers and western cowboys possessed by a dream of extracting a living from the land.

As population in any urban area grows, outward spreading occurs as a "natural" and inevitable process. Suburbanization in the U.S. after World War II progressed at an extraordinary pace—exceeding anything that could be called "natural" with its emptying out of the bulk of the white middle class from the central city. This outward movement was as much driven by public sector innovations in transportation and housing finance as it was by any quest for rural values. The creation of the Highway Trust Fund, with its earmarked source of revenue from fuel taxes, and the formation of a low-cost, publicly backed mortgage financing system provided the critical spark and fuel that ignited a boom in suburban housing construction across the U.S. beginning in the 1950s and continuing into the 1970s.

No single public works financing arrangement has done as much to reshape the urban landscape as the creation of the Highway Trust Fund by the Highway Act of 1956. This act authorized the construction of the Dwight D. Eisenhower National System of Defense and Interstate Highways and its funding with a variety of federal user fees including a gasoline and diesel fuel tax. These fees and taxes were to flow into the Trust Fund where they could be used only for roads and highways. Federal aid to states continued for primary, secondary, and urban roads on a 1 to 1 matching basis as in the past, but an amount exceeding these three categories together went to the construction of the Interstate system with a much more lucrative match of 9 federal dollars for every state or local dollar. While state and local governments had limited-access expressways on the drawing boards, such a lucrative match dramatically accelerated the pace of construction starting with a federal allocation of $1 billion a year initially that quickly climbed to $2 billion a year. The intention of the Interstate System was to connect the country's metropolitan areas, not to improve transportation within cities. Nonetheless, the impact of the Interstate System within urban areas was to dramatically improve transportation between central cities and their surrounding suburbs. Local residents who lived on a central city's outskirts, owned a car, and commuted to the center benefited directly and substantially from construction of the Interstate System.

A half century of political lobbying by highway construction advocates culminated in the creation of the Trust Fund and construction of the Interstate System. At the beginning of the Twentieth Century, America's roads suffered from serious neglect largely because of the dominance of the railroad for transporting goods and people around the country. Bicyclists started the Good Roads movement to pressure government to do something about the terrible state roads were in before the motor vehicle became a significant presence, but once Henry Ford's Model-T transformed the industry into a serious engine of economic growth by making cars available to the masses, the motor vehicle industry took over leadership of the road-improvement movement. A variety of newly empowered economic interests came together to form what became the "highway lobby." These interests included such industries as motor vehicles, petroleum, rubber tires, highway construction and engineering, and trucking. They pressured local and state as well as the federal government to spend money on road improvements but to avoid taxing motor vehicles or fuel to fund such efforts. The lobby experienced its first major victory in the passage of the Federal-aid Highway Act in 1916. The act established the precedent of distributing highway aid to states through a federal bureaucracy, the Bureau of Public Roads, controlled by experts in highway engineering. The formula for aid created a strong bias that favored sparsely settled rural states and much of the aid went to primary and secondary roads outside of urban areas. Farmers lobbied for improved roads so they could break the local monopoly many railroads had on transporting agricultural goods. Because of the power of the highway lobby, gas taxes and other user fees were kept to a minimum and most road construction was funded out of general revenues at both the state and federal level. Motorists contributed less than a fourth of the $21 billion spend on roads and highways between 1921 and 1932. Those who didn't own cars or trucks subsidized those who did. During the Great Depression, the federal government picked up the highway spending ball dropped by cash-strapped state governments with $5 billion in New Deal projects for roads. One could argue that the highway lobby was a cabal of special interests aimed at sucking resources from government treasuries, but American's had begun their love affair with the automobile. Many ordinary Americans owned automobiles even in the Depression, and many more wanted them. Highway projects brooked little opposition amongst the general public.[18]

After the war, the highway lobby was in disarray. The automobile and petroleum industry, American Automobile Association, and truckers wanted free limited access highways, but states were using tax exempt bonds to construct toll roads. Highway bureaucrats wanted gas tax increases to fund roads, but the highway lobby opposed this idea. Incoming President, Dwight D. Eisenhower, became the white knight of the highway movement by breaking the impasse and bringing to fruition a 42,000 mile, National System of Defense and Interstate Highways paid for from a trust fund fed largely by taxes on fuel. The highway lobby lost the battle on a gas tax but won struggle to make sure the tax would always go to highways and could not be redirected by Congress to other purposes and that access to the Interstate System would be free. Eisenhower's support for an interstate system undoubtedly solidified as a young army officer in 1919 when he participated in the Army's First Transcontinental Motor Convoy. The Convoy of close to 300 men and a number of new military vehicles managed an average speed of six miles an hour coast to coast reinforced the need for a system of national highways to facilitate not only military movement but both commerce and the settlement of sparsely populated parts of the country. In the next ten years after the passage of the 1956 Highway Act creating the Highway Trust Fund, spending on federally aided highways increased more than fourfold. Completed in 1992, the 47,000 mile system ended up costing $114 billion.[19]

The funding of freeways opened up access to land on which single family homes could be built, but more was needed. The dream of homeownership itself had to be financed. To afford homeownership, working families who wanted to move to the suburbs needed the ability to borrow money for an extended period at low interest rates. The invention of the 30-year mortgage and the creation of a government-backed system of finance accompanied by significant income tax breaks made all this possible. The birth of the Federal Housing Administration (FHA) with the National Housing Act of 1934 marked the beginning of the housing finance system we know so well today. The FHA expanded the use of the 30 year, low-down payment, low-interest, fully amortized mortgage invented by an earlier federal creation to forestall Depression induced mortgage defaults, The Homeowners Loan Corporation. The FHA greased the mortgage market skids by insuring mortgages in return for a small premium. Mortgage insurance removed the element of risk from mortgages, bringing down both interest rates and down payment requirements. The FHA also established minimum housing quality standards verified by an inspection before the insuring of a mortgage. An unfortunate side-effect of FHA quality standards was the creation of a bias in favor of suburban detached bungalows and colonials with yards and driveways and against multifamily units in densely packed central city neighborhoods. Despite the presence of many single family housing units in some central cities, FHA mortgage insurance went disproportionately to the newly developing suburbs on the outer fringe. FHA standards for many years caused clear discrimination against insuring mortgages in central city black neighborhoods and areas where whites and blacks lived in immediate proximity. After the war, the Veterans Administration provided mortgages on the FHA model to returning veterans with the added benefit of a zero down-payment option. The availability of these loans at such a low cost, along with the federal income tax deductibility of mortgage interest and property taxes, made homeownership cheaper than renting, and as a result the march to the suburbs by the white middle class began. This in turn sparked an unprecedented boom in large scale suburban housing construction that increased the homeownership rate from 44 percent of households in 1934 to 63 percent in 1972.[20]

Living Compactly: Paris

The French, like Americans, love their cars. Anyone who visits Paris and experiences its traffic, especially around the Arc de Triomphe, knows that Parisians feel a passionate connection to their vehicles—to put up with the city's traffic and parking challenges, they must. The French also contend with gasoline prices at least double those in the U.S. The French government sees fuel taxes as a revenue source and uses them extensively as such. Higher gasoline prices due to higher fuel taxes encourage the French to drive smaller, more fuel efficient cars and to drive less than Americans. Visitors to Paris also know that the city and its surrounding suburbs have perhaps the best urban public transportation system in the world. Getting from any one point to any other within Paris' city boundaries seldom takes longer than a half hour. A mixed underground and surface rail system, the RER, connects the residents of the Paris metropolitan area to the city and all of its major suburbs. To navigate Paris with ease, one is probably better off without a car.

From 1954 to 1982, the Paris metropolitan population increased from about 7 to 10 million, driven by international immigration and a movement from the country to the city within France. In the 40 year period after World War II, France was transformed from a predominantly rural to a truly urban society. The added residents of the Paris area found their new homes in the suburbs, not the city which shrank slightly in population over the period. The Paris metro area spread out. Parisian planners, enthralled with the motor vehicle, built an extensive system of expressways beginning in the 1960s, but they didn't run them through the   city center as was commonly done in American urban areas.   Instead, peripheral expressways serve the Paris region, notably the Boulevard Péripherique which follows the last wall around Paris and, farther out, the Ile de France ring-road.   The French avoided putting all of their eggs in the motor vehicle basket.   They modernized Paris' subways, built the regional RER commuter train system, and constructed high-speed intercity rail lines with trains that zip along at 150-plus miles per hour.   Before World War II, development outside the Paris city boundary occurred in an unplanned fashion.   Housing estates were put up without roads, sewers, waterlines, or public facilities of any kind. Following World War II, the French government had to play catch-up in supplying local government services to such developments along with recovering from destruction caused by the war.   Full fledged planning in the Paris metropolitan area didn't really get underway until the 1960s.   Realizing the need to deal with an exploding population, the French central government instituted topdown planning in the Paris region and began to invest heavily in a new office center, La Défense, and new towns which together took on the brunt of development and population expansion up to the 1980s.   The goal was to create a polycentric urban form with numerous auxiliary business and residential centers to augment Paris itself.   La Défense on Paris' western edge is the most successful for its brute economic effect, and the five new towns farther out have emerged as key centers of employment and population concentration.[21]   La Défense visually causes one to take pause.   How could the French allow the construction of such a huge collection of nondescript but alienating glass, steel, and concrete towers centered on a huge but artless arch next to the most beautiful city in the world?

After the war Parisians suffered from an acute housing shortage.   This reality, along with a burgeoning urban population, drove French urban planning from the 1960s to the 1980s.   France's first response to this problem was to construct high-rise public housing in the suburban ring just outside of the Paris city boundary.   Feeding the French desire for home ownership rooted in its recent rural past, the French government soon shifted to subsidizing construction of private housing in suburban estates.   The original high rise public housing today is where France's poorest citizens, many of whom have immigrant backgrounds, now live in graffiti-ridden squalor. Although the city of Paris has experienced a reduction in population since World War II (2.8 down to 2.1 million), it remains an affluent and vibrant center of economic and cultural activity.[22]   In short, French government policy encouraged an American style suburbanization based on the motor vehicle, while at the same time directing development to new towns, investing in the renewal of existing urban centers, and creating a sophisticated public transit system oriented on central cities such as Paris. Urban populations spread outward around French cities, but at rates much below those experienced by their American counterparts.   The amount of land per person in France amounts to 8,800 square meters, or a bit more than a football field and a half.[23]   The same figure for the U.S. lower 48 states is

25,500 square meters, or not quite five football fields (a football field is about 5,500 square meters).[24] The French as a society live at higher densities than Americans. Parisians get a mere 50 square meters each within the city boundaries, in contrast with the 203 square meters available to the residents of the City of Chicago, to provide a point of comparison. In the larger Paris urbanized area, the amount of land per person is 282 square meters, while the comparable figure for Chicago is 661 square meters.[25] The French live compactly; Americans live expansively.

Land in the U.S. is abundant, making it comparatively cheap, while land in France is relatively scarce, causing land to be comparatively costly. Expensive land in itself encourages more limited land consumption and living at higher densities. Add to that the higher relative cost of motor vehicle transportation in France and the relative ease of using public transportation, the trend to suburban living is bound to be more moderate in France than the U.S. The most attractive locations to live where public transit predominates will be within easy walking distance of transit stations. The bidding up of rents close to stations will stimulate the construction of multistory dwellings and relatively higher densities than would prevail in a land-using, auto oriented suburban-style setting. Land close to stations will be limited in supply and will carry with it a relatively high price, stimulating an economizing on land by the vertical orientation of dwellings, as opposed to the horizontal orientation we see in the suburbs where land is comparatively cheap.

While we Americans have never been too excited about French haughtiness on the global political and cultural stage, we love to visit France, especially Paris. Since we have a passion for Paris, and because it is one of the densest cities in Europe, contrasting the economy of urban space in the U.S. and Paris is an interesting and instructive exercise about different possibilities for the spatial shape of how we live. After World War II, we as a society opted to live at extremely low population densities and we accomplished this through public investment in freeways, a government backed mortgage lending system, and tax subsidies for homeownership. As the case of France demonstrates, we could have chosen differently—a mix of public and private transportation and higher densities—but we did not. Economic interests, namely the highway lobby, through its exercise of political clout, effectively made the choice for us, but we seemed quite happy with the decision and quickly bought up automobiles and suburban houses. Economic interests at the time coincided with the American rural ideal and the suburban dream. One could as easily claim that the French government made a comparable choice for its citizens to pursue an urban ideal, with which most Parisians are probably not displeased. Certainly, those who can afford it love living in Paris just as the residents of suburban housing estates around Paris are probably content with their bit of country paradise combined with ready access to one of the world's greatest cities. The French too have a rural ideal buried in their historical peasant psyche, but they seem to nonetheless love their city centers more than we Americans.

Living beyond the Urban Boundary versus Moving Back to the Urban Center

Crested Butte, Colorado, an entirely different sort of place than Paris, France, lies in the Rocky Mountains at the head of the beautiful, grassy, open East River Valley about 40 miles north of Gunnison which is roughly a four hour drive from Denver. Once a remote mining town, Crested Butte today is a ski resort, Mecca for mountain bikers, and jumping off point for high-mountain hikers and climbers. As one drives up the valley from Gunnison to Crested Butte, dwellings visible from the highway are sparse at first, but more soon come into view. Land in the upper valley that may have sold for a few hundred dollars an acre 25 years ago when cattle ranching dominated the landscape, now often goes for half a million or more. Not many dwellings can be found in the area today for less than a million dollars—this is what old miner's houses in town have sold for recently. You might think these prices are driven solely by second homeowners and retirees looking for their piece of paradise in which to spend their leisure, but young families are also moving to the area permanently and bringing the means of making a living with them. This is a new trend throughout much of the mountain west made possible by revolutionary change in the way we compute, communicate, and move ourselves and our goods about the planet.[26]

Today, information travels around the world almost immediately and at an infinitesimal cost per unit. One can play the stock market just as well from an office in Manhattan or a country cabin in the Rocky Mountains near Crested Butte where the world of finance is just a mouse click away. Also today, goods can be moved around the world overnight. The global consumer economy can be accessed quickly from almost anywhere with the internet and express delivery. If we have to, we can even move our physical selves almost anywhere in the world within a matter of hours, especially if we are wealthy and can afford the corporate jets that fly in and out of the Gunnison Airport. Simply put, cheapening and speeding up the movement of knowledge, goods, and people expand the possibilities for choosing where to live. We are no longer tied to urban centers for either work or consumption. Today people and businesses are able to locate almost wherever they desire. Movement through space is not at all free, but it certainly has become very cheap. Increasingly, affluent professionals have a choice. They can live in either the spatially expansive beauty of remote mountains, or else in the excitement of densely packed cities, such as San Francisco, New York, Paris, Tokyo, or Rome, or even somewhere in between. Just a hundred years ago, almost everyone in the pursuit of economic success needed to live in immediate proximity to urban industrial centers. Economic necessity dictated spatial compactness. With the collapse in the cost of movement, the freedom to choose where to live and how to use space has vastly expanded.

Despite this new freedom, the essential lesson of spatial economics remains: private space in a market economy goes to the highest bidder and what exists around that space largely establishes its ultimate value. As the realtors say, the determining force in real estate prices is "location, location, and location." As a particular locality becomes more popular, competition bids land values up, and as a place becomes less popular, land values decline. In the last 20 years, land prices in the inner city of Detroit, Michigan have collapsed to near zero in some neighborhoods due to serious economic and social decline, but property values have exploded in popular suburbs around the country, such as Scottsdale, Arizona, or in fashionable mountain getaways such as Aspen, Colorado or even in less fashionable Crested Butte. Where to live and how much space to take up in a high-technology, affluent world is increasingly a matter of personal choice.

When I moved to Milwaukee, Wisconsin back in the 1970s to take my first job as a professor, the city's downtown Third Ward contained a collection of rundown, turn-of-the-century, five to eight story, wonderfully designed and constructed, brick buildings used mainly for wholesaling produce and other goods. The area didn't look to have much of a future and its property values were in decline. Today the Third Ward is undergoing a boom in condo construction and is the home of theaters, good restaurants, art galleries, stuff shops, a public market, a brew pub, a beautiful river walk, numerous professional offices, a school of art and design and much more. Young professionals and empty nesters are moving back to the Third Ward and other neighborhoods surrounding downtown Milwaukee in droves. Even though the "rural ideal" and its emphasis on spatial expansiveness has dominated our choice of where to live in the past century, hope for an "urban ideal" rooted in spatial compactness lives on and seems to be in resurgence. For the first time we truly have a choice in deciding how compactly we are to live. We can spread out over the landscape as do the recent arrivals around Crested Butte or the suburbanites in Brookfield, or we can choose to live densely as do the residents of Milwaukee's Third Ward.

Steaks, Consumer Goods, and the Land Use Pyramid

Take a moment to think about steaks. The cow from which steaks come starts life somewhere on a ranch out west, maybe near Gunnison, Colorado or on ranchland protected from development by a conservation easement near Crested Butte (otherwise the cows would have been crowded out by now). Cattle pasture takes up a substantial amount of space, at least 10 acres per head, but this is only the beginning of the story. At about 8 months of age, our cow moves to a feed lot where it eats mainly corn for the rest of its life—about eight pounds for each pound of weight added before facing the butcher. The feed lot itself, unpleasant as it may be to human sensibilities, uses relatively little space, but it takes a lot to grow the corn needed to feed our cow. We Americans consume roughly 11 billion bushels of corn per year using some 75 million acres of land, or about 11,000 square feet (1,000 square meters) for each of us. About sixty percent of this corn goes into meat production—beef, pork, chicken, and turkey—and the rest into a surprising range of other food products, from Twinkies to Coca Cola.[27] We indirectly use much space for our food, more than we might think, and corn is just one example. The space we require to support our diet goes well beyond what we personally experience on a daily basis. Thing about all the pasta, breads, bakery, fruits, and vegetables you eat in a day and everything else. It all requires land on which to grow. The food that we eat, we will see, requires a huge amount of space to grow.

Now think about all the paper we use both at home and work and on our shopping expeditions—bags, cardboard boxes, and reams of printer paper, newspapers and magazines. Per capita paper products consumption in the U.S. amounts to about .27 metric tons a year (or about 600 pounds), requiring around 16 cubic feet of newly harvested pulpwood on top of the 55 percent of the raw material for paper products that comes from recycling.[28] Paper consumes about a third of our annual timber harvest in this country. Most of the rest goes into wood and other materials for the construction industry, and most of that goes into new homes. To take care of all of our wood fiber consumption of roughly 52 cubic feet per year each, we would need at least an acre (43,000 square feet or 4,000 square meters) of forestland per person to grow enough.[29] In any given year for you personally this figure could be much larger, especially if you built a new single family house of average size. This would cause you to consume the amount of wood obtained by clearcutting an acre of forestland (about ¾ of a football field), a bit more than 1,600 cubic feet.[30] For this amount to grow back would take about 32 years.

The point is simple. We indirectly use substantial amounts of land area out of our immediate view in the production of food, paper products, new homes, and a variety of other consumer goods. Developed land—the kind we urban dwellers see around us on a daily basis—lies at a relatively small peak of our total "land use pyramid." We live at the top, but the bulk of the land we need for those things we enjoy in our economic being is at the bottom of the pyramid. Material goods and energy flow upward in the pyramid to the urbanized peak from a base of cropland, pasture, forestland, mines, and oil and gas fields. We residents of the lower 48 states on average use 1,500 square meters for development at the pyramid peak (.15 hectares), and this is mostly what we see around is in our towns, cities, and suburbs. Of the total developed land each of us uses, 73 percent about 1,100 square meters is found within the boundaries of our major urban areas. Our rural highway system including the Interstate and small towns account for the rest.[31]

A Note on Numbers and Space

Numbers can be mind-numbing, especially if we can't easily get a sense of what they mean. Unfortunately, we can't talk about space without them. We will try to ease the task by referring to an amount of space familiar to most of us, an American footfall field. Even if you hate football, you have no doubt come across a Sunday game while channel-surfing for something to watch. Next time, stop for a minute and get a sense of a football field's spatial extent.   This will allow us to talk about our measures of space in football field equivalents.   You will notice that I make use of the metric system here, something that scientists and other countries in the world do as a matter of course.   I am doing so too not so much because it's what we will all do eventually, but because of the system's ease of use.   A meter is 3.28 feet, a messy number, but within the metric system, all is simplicity.   A square kilometer is 100 hectares and a hectare is 10,000 square meters.   Since our topic is space, we have to make use of spatial measures.   Again, I like thinking about space in terms of American football field equivalents.   A football field is about 5,500 square meters in area.   Now we are ready to talk about the space we each occupy and use on the American landscape.

Back to the Land Use Pyramid

The land area available to each of us in the lower 48 states is 2.55 hectares, or 25,500 square meters.   Simply put this is the amount of land (excluding water) in the contiguous continental U.S. divided by population (I use 300 million for population, roughly the 2006 figure).[32]   The average for each of us amounts to a little less than five football fields (4.6 to be more exact).   On top of 1,500 square meters for development at the peak of the "land use pyramid," we each also *indirectly* use an average of 7,000 square meters for cropland and pasture lower down the pyramid.   I say indirectly, because we personally don't spend any time on it, but farmers farm it on our behalf.   We still need that land to live and enjoy life's material fruits.   On it the bulk of our food is produced, although a small portion comes from other countries and a small share of our own output is sold overseas. We also devote 5,500 square meters each to privately and state-owned forestland in this country, of which roughly 4,200 is needed for wood fiber production. We each employ another 100 square meters or so of federal lands to support our consumption of wood-based products (This figure is substantially below the historical peak because of recent dramatic declines in harvests from federal lands).[33]   The total of other uses on private lands equals about 700 square meters per person, and includes mining and oil and gas production and farmsteads.   On top of this, we as a society own 5,400 square meters each of federal lands, and we use it for a variety of purposes, including, logging (remember we are already currently using 100 square meters or so for wood fiber production), grazing, oil and gas production, mining, recreation, and habitat protection. About half of federal lands in the lower 48 states are relatively undeveloped and currently free of any kind of commodity production (i.e. they are roadless or protected from exploitation in some way) and contain some of the largest remaining expanses of natural habit for our fellow nonhuman species.[34]   The one remaining major land use category we have yet to mention is privately owned rangeland, about 5,500 square meters for each of us, a portion of which is used for grazing.   Some of this is covered with nonnative grasses, but much of it remains in native vegetation.[35]

To sum up, each of us directly and indirectly uses 1,500 square meters of developed land and 11,300 square meters for food and fiber with a small amount (700 square meters) for mining, oil and gas extraction, and other rural uses adding up to 13,500 square meters. This is the total amount of space in our personal land use pyramid. Again what we see and use personally is the top 1,500 square meters. The rest we seldom if ever step foot on but depend on for our material sustenance. Again, all these numbers are averages. In practice some of us use more, and some use less. With each of us directly and indirectly making intensive use of 13,500 square meters on average in our land use pyramids, this means that a bit less than half (12,000 to be exact) of our 25,500 total square meters each in this country remains outside of substantial landscape-modifying human use and largely in natural vegetation.[36] Some of this land is degraded by grazing, recreation, and extensive road systems, but much of it still functions as natural habitat for native plants and animals. The majority of such land does occur in harsh landscapes that naturally possess relatively low species diversity, what one historian called worthless lands.[37] These are areas in which we typically don't live and lands that we don't find very economically productive. The richest biological habitats in this country, where the largest numbers of native plant and animal species would live absent human disturbance, occur on the country's most productive agricultural and commercial forest land and the most desirable urban, suburban, and exurban landscapes. Human use of these spaces has largely crowded out use by native flora and fauna. Old-growth forests and tallgrass prairie landscapes, for example, are among the rarest remaining in the lower 48 states, and species that find their home there tend to be among the most threatened in the country.[38] The same is true for riparian and wetland habitats which tend to be substantially degraded by economic activities of various kinds, such dams on rivers and the draining of wetlands for agriculture, dwellings, or commercial buildings. The point is, while much natural habitat continues to exist in this country, remaining rare habitat types are often insufficient for the protection of threatened and endangered species, about which we will be saying more.

The land use pyramid, with energy and materials flowing upward from sparsely populated rural areas to dense urban centers, is an ecological idea, not an economic one. An economist would simply point to the return flow of high value goods and services to rural producers in return for their low value per unit-high volume natural resources. All exchange in a market context ultimately involves economic equivalents. An economist who focuses on the workings of markets alone would refrain from giving any special attention to the idea of rural land exploitation supporting life in urban centers and how the urban use of space and urbanite consumption patterns indirectly affects the way rural land is used. If space becomes scarce economically, then its price will be bid up, and consumer behavior will adjust. If we care about ecology and nature's need for space, then we will have to take a step beyond economics, and the land use pyramid will make sense, as we will see in the pages to follow.

The land use pyramid is the key take away idea to remember from this chapter.   We human beings in the good old "United States of America" consume vastly more space than we might think.   Our spatial expansiveness turns out to be a critical problem for our friends out there in the natural world.   Again the size of our personal space pyramid is about 13,500 square meters, or about 2.4 football fields.   We will also see in the pages to follow that an intimate connection exists between how we use space, our consumption of energy resources, and a changing global climate.   We will also see that both space and the global climate substantially affect our global ecology, but before we get to this issue we need to understand the linkage between space and ecology.   Not only is the economy of space a big deal, but so is the ecology of space.

The Ecology of Nature's Space

Life for a longleaf pine tree, a native of the southeastern U.S., plays out in a spatial context. A longleaf pine sapling in a northern Florida dry-forest requires unoccupied space on the forest floor where its roots can find their way into the soil subsurface to extract moisture and chemical nutrients. The roots also serve as the foundation for the upward growth of the trunk necessary to put branches and needles in the bright sunlight where the production of chemical energy needed to keep the tree alive can take place through photosynthesis. The vertical orientation of a pine tree also allows it to send out pollen on the wind to other trees and receive the same for the fertilization of its own ovules so that seeds can be produced and serve as the source of the next generation of trees. Ironically, the destructive force of surface fires burn off the forest ground layer in a longleaf pine forest from time-to-time and create the bare soil needed for seeds to take root.[39]

A mature longleaf pine in turn serves the needs for both food and a refuge for reproduction for other species. As a general ecological rule, about 10 percent of a tree's biomass and photosynthetic energy might be passed onto a herbivore, such as a bark beetle or gypsy moth. A fairly famous occupant of a longleaf pine forest is the endangered Red-cockaded Woodpecker, a good sized bird with a wingspan of 35 centimeters (14 inches) and a length of 22 centimeters (9 inches). Red-cockades possess the black and white pattern wings common to many woodpeckers, but their black caps and white cheeks with a little red streak along the base of the cap for the male distinguish them from other species.   A male will carve out a roost cavity in a large pine where his mate will lay three or four eggs.   Male fledglings generally stick around for a year or so to help raise the next season's brood. A male and female form a monogamous bond lasting up to several years.   A woodpecker's typical diet includes ants, beetles, cockroaches, caterpillars, wood-boring insects, spiders, and sometimes fruits and berries. Again, these animals may get about 10 percent or so of the energy contained in the plants they feed on, and they will pass on no more than 10 percent of the energy in their own body mass to their predators such as the Red-cockaded Woodpecker.

Red-cockades like tall old-growth pines and excavate cavities out of living trees, unlike many other woodpeckers who stick with the softer, rotting wood of dead snags. Territory is important and will be defended during breeding season. The amount of land a breeding pair will range over varies from 50 to as much as 250 hectares of old-growth longleaf pine forest. At the low end this amounts to about a hundred football fields. The space requirement for woodpeckers is substantial. This of course is shared space. Longleaf pine forests are species-rich habitats. A range of species actually end up using Red-cockaded cavities, including chickadees, bluebirds, titmice, other woodpeckers, Eastern Screech Owls, Wood Ducks, flying squirrels, and a variety of reptiles, amphibians, and insects. The total population of Red-cockaded Woodpeckers is down to about 5,000 breeding pairs, around 1 percent of its original population. The source of population decline is largely habitat loss and habitat fragmentation. Fragmentation occurs when human use or development of the landscape breaks it up into pieces to small to be of any value to woodpeckers. To stay in the business of successful reproduction over the long haul, the Red-cockaded needs a large, contiguous landscape that will support at least 500 breeding pairs. A breeding population of this size will avoid the in-breeding problems and demographic accidents that would plague a smaller group. Because the total population is so small and many sub-populations fall below viable minimums, the Red-cockaded woodpecker has been designated as an endangered species by the U.S. Fish and Wildlife Service giving it protection under the Endangered Species Act.[40]

We can now make some points about nature's space requirements. A tree, capable of producing its own chemical energy, doesn't need very much space and a bark beetle even less. Again, the later passes on no more than at most 10 percent of its energy-containing biomass to herbivores such as the bark beetle that feed on it. Finally, the woodpecker gets no more than 10 percent of the biomass of the bugs it preys on. Clearly, a woodpecker will have to range far and wide, punching holes in many different trees, in order to find enough biomass energy to live on and reproduce. Big organisms need a lot more space than little ones, and animals more than the plants or pieces of plants they feed on. There is an energy pyramid extending up the food chain from the plant base with each block about a tenth of the previous one. This means that large predators at the very top of the chain need huge amounts of space. This also means the biomass of the plants at the bottom of the pyramid must be huge compared to the biomass of the large carnivores at the top. In short, a huge amount of undivided longleaf pine habitat is needed to support a viable population of Red-cockaded woodpeckers, as much as 125,000 hectares. Protecting this amount of habitat will be good for numerous other species as well whose habitat needs fit under the umbrella of the Red-cockaded Woodpeckers spatial needs. Bigger chunks of undivided and undisturbed habitat will mean more species. Cut such chunks up with housing development or roads, fewer species will be present. Chop down large trees and stop ground-layer fires, then longleaf pine will be replaced by oaks and other species that flourish where fire does not occur and the ground layer becomes thick and shady. Pine saplings need sunny, open soils created by fire, and they of course originate from the pine cones supplied by big, old, widely space pine trees resistant to low-level fires. Taking away the pines will take away the food base for many longleaf pine forest animals. In short, for survival, some species and the spaces they occupy need to be free of human disturbance and exploitation.

All this makes apparent a key difference between a natural ecosystem and the human economy. Natural ecosystems run with rare exceptions on the energy of the sun. No sunshine, no life. Except for food production on farms and ranches and wood fiber production in the forests, the human economy runs mostly on fossil fuel energy. Fossil fuels, as their name implies, originate from plants that stored photosynthetic energy from the sun, died, and were buried under the earth's surface millions of years ago. These underground stocks contain those fuels—petroleum, natural gas, and coal—that supply the motive power for our economy. While currently abundant, these energy sources are finite and their production rates will start shrinking comparatively soon. In contrast, solar energy, which powers our global ecosystems, is available everyday the sun shines. As we all now also know, burning fossil fuels causes carbon dioxide to accumulate and act as a climatic blanket, raising the earth's temperature.

Notes

[1] William Howard Adams, *The Paris Years of Thomas Jefferson* (New Haven: Yale University Press, 1997).

[2] Ibid.

[3] Ibid.

[4] Ibid.

[5] Merrill D. Peterson, *The Portable Thomas Jefferson* (New York: Viking Press, 1975).

[6] Eugene Hargrove, "Anglo-American Land Use Attitudes," *Environmental Ethics* 2 (1980).

[7] Peterson, *The Portable Thomas Jefferson.*

[8] Paul W. Gates, *The Jeffersonian Dream: Studies in the History of American Land Policy and Development* (Albuquerque: University of New Mexico Press, 1996).

[9] U.S. Bureau of the Census, *Historical Census Statistics on the Foreign-Born Population of the United States: 1850-1990* (U.S. Bureau of the Census, 1999 [cited April 8, 2009]); available from http://www.census.gov/population/www/documentation/twps0029/twps0029.html.

[10] Sam B. Warner, Jr., *Streetcar Suburbs: The Process of Growth in Boston, 1870-1900* (New York: Atheneum, 1974).

[11] Ibid.

[12] Ibid.

[13] For my own city, Milwaukee, a number of good histories document city improvement. See Douglas E. Booth, "Municipal Socialism and City Government Reform: The Milwaukee Experience, 1910-1940," *Journal of Urban History* 12, no. 2 (1985). You can find similar histories I am sure for your own home town.

[14] Jane Jacobs, *The Death and Life of Great American Cities* (New York: Vintage, 1961).

[15] Ian L. McHarg, *Design with Nature* (Reading, MA: Addison-Wesley Publishing, 1973), 19. We will take up the question of meaning and its connection to the natural world in much more detail later on.

[16] For information on Brookfield, see City of Brookfield, *2020 Master Plan* (City of Brookfield, 1999 [cited April 21, 2009]); available from http://www.ci.brookfield.wi.us/index.asp?NID=237; City of Brookfield, *Fact Book 2007* (City of Brookfield, 2007 [cited April 21, 2009]); available from http://www.ci.brookfield.wi.us/DocumentView.asp?DID=6. Joel Garreau would call such a place an "edge city." See Joel Garreau, *Edge City: Life on the New Frontier* (New York: Doubleday, 1991).

[17] Demographia, *Large USA Urban Areas: 1950 to 2000* (Demographia and the Public Purpose, 2005 [cited April 21, 2009]); available from http://www.demographia.com/db-uza2000.htm.

[18] Owen D. Gutfreund, *Twentieth-Century Sprawl: Highways and the Reshaping of the American Landscape* (New York: Oxford University Press, 2004).

[19] Ibid.

[20] Kenneth T. Jackson, *Crabgrass Frontier: The Suburbanization of the United States* (New York: Oxford University Press, 1985).

[21] Richard Shearmur and Christel Alvergne, "Regional Planning Policy and the Location of Employment in the Ile-De-France: Does Policy Matter?," *Urban Affairs Review* 39, no. 1 (2003).

[22] Hans van der Cammen, ed., *Four Metropolises in Western Europe: Development and Urban Planning of London, Paris, Randstand Holland and the Ruhr Region* (Amsterdam: Van Gorcum, Assen/Masstricht, 1988); Harry W. Richardson and Chang-Hee Christine Bae, eds., *Urban Sprawl in Western Europe and the United States* (Burlington, VT: Ashgate, 2004).

[23] U.S. Central Intelligence Agency, *World Fact Book* (U.S. CIA, 2009 [cited April 39, 2009]); available from https://www.cia.gov/library/publications/the-world-factbook/geos/fr.html#People.

[24] U.S. Bureau of the Census, *American Fact Finder* (U.S. Bureau of the Census, 2009 [cited April 27, 2009]); available from http://factfinder.census.gov/home/saff/main.html?_lang=en; USDA National Resources Conservation Service, *National Resources Inventory: 2003 Annual NRI* (Natural Resource Conservation Service, 2003 [cited April 27, 2009]); available from http://www.nrcs.usda.gov/technical/NRI/2003/national_landuse.html. Water area is excluded. I like to use the American football field area to provide an order of magnitude. Most of us know visually how big a football field looks. The American football field is about 6,400 square yards, or 5,400 square meters. Ultimately we will all be using the metric system, which is really easy to work with, so we might as well get used to it. Remember, a square meter is a bit more than a square yard. Everything increases in some multiple of 10 as things get bigger. A hectare contains 10,000 square meters, and a square kilometer possesses 100 hectares.

[25] Demographia, *Large USA Urban Areas: 1950 to 2000* ([cited]); Demographia, *Paris Arrondissements: Post 1860 Population & Population Density* (Demographia and the Public Purpose, 2005 [cited]); available from http://www.demographia.com/db-paris-arr1999.htm; Demographia, *Paris Urban Area: Population, Area & Density from 1807* (Demographia and the Public Purpose, 2005 [cited); available from http://www.demographia.com/db-parisua.htm; U.S. Bureau of the Census, *American Fact Finder* ([cited]). The woodlands, Bois de Bolgna and Bois de Vincennes, outside of Paris proper, but owned by the city, are not included in the density calculation. If they were, each Parisian would have access to more like 50 square meters of land area. The data is all 1999-2000.

[26] Douglas E. Booth, *Searching for Paradise: Economic Development and Environmental Change in the MountainWest* (Lanham, MD: Rowman and Littlefield, 2002); Stephan Weiler and David T. Theobold, "Pioneers of Rural Sprawl in the Rocky Mountain West," *Review of Regional Studies* 33 (2003).

[27] Michael Pollan, *Omnivore's Dilemma: A Natural History of Four Meals* (New York: Penguin Books, 2006). U.S. Bureau of the Census, *The 2007 Statistical Abstract* (U.S. Bureau of the Census, 2007 [cited January 4, 2007]); available from http://www.census.gov/compendia/statab/.

[28] American Forest & Paper Association, *Country Report: United States of America* (FAO Advisory Committee on Paper and Wood Products, 2008 [cited April 29, 2009]); available from http://www.fao.org/forestry/media/ 15367/1/0/; W. Brad Smith et al., "Forest Resources of the United States, 2002," (St. Paul: USDA Forest Service, North Central Research Station, 2002).

[29] Smith et al., "Forest Resources of the United States, 2002." The calculations are based on forest productivity data in this report.

[30] Wood Products Council Market Research, *Wood Used in New Residential Construction: U.S. And Canada* (NAHB Research Center, 2005 [cited April 27, 2009]); available from http://www.fpl.fs.fed.us/documnts/pdf2005/ fpl_2005_mckeever002.pdf.

[31] USDA National Resources Conservation Service, *National Resources Inventory: 2003 Annual NRI* ([cited]); USDA Natural Resources Conservation Service, "2001 Annual NRI: Urbanization and Development of Rural Land," (Washington D.C.: Natural Resources Conservation Service, 2001).

[32] U.S. population is growing at about a percent a year. See U.S. Bureau of the Census, *The 2009 Statistical Abstract* (U.S. Bureau of the Census, 2009 [cited April 29, 2009]); available from http://www.census.gov/compendia/ statab/.

[33] These calculations are based on data found in Smith et al., "Forest Resources of the United States, 2002." The federal and private forestland requirement is calculated as the amount of land needed to re-grow the current volume of wood harvested in a year based on current forest growth rates. For the 1970 peak harvest on the national forests, the land requirement would be 700 square meters per person instead of 100 square meters. For the harvest data see Richard W. Haynes et al., "The 2005 RPA Timber Assessment Update," in *PNW-GTR 699a* (Portland, OR: USDA Forest Service, Pacific Northwest Research Station, 2005).

[34] We will have more to say later on this topic. For a couple of good references see J. Michael Scott et al., "Nature Reserves: Do They Capture the Full Range of America's Biological Diversity?," *Ecological Applications* 11, no. 4 (2001); David S. Wilcove et al., "Rebuilding the Ark: Toward a More Effective Endangered Species Act for Private Land," (New York: Environmental Defense Fund, 1996).

[35] U.S. Bureau of the Census, *American Fact Finder* ([cited)]; USDA National Resources Conservation Service, *National Resources Inventory: 2003 Annual NRI* ([cited).

[36]As we will discuss later, this 12,000 meters per person outside the intensive human use pyramid is by not at all free of human influence. In particular a significant amount is degraded by oil and gas production, clearcut timber harvests, mining, and overgrazing.

[37] Alfred Runte, *National Parks: The American Experience*, 2nd ed. (Lincoln: University of Nebraska Press, 1987).

[38] We will offer up evidence for this proposition later.

[39] Carolina Sandhills National Wildlife Refuge, *The Longleaf Pine/Wiregrass Ecosystem* (U.S. Fish and Wildlife Service, Carolina Sandhills National Wildlife Refuge, 2005 [cited October 12, 2005]); available from http://www.fws.gov/carolinasandhills/longleaf.html.

[40] R. Todd Engstrom and Felicia J. Sanders, "Red-Cockaded Woodpecker Foraging Ecology in an Old-Growth Longleaf Pine Forest," *Wilson Bulletin* 109 (1997); National Wildlife Federation, *Red-Cockaded Woodpecker* (National Wildlife Federation, 2005 [cited October 7, 2005]); available from http://www.nwf.org/wildlife/redcockadedwoodpecker/; J.M. Reed, P.D. Doerr, and J.R. Walters, "Minimum Viable Population Size of the Red-Cockaded Woodpecker," *Journal of Wildlife Management* 52 (1988).

Chapter 2
Fossil Fuels and the Space Subsidy

The ultimate modern American consumer love affair is with energy. Our immediate passion is for cars and consumer gadgets, but they all run on energy, of which in our consuming lives each of us absorbs about 360 gigajoules annually (on average). Technically, a joule is the energy needed to produce one watt of power for one-second, a fairly small amount (a 60 watt bulb needs 60 joules each second). Since we each use many multiples of this, mega- or giga- usually appears in front of joules (mega stands for million and giga for a billion).

Numbers for measuring energy can be even more mind-numbing and challenging than for measuring space. The numerous different units of measurement—joules, watts, BTUs, and calories—increase the challenge of getting a quantitative handle on energy. Just as we will use football-field equivalents to simplify our measurement of space, we will use gasoline-equivalents for our measures of energy. We all have a rough idea what a gallon of gas looks like and about how many miles it will take us in our car.

A gallon of gas contains around 130 megajoules (million), meaning that we each burn up the amount of energy contained in 2,800 gallons of gasoline in a year. If we used energy for nothing but driving, we could all go roughly 70,000 miles annually at 25 miles to the gallon. We use quite a bit, but certainly not all, of our energy for getting around. While transportation absorbs around 28 percent of our energy consumption, the rest goes to residential, commercial, and industrial uses. We are especially lucky to have a highly concentrated source of stored energy in the form of fossil fuels providing us with what I will call a "space subsidy."[1]

Think about our situation if we lacked the presence of fossil fuels. We would then need to get our energy from the sun just like the rest of nature.[2] If we each had to capture 360 gigajoules of energy per year directly from photosynthesis by plants, we would need a huge amount of land. The most energy we are likely to ever be able to capture annually from plants for biofuels is about 100 gigajoules per hectare, meaning that each of us would need 3.6 hectares (36,000 square meters or almost 7 football fields) to feed our energy habit, but this would add up to more land than we have, 2.6 hectares each (25,500 square meter or not quite 5 football fields) in the lower 48 states.[3] Thank God for fossil fuels, which provide us with a substantial space subsidy, to the tune of about 7 football fields.[4] To recreate through nature's gift of photosynthesis an amount of energy equal to what we each use in a year cannot be done. We simply don't have enough land on which to do it.

The problems with the space subsidy given to us by fossil fuels are two: first, fossil fuels reserves will reach their practical limit in this century; second, fossil fuel emissions cause damaging global warming (as well as other harms such as ozone pollution). Millions of years ago photosynthesis combined with geological forces to remove billions of tons of carbon from the earth's atmosphere and store it beneath the earth's surface. By extracting this carbon back out today as fossil fuel and burning it up, we are suddenly re-injecting huge amounts of carbon into the earth's atmosphere, carbon that in effect functions like a global tea cozy. Physical and natural systems that have adapted over centuries to a relatively stable climate are reacting to a warmer world in ways that hurt both us human beings and our non-human evolutionary relatives—melting ice caps, declining polar bear populations, disappearing tundra habitats, rising sea levels, more droughts and hurricanes, to name just a few of the harms. If we want to limit these, we will have to halt the use of fossil fuel long before supplies run out. In short, the space subsidy will have to go away sooner, or it will on its own later. We will need to generate most of our energy somehow directly from the sun, and this will require space. Our human footprint on the earth's surface will inevitably grow. If we don't contract our footprint in other arenas, we will be forcing the shrinkage of nature's space—the land area in natural habitat needed for the survival of the earth's nonhuman species. Total reliance on plant energy through biofuels simply won't work—too much land would be taken up. We do have other solar options that use land more efficiently including the generation of electricity using wind or tidal flows, photovoltaic cells, or hot water thermal solar systems with mirrors to concentrate the heat of the sun. We also have the highly space conserving option of nuclear power—this is the method France uses for generating most of its electricity—although some would consider this to be a Faustian bargain because of the resulting radioactive wastes that will be toxic for thousands of years and create a huge storage problem. Nuclear energy amounts to a new kind of "space subsidy," one that comes with its own unique set of environmental dangers.

Let's do some 'back of the envelope' calculations to see about how much space for solar energy we would need to replace our current consumption of fossil fuels. Again, each of us consumes 360 gigajoules of energy annually (think 2,800 gallons of gasoline) of which 85 percent or so comes from fossil fuels (the rest is mainly nuclear and hydroelectric).[5] For the moment, let's assume that in the long haul we desire to return dammed streams to nature and retire our nuclear plants. We will explain the logic of this later. In short, we will want to replace all the energy currently consumed with the clean, renewable kind. Experts tell us that with serious attention to conservation, we can probably reduce our energy consumption by about 30 percent at a zero net cost, meaning what we save by buying 30 percent less roughly pays for the efficiency gains.[6] Up to this point, energy conservation would essentially be a free lunch. This means we need to find 360-.3x360=252 gigajoules of clean energy each to get unhooked from fossil fuels (and nuclear and hydro). Experts also suggest about 20 percent of our energy could come from wind, and wind power on agricultural lands and grasslands would have a pretty modest spatial footprint, taking very little land out of production. The cost of wind is converging on the cost of electricity from coal today, so it should be even more affordable down the road. So this would leave us with 252-.2x252=201.6 gigajoules each in additional clean energy required. At a 15 percent conversion efficiency rate and an annual 6.5 gigajoules of energy hitting each square meter of surface on average in the U.S. annually[7], 200 square meters of photovoltaic cells (201.6/.975=206.8, but let's round down for simplicity) would produce the added clean energy we each need. Conversion efficiency in the long run will probably be higher, more like 20 percent, so the solar cell area estimate may be too large.[8] On the other hand, a portion of the solar energy would have to be converted from electricity to a form that can be stored and used in vehicles, such as hydrogen. Hydrogen production would itself absorb energy, increasing the solar cell requirement. Adopting a 15 percent solar cell conversion efficiency instead of 20 percent adds some wiggle room to account for any extra energy absorption in producing hydrogen. On top of the solar cells, extra space will be required for equipment that distributes or stores electrical energy or converts it into hydrogen. Let's assume that 200 square meters of solar cells will use 400 square meters of land area, accounting for all the space needed by the total solar system. While roofs of buildings and other underutilized spaces could accommodate some of the solar facilities, probably most would displace other land uses, adding let's say 300 square meters for solar production to the 1,500 square meters of developed land we each already inhabit, or another 20 percent and a grand total of 1,800 square meters each. The same amount of energy from biofuels by contrast would require roughly 20,000-plus square meters (2 hectares) of land for plant growth per person (at 100 gigajoules per hectare), or almost 4 football fields. Remember we only have about 5 football fields available per person in the lower-48 states. To produce our energy requirements through plant growth for biofuels would be infeasible since we wouldn't have nearly enough land left for food and fiber production much less for the survival of the rest of the natural world. Photovoltaic cells are spatially speaking much more efficient than plants for producing usable energy. If photovoltaic solar cells can feasibly replace fossil fuels, then the fossil fuel space subsidy for each of us in effect shrinks to about 300 square meters, or a bit more than 5 percent of a football field.

Whether we could ever afford 200 square meters of photovoltaic cells per person is another question. At today's prices of four to eight times the cost of coal fired electricity for solar energy, the answer is an unqualified no, but this isn't the end of the story. Historical economic experience suggests that when one does more of something it gets cheaper. Catalytic converters on motor vehicles to cut pollution emissions by 90 percent became very affordable because the government required one on every new motor vehicle produced. Economies of scale inevitably bring costs down. Studies by the Department of Energy suggest that solar should be competitive with fossil fuel generated electricity by 2020 at the latest, costing 10 cents per kilowatt hour or less.[9]

These 'back of the envelop' calculations should not be taken as gospel until we look into the reality of solar energy, something we will do in chapters to come, and we will revisit these numbers later to see how they stand up. The numbers do give us a sense of optimism about the feasibility of cooling the climate by getting out from under the tyranny of fossil fuels.

The space subsidy goes away without fossil fuels, but the land area requirements for solar are not at all outrageous. We will all have to live a little more compactly, but by the end of the book I hope to convince you that this is a good thing in itself.

To sum up, with a shift to solar, each of us would directly and indirectly use a total of 13,800 square meters of land space for the following uses: development (1,500), solar energy (300), food and wood fiber (11,300), and other rural (700). This is out of a total of 25,500 square meters per capita in the lower 48, leaving 11,700 square meters per person for nature. Nature gets not quite 2 football fields for each of us while our personal land use pyramid includes almost 2.5 football fields. This unrealistically assumes population stability. If our human population expands, and each of our land pyramids remains the same, the amount of land for nature will inevitably shrink. In the next forty years if each one of us in effect becomes 1.5 persons (population is predict to increase in the U.S. by almost 50 percent), then nature's space will contract by more than one half. For anyone who cares about protecting species diversity, this is thought-provoking. We will revisit this issue later.

Notes

[1] U.S. Department of Energy, *Annual Energy Review, 2008* (U.S. Department of Energy, 2009 [cited December 18, 2008]); available from http://www.eia.doe.gov/aer/pdf/aer.pdf.

[2] Set aside for the moment nuclear whose potential for energy supply has inherent limits.

[3] Andrew R.B. Ferguson, "The Logical Foundations of Ecological Footprints," *Environment, Development and Sustainability* 1, no. 2 (1999).

[4] Shortly we will see that space requirements for solar can be cut substantially by using wind generators and photovoltaic cells and other measures. For now, lets take biofuels—nature's way of producing energy—as our point of departure for talking about energy and space.

[5] U.S. Department of Energy, *Annual Energy Review, 2008* ([cited]). Per capita energy consumption has been stable for the last 15 years. We have no reason to expect this to rise in the future, especially at a time of rising energy scarcity and prices.

[6] D. Pimentel et al., "U.S. Energy Conservation and Efficiency: Benefits and Costs," *Environment, Development and Sustainability* 6 (2004).

⁷ U.S. Department of Energy, *Solar Energy Technologies Program: Multi-Year Program Plan* (U.S. Department of Energy, 2007 [cited December 8, 2008]); available from http://www1.eere.energy.gov/solar/pdfs/set_myp_2007-2011_proof_1.pdf.

⁸ U.S. Department of Energy, *Solar America Initiative: A Plan for the Integrated Research, Development, and Market Transformation of Solar Energy Technologies* (U.S. Department of Energy, 2007 [cited December 8, 2008]); available from http://www1.eere.energy.gov/solar/solar_america/pdfs/sai_draft_plan_Feb5_07.pdf; U.S. Department of Energy, *Solar Energy Technologies Program: Multi-Year Program Plan* ([cited]).

⁹ U.S. Department of Energy, *Solar America Initiative: A Plan for the Integrated Research, Development, and Market Transformation of Solar Energy Technologies* ([cited]); U.S. Department of Energy, *Solar Energy Technologies Program: Multi-Year Program Plan* ([cited]).

Chapter 3
Taking up Less Space: The Joys of Compact Urban Living

French author and philosopher, Jean-Paul Sartre, entered the elite Ecole Normale Superieure, located in the 5th Arrondissement on Paris' left bank near the famous Pantheon, in 1924 at age nineteen. Already a winner of academic prizes from his pre-college schooling, at the Ecole Normale Sartre honed his skills as a writer and philosopher. Completing a two year stint in the army, Sartre took a job teaching high school age students in Le Havre in 1931. After Paris, Le Havre amounted to banishment to an intellectual wasteland. It is here that he took to writing and passing time with his students in a local cafe, an experience that provided some of the raw material for his first and most famous novel, *Nausea*. Not until 1937, when Sartre received a new teaching assignment at the Lycee Pasteur, could he return to the Parisian life. He amused his students at the cafe Sabot Bleu across the street from the Lycee, and, with the publication of *Nausea*, became a star, and gathered an expanded coterie of intellectuals around him for drink and conversation. World War II intervened, resulting in Sartre being shipped off to the army, and his eventual captivity and internment in a German prison camp. He came back to Paris in 1941 after being released from the camp under the pretense of medical ills. He returned to his teaching job at the Lycee Pasteur and spent his spare time next to the stove at the then seedy Cafe de Flore near the Sorbonne (only cafes could get coal for heat during the war). Through much of the 1940s, the de Flore served as Sartre's headquarters where he wrote and commiserated with fellow intellectuals such as Albert Camus, Maurice Merleau-Ponty, and, his longtime companion, Simone de Beauvoir.[1] Today only affluent tourists can be found in the de Flore. Bohemian intellectuals who become famous inadvertently make such places fashionable and ultimately unaffordable to their own kind.

In the war years, Sartre wrote his philosophical tome, *Being and Nothingness*, and plays and works of fiction that set out his existentialist philosophy.[2] In October of 1945, Sartre was invited to defend his philosophical views by the Club Maintenant near the Grand Palais and the Champs-Élysées. The event was an overwhelming success, drawing a huge crowd that pushed and shoved to get the limited seating available.[3]

Sartre's writings bear the influence of not just his study of philosophy and literature at the Ecole Normale, but also his experiences of life around him at the cafes and on the streets of Le Havre and Paris. At one point in *Being and Nothingness*, he proclaims, "the cafe by itself with its patrons, its tables, its booths, its mirrors, its light, its smoky atmosphere, and the sounds of voices, rattling saucers, and footsteps which fill it—the cafe is fullness of being." Sartre's success as an intellectual benefited from not just his depiction of Parisian life around him, but an interested public ready at hand in the city to attend his plays and lectures and to buy, read, and discuss his books. Intellectual ferment of the kind cultivated by Sartre finds a special fertile ground in dense and stimulating urban environments such as Paris.

Sartre is just one of many writers who flourished in the Parisian cultural hothouse. Among them celebrated American authors who made their mark on the city include Ernest Hemingway, F. Scott Fitzgerald, and Gertrude Stein. The city is also famous for its avant-garde artists such as Henri de Toulouse-Lautrec, Amedeo Modigliani, Juan Gris, and Pablo Picasso who populated right-bank, Montmartre, towered over by a beautiful church, the Sacré Coeur, on Paris' highest hill. A sense of the unconventional cafe and nightlife loved by these artists can be gotten from Toulouse-Lautrec's many paintings, but especially *A Corner of the Moulin de la Galette*. Today the narrow streets of Montmartre and the left-bank Boulevard St. Germaine des Pres fill with tourists (I have been in the crowd) who are trying to get a feel for what daily life must have been like for Paris' cultural luminaries.

Why Does Everyone Love Paris?

Americans have a special place in there hearts for Paris, as do many others around the world. The hotels of Paris chalked up more than 15.4 million individual arrivals in 2006 of which 8.8 million came from outside of France and 1.5 million from the U.S.[4] Paris is amongst the most visited cities in the world. Why do so many people want to visit such a densely packed, crowded city? After all, Paris itself covers only a bit more than 105 square kilometers of land but contains almost 2.2 million residents. Scottsdale, Arizona, one of my favorite upscale American suburbs, possesses 480 square kilometers and has just 220,000 residents. Visitors come to Paris of course to see its unmatchable attractions, such as the Notre-Dame Cathedral, Sacré-Coeur Basilica, the Louvre, and the Eiffel Tower. Paris contains so many attractions that scores of tourists visit repeatedly to take them all in. It is not just the museums, the shopping areas such as the Champs-Élysées, the architectural wonders, or the grand boulevards that people want to experience. They also want to enjoy Paris's restaurants, cafes, colorful markets, parks and open spaces, walkways along the Seine, neighborhoods with their intimate lanes and squares, impromptu cultural events and street entertainments, and creative nighttime lighting. Most of all, people want to gain a sense of what it's like to live in a place like Paris. This is especially the case for visitors who return to the city multiple times. Surveys of tourists suggest that repeat visitors work hard at avoiding the touristy parts of the city and devote their efforts to getting out into the neighborhoods and experiencing the everyday Parisian life. They want to "enjoy the atmosphere and environment of the city." Instead of rushing around to see the major sites, the experienced visitor adopts a more relaxed pace, taking time to search out the interesting details of Paris's cityscape.[5] Guidebooks, such as *Rick Steves' Paris 2006*, devote considerable space to Paris's main attractions, but they also usually offer suggested walking tours that give one a taste of the city's neighborhoods. Steves' guidebook supplies an introductory window into Parisian streetlife. If you read through his walking tour for the popular right-bank Marais neighborhood, you gain a sense of the features that many people enjoy in a city. As Steves emphasizes, the Marais contains more pre-Revolutionary narrow-lanes and buildings than most other Paris neighborhoods. The street-level scale of Marais appeals more to most than the wide, traffic-clogged boulevards blasted out in the mid-1800s under the direction of Baron Georges-Eugene Haussmann, someone will have more to say about shortly. Luckily Marais managed to avoid 'Haussmannization.' Steves' takes you to the key historic sites in the Marais, such as Place de la Bastille, but he also leads you through intimate courtyards containing interesting architectural details and to the park-like setting of Place des Vosges with sandboxes for children, benches for lovers, fountains for pigeons, and shaded trees for all to escape from the summer heat. He also takes you to blocks lined with not just fashionable boutiques, but with antique shops, cafes, interesting eateries, and food shops that reflect the area's Jewish and Muslim heritage, two groups that seem to have little trouble living here side-by-side. Parisian's love there markets, and Steves' ends the tour at rue Montorgueil across the border into Montmartre where a daily market flourishes in a traffic-free setting.[6] The one problem with Marais today is the invasion of hoards of high-fashion boutiques that displace boulangeries, cafes, and other businesses that make for a functional and interesting street life. The local Jewish community appears to be under siege from the influx of money driving up local real estate prices.

The walls around Paris defined and shaped its pattern of growth over time. Containment within walls historically meant growth in population density to the bursting point, construction of new walls farther out, and a repetition of the cycle. The final Eighteenth Century "Farmer's-General" wall, encompassing much of modern Paris, allowed the city's rulers to collect taxes on all the goods entering the city, which Thomas Jefferson, by the way, found appalling. Today the *boulevard Péripherique* replaces the wall as a barrier defining the city's boundary, and the outer boundary of Paris' suburbs extends well beyond the city itself, encompassing just over 12,000 square kilometers and 6.4 million residents.[7] Recall that Paris itself covers just 105 square kilometers and possesses a population of 2.2 million individuals. The growth of Paris and its extraordinary density caused the city to be in a state of crisis by the end of the Eighteenth Century. The city lacked a functional circulatory system—navigating the crooked and narrow streets of Paris made life unpleasant to say nothing about the problems posed by sewage and accumulating garbage.

The modern transformation of Paris began under Napoleon I, but it didn't really get moving until George-Eugéne Haussmann became the prefect of the Seine (1853-1870) under the rule of Louis-Napoléon Bonaparte, or Napoléon III, nephew of Napoleon I. By this time, Paris had become an industrial powerhouse along with being France's center of government and finance. Haussmann's charge was to bring order to the streets of Paris, and he did so at great expense by punching grand boulevards through the city's decrepit and overcrowded neighborhoods. He went so far as to have torn down the house of his own birth when he cut the boulevard that bears his own name.

He was borne George-Eugéne Haussmann in 1907 in a family of military officers and politicians who served under the Emperor Napoleon. While his name has German roots, his family had lived in France for four generations. His paternal grandfather made money in the cloth trade, and his maternal grandfather was given the title of Baron of the Empire as a reward for service to the Emperor Napoleon. For this reason Haussmann referred to himself later in life as "Baron" instead of just the more technically correct "Monsieur." He studied law and attended courses on the side at the Sorbonne in philosophy, mathematics, and geology. Through astute political maneuvering and a record of success in the government bureaucracy, he worked his way up to prefect of the Seine under Napoleon III.[8]

The funds needed to carry out the renewal of Paris were borrowed on the expectation that new development and increased commerce would ultimately generate more than enough new tax revenues to pay off the resulting debt. The process didn't always work this way, and financial problems emerged periodically, but Haussmann's reshaping of Paris continued anyway. Along with most of the grand boulevards we see in Paris today, much of the city's green space, and its water supply and sewer system, originated with the work of Haussmann. Street width was one of his obsessions—he doubled the average width of streets in the older part of Paris from 39 to 79 feet. Wider streets not only improved vehicular and pedestrian circulation within the city, but accommodated trees and improved air circulation. Some argued that wide boulevards eased the task of moving troops into neighborhoods to suppress urban rebellions. Unlike many large cities in the U.S. with their monocentric business cores, Paris today contains multiple hubs connected by boulevards, most of which were planned by Haussmann to visually terminate in a monumental building or structure, the classic example being the ending of the Champs-Élysées at the Arc de Triomphe. Haussmann's influence on the Paris cityscape remains today in expansive, tree-lined boulevards emanating like spokes on a bicycle wheel from "places" (open areas usually centered around a monument); uniform facades of buildings no more than six stories in height with classically styled decorative elements, mansard roofs, and four foot windows frequently with parapets set four feet apart; extensive tree-lined gardens and green spaces with paths for strolling and relaxing; uniformly designed street furnishings; and numerous public buildings including hospitals, local city halls, and churches. Haussmann's head architect, Gabriel Jean Antoine Davioud, inadvertently invented "street furniture" by filling Paris's public spaces with artfully decorated fountains, tree grates, benches, street lighting, trash receptacles, kiosks, and urinals.

The reshaping and opening up of Paris' cityscape under Haussmann came at a high price. Haussmann's numerous critics lamented his destruction of human scaled, intimate medieval neighborhoods that lay in the path of his boulevards, the displacing of the poor to slums in the outlying neighborhoods, and the creation of boring, repetitive blocks of high-end residential and commercial buildings. With the arrival of the automobile, some of the Haussmannized boulevards and places have become noisy, traffic-clogged areas pedestrians frequent at their discomfort if not peril, especially Place Charles De Gaulle, the home of the Arc de Triomphe.[9]

Paris since Haussmann has benefited especially from the construction of the Metro, an underground subway system that will deliver you within a few blocks of wherever you want to go anywhere in the city. The Metro is a marvel of urban transportation efficiency, except of course when the transportation unions call a strike in protest of an attack by government on their own or other workers' standard of living or conditions of labor. The impact of traffic-laden boulevards on pedestrians have been softened somewhat by wider sidewalks, bike and bus lanes, bus shelters, and rows of trees and parking that separate and buffer walkers from fast-moving vehicles. Parisians love their cars just like Americans, but high gasoline taxes along with parking limitations motivate the French to choose smaller models and to own fewer per household. The Parisian planners in recent years have become experts at separating motor vehicles from pedestrians, making extensive use of bollards—short cement rectangular columns or round iron stanchions—to keep cars out of pedestrian territory. Planners have even gone so far as to close numerous shopping streets to all vehicular traffic except for delivery vans, which have the magical ability of making the bollards retract before your eyes. Paris has not been immune from human-scale killing skyscrapers, ugly public edifices, and stultifying high-rise apartment complexes. Despite such errors, much of Paris continues to be an easy-to-navigate pedestrian paradise with visual delights at almost every turn. The recent implementation of a bicycle rental system with numerous stations throughout the city has proven to be a popular addition to the city's transportation system. Simply rent a bike at one location, after swiping a credit card in a reader to unlock it, and return at another. A second recent environmentally friendly trend in the city is the explosion in the use of fuel-efficient motor bikes. Sadly, the ability to park them on sidewalks and the need to dodge them crossing streets adds to pedestrian woes.

The special advantages of compact living in a place like Paris include proximity, diversity, and scale. The Parisian cafe life, which proved so fascinating and stimulating to Sartre, depends for its survival on a sufficiently large clientele who live within walking distance. Cafes enable both vicarious and actual social engagement and thrive on the diversity of personality and cultural type they attract. We don't want to hang out in a cafe to look only at people just like us. We instead desire the opportunity to fantasize about what another's life very different from our own might be like, or perhaps to look askance at someone of whom we don't approve. In the same vein, a diverse street life makes wandering through Paris especially interesting with different sorts of people hurrying about pursuing a diversity of purposes and goals. Someone like Sartre depended as well on the scale of a variety of activities made possible by compact living in a large city. The ability for him to successfully write and have performed his somewhat esoteric plays, or to give lectures on philosophy, requires a large, concentrated population in order for there to be an audience of sufficient size. Writers and artists naturally migrate to large, dense cities with there ready access to libraries, universities, publishers, bookstores, theaters, art museums and galleries, cheap living space, cafes, and self-selected communities of the like-minded. Compact living has its own inherent virtues, but is made especially pleasant by pedestrian friendly streetscapes and green spaces that a place like Paris has to offer. Tourists and residents alike find a special joy in the streets, parks, and squares of Paris.

Life in a compact world can be good, but it isn't all a bed of roses. A price is to be paid for compactness—noise, crowds, traffic congestion, and threatening people. The ultimate limitation of compact living is space. Paris covers roughly 105 square kilometers and contains within its boundaries 2,168,000 residents, meaning that each gets not quite 50 square meters. Of Paris' total land area, parks, gardens, squares, and other open spaces cover roughly just 1.5 percent, but when we add the huge Bois de Boulogne and Bois de Vincennes, expansive parks and woodlands on the city's west and east edges, the figure goes up to 17 percent.[10] Streets, boulevards, sidewalks, and service roads bring the total area covered by public spaces to nearly 30 percent. The remainder is left for Paris' businesses, public buildings, and dwellings. Each Paris dwelling on average has a useful floor area of roughly 58 square meters (600+ square feet), giving each resident an average of about 31 square meters (Paris' average household includes 1.87 individuals).[11] For France as a whole, the average householder enjoys about 37 square meter of floor space.[12] By American standards living in France would not be considered very spatially expansive. The median dwelling in the U.S. includes about 160 square meters (1,700+ square feet), or roughly 62 square meters per occupant (assuming 2.6 individuals per household).[13] The typical Parisian lives in about half the space of the typical American. The virtue of compact living in Paris is ready access to the city that everyone, especially Americans, loves to visit.

We know from the Parisian experience people readily fall in love with compact cities that have certain qualities. There is no better place to go than the writings of Jane Jacobs to discover those qualities that make for attractive urban spaces. In her classic work, *The Death and Life of Great American Cities*, Jane Jacobs offers powerful arguments for high density cities as we have already pointed out, but she bears repeating.[14] Her emphasis is on the importance of vibrant neighborhoods. According to Jacobs: (1) a city's neighborhoods should serve more than one primary function, ideally more than two; (2) most blocks should be short and the opportunity to turn corners should be frequent; (3) neighborhoods should mingle buildings that vary in age and condition and should include older buildings; and (4) the density of population must be sufficient to support the purposes for which people are attracted to a neighborhood. For streets to be successful and offer a sense of security and safety, people must appear on them throughout the day, a phenomenon that commonly occurs in neighborhoods having several different primary uses. Neighborhood streets are active all day if people come to work in the neighborhood in the morning, spill out on the streets for lunch, and go home again at night; if local residents come out to shop in between; and if people come to the area in the evening for the restaurants or entertainment. Streets that are used steadily are safe for adults and children alike, and are attract casual social contacts. Short blocks create a variety of paths through a neighborhood to the benefit of pedestrians, but long blocks are isolating and less used by neighborhood residents. A city needs a mixture of older buildings to attract an assortment of new businesses that can't afford very high rents. Older buildings with low rents can often be cleverly adapted to new uses and serve as incubators for new enterprises. These are the features Jacobs envisions for a socially successful city and they are exactly the features one finds in the neighborhoods of Paris.

Visitors marvel at the efficiency of Paris's underground subway system. One can get from any neighborhood in the city to any other in less than 30 minutes, as already noted. The importance of efficient urban transportation cannot be overemphasized and bears repeating. Every neighborhood in a large city benefits from ready access to every other neighborhood. Automobiles in a city like Paris continue to play a critical role in the Paris's urban matrix—Parisians like everyone else love cars—but space for motor vehicles in a successful high density city must be balanced against the needs of pedestrians and bicyclists. Traffic calming, helps attain this goal using wider sidewalks, center islands on streets and boulevards, and traffic circles. Traffic calming can be combined with landscaping on the widened sidewalks, center islands, and traffic circles to make streets increasingly attractive to pedestrians. People have left central cities for the suburbs in part because city life has often been given over to the automobile. Long unbroken streets with high speed traffic, narrow sidewalks, and a lack of landscaping are unappealing to pedestrians as are acres of parking lots or large, noisy freeway structures. Conversely, high density, pedestrian friendly cities combined with convenient public transportation are likely to win converts back to a less auto oriented way of life. This doesn't mean giving up cars completely, it just means balancing there use against other ways of getting around, as do Parisians.

Are Consumerism and Compact Living Compatible?

Americans need little tutoring on the virtues of suburban living: the opportunity to own a detached dwelling on a large lot; local control of schools and other government services; social and economic homogeneity; ready access to open spaces; convenience, comfort, and versatility of private motor vehicle transportation; ready access to a consumer wonderland in the form of shopping malls and big box retailers; and convenient commuting to suburban employment in the comfort of one's car. Americans who visit Paris become quickly aware of the merits of high density urban living but may not even think of applying them to their own personal circumstances at home. Judging from the recent condominium construction boom in many older U.S.

cities, at least some Americans are beginning to reconsider what can be gained by a return to central city living.

Admittedly, suburban life excels at serving the dream of access to the riches of a consumer society. Nonetheless, one cannot sell the densely packed city short in this regard. A consumer society is all about acquiring material possessions, and the central quest is to gain ownership of those goods that communicate to the world who we are and provide us with new and novel comforts and pleasures. I thoroughly enjoy visiting Scottsdale, Arizona on my annual trek to camping in the desert. Scottsdale, a high-end suburb next door to Phoenix, features the best of the modern consumer society with immediate access to Sonoran desert mountain landscapes thrown in as a special bonus. Is spatially expansive Scottsdale, Arizona any more, or less, of a consumer paradise than spatially compact Paris, France? In Scottsdale, acquiring new and novel consumer goods offers a special joy in its ease. Need a new Cadillac Escalade, just drop on down to the motor mile on Scottsdale Boulevard. Need a new Channel handbag or Cartier diamond, just head for the Fashion Square shopping mall.

Of course, Scottsdale can't even come close to the Champs-Élysées as a consumer heaven. In Paris, where cars are tiny, streets are often very narrow, and parking spots scarce by comparison to Scottsdale, one would not want a Cadillac Escalade, but plenty of other goods can be bought to advertise one's status or to experience the new and the novel. Paris, after all, is the global capitol for the production of fashion and luxury. As a Parisian, one can be a spatially compact consumer by living in a vertically stacked apartment where you can still have plenty of floor space if you are willing to pay for it and by owning a compact luxury car to get around the city. Luxury can take a compact form through an emphasis on the style of one's apparel (as the French do), on where one spends time (expensive restaurants, art galleries, operas, the theater, the symphony, expensive resorts), or on what one collects (art objects can be displayed in one's spacious, but compactly arranged luxury apartment). While one would not be able to buy a single story ranch-style house with a swimming pool and mountain views in Paris, you could acquire a stylishly appointed apartment near the River Seine, art museums, theaters, and fashionable restaurants and cafes. Hedonism and the pumping up of happiness that goes with constant additions to consumption are obtainable in both spatially expansive Scottsdale and spatially compact Paris. The point is simple—a form of life rooted in consumption is feasible in both low-density, auto-oriented suburbs such as Scottsdale and spatially compact cities such as Paris. Consumerism doesn't discriminate in providing opportunities between those who live in the suburbs and those who live in highly dense cities.

The affluent consumers of Scottsdale and Paris fall at the extreme high end of the global wealth distribution, but there is no reason to believe that the middle ground of consumption would obey different behavioral rules. If the middle class shifts to high density living, the consumer economy will adapt since that is where the bulk of its profits reside. Consumerism as a social phenomenon is independent of spatial compactness. Affluent middle class Europeans who live at high densities enjoy no less of a consumer economy than their spatially expansive American counterparts.

The projects we choose in life influence the way we use space. If, like Jean-Paul Sartre, we choose to pursue a life of the intellect and care little about accumulating material wealth—for many years Sartre lived in cramped hotel rooms and spent his days writing and conversing in cafes—then we would use little space. If we choose the path of the modern consumer of the kind found in Scottsdale, Arizona—living in a 10,000 plus square foot house (930 square meters) on a large lot, driving a large luxury motor vehicles, and enjoying the many shopping and dining opportunities Scottsdale has to offer —then space will be used more expansively. If we can afford to live in Scottsdale, we could also afford to live in Paris where a consumer economy is also readily available, although of a different kind.

In the Paris area, we will now see that one can actually enjoy the benefits of compact living along with those things we love about suburbs.

Compact Living in a Parisian Suburb

Saint-Quentin-en-Yvelines is a "new town" built on 7,000 hectares of land 20 kilometers west of Paris near Versailles. Having once served as an outdoor playground for the French aristocracy, the land on which the town sits retains a mix of beautiful woodlands and numerous ponds. The town as a whole includes seven different municipalities (communes) which add up in population to 147,000.[15] The population density of the town equals 2,100 individuals per square kilometer which amounts to about 476 square meters per person, or more than twice the same figure for the Paris urbanized area as a whole. The fairly high density "streetcar" era suburb where I live, Shorewood, Wisconsin, has 301 square meters of land surface per resident, a modest amount by American standards (the average for 13 large urbanized areas in U.S. is 700 square meters per person). Saint Quentin on its face looks like a fairly low density, spread out suburb, not that much different from the American experience.[16]

A closer look at the town's spatial arrangement tells a somewhat different story. Within its boundaries, more than 40 percent of Saint Quentin's surface area is devoted to woodlands, water, and other kinds of open space. In short, population density for the land in strictly urbanized use is more like 3,500 individuals per square kilometer yielding a per capita surface area of 285 square meters, somewhat less than what I get in my home suburb. Essentially, what Saint Quentin has done is retain much of its landscape in a natural condition and concentrate business and housing development at fairly high densities. This is confirmed in a tour around the town by the presence of significant numbers of three and four story multiunit residential buildings. The downtown pedestrian-only retail mall is also at fairly high density with 2-4 story structures surrounded by taller office buildings. Wherever one is in the town, woods and water are never very far away. The virtues of high density are gained without sacrificing access to green space. Many of the buildings are standard modernist architectural fare but have been designed on a human scale, and a number originated from some of France's leading architects who have sometimes given their works here an eye-catching if controversial whimsical quality.

Saint-Quentin-en-Yvelines is a product of France's 1960s new town movement, an effort to solve critical social problems that became apparent in the wake of World War II—urban crowding and a housing shortage worsened by rapid population expansion in the Paris region. From the beginning, new towns were a product of central planning. As the story goes, Charles de Gaulle took his head urban planner, Paul Delouvrier, for a helicopter ride over the Paris area in 1961 and told him to bring a bit of order to all that they could see below. This is exactly what happened. A plan for the Paris region established La Défense just outside the city boundaries as the region's second central business district and five new towns which were to absorb the bulk of the region's population and employment growth. La Défense, with its high-rise glass office towers and its stark rectangular memorial arch, stands in sharp contrast to the classic beauty and human scale of historical Paris right next door. At the same time the five new towns were being developed, a regional passenger rail system, the RER, was constructed to connect them to the Paris area as a whole. On top of dealing with the effects of rapid population growth, part of the strategy for creating distinct concentrations of population and employment rather than a general spreading was to protect the green spaces in between. In the 1970s and 1980s, Saint Quentin grew rapidly and became a family oriented bastion of the French middle class with numerous young families, many of who derive their income from employment in the professions or as managers.[17] The town has attracted its share of high-tech employment, including Renault's technology center.[18]

Today in the U.S. members of the middle class see two distinct possibilities in choosing where to live. Either one can enjoy the rural ideal with its spacious living and close access to the countryside in the suburbs, or one can live according to an urban ideal and take pleasure in the cultural amenities ready at hand in a spatially compact central city. In Saint-Quentin-en-Yvelines one appears to be able to satisfy both ideals simultaneously. Residents have access to both urban amenities that come with compact living and beautiful nearby rural open spaces within their "new town" boundaries.

Notes

[1] Annie Cohen-Solal, *Jean-Paul Sartre: A Life* (New York: New Press, 2005).

[2] Jean-Paul Sartre, *Being and Nothingness: A Phenomenological Essay on Ontology* (New York: Washington Square Press, 1992).

[3] Cohen-Solal, *Jean-Paul Sartre: A Life.*

[4] Paris Office of Tourism, *Tourism in Paris:2006* (Paris Office of Tourism, 2007 [cited April 30, 2009]); available from http://www.parisinfo.com/uploads/bd//chiffres_cles_2007_2.pdf.

[5] T. Freytak, "Making a Difference: Tourist Practices of Repeat Visitors to the City of Paris," *Social Geography Discussions* 4, no. 1 (2008); Douglas G. Pearce, "Tourist Districts in Paris: Structure and Functions," *Tourism Management* 19, no. 1 (1998).

[6] David Downie, *Paris, Paris: Journey into the City of Light* (Fort Bragg, CA: Transatlantic Press, 2005); Rick Steves, Steve Smith, and Gene Openshaw, *Rick Steves' Paris 2006* (Emeryville, CA: Avalon Travel Publishing, 2005).

[7] Paris Office of Tourism, *Tourism in Paris:2006* ([cited).

[8] David P. Jordan, *Transforming Paris: The Life and Labors of Baron Haussmann* (Chicago: University of Chicago Press, 1995).

[9] Ibid.

[10] Michel Carmona, *Haussmann: His Life and Times, and the Making of Modern Paris* (Chicago: Ivan. R. Dee, Inc., 2002).

[11] Alfred Dittgen, "Housing and Household Size in Local Population Dynamics: The Example of Paris," *Population* 60, no. 3 (2005).

[12] Department of Housing Walloon Region of Belgium, *Housing Statistics in the European Union 2002* (Walloon Region of Belgium, Department of Housing, 2002 [cited April 30, 2009]); available from http://mrw.wallonie.be/dgatlp/dgatlp/Pages/Log/DwnLd/Stats2002/housingStats2002.pdf.

[13] U.S. Bureau of the Census, *The 2009 Statistical Abstract* ([cited]).

[14] Jacobs, *The Death and Life of Great American Cities*.

[15] Saint-Quentin-en-Yvelines, *Observatoire De La Ville: Fiche Population* (Saint-Quentin-en-Yvelines, 2008 [cited November 4, 2009]); available from http://www.saint-quentin-en-yvelines.fr/fileadmin/portail/MEDIA/Decouvrir/SQY_en_chiffres/Thematiques_de_territoire/Demographie/Agglom%C3%A9ration%20-%20demographie.pdf.

[16] European New Towns Platform, *Home Page for St. Quentin En Yvelines* (Europeans New Town Platform, 2009 [cited November 4, 2009]); available from http://www.newtowns.net/Members/st-quentin-en-yvelines/home-page-for-st-quentin-en-yvelines.

[17] Shearmur and Alvergne, "Regional Planning Policy and the Location of Employment in the Ile-De-France: Does Policy Matter?"

[18] Institut National de la Statisque et des Etudes Economiques, *Les Villes Nouvelles: Atlas Statistique, 1968-1999* (Insee, 2004 [cited November 5, 2009]); available from http://www.insee.fr/fr/themes/document.asp? ref_id=9056.

Chapter 4
Happiness and Compact Living

Researchers have found a new holy grail for investigating the age old question of how we attain happiness in our lives. The simplicity of the approach is ingenious—just ask people about how happy they are about their lives. The standard question for doing this has the following form: "Taking all things together, would you say you are very happy, rather happy, not very happy, or not at all happy?" Surveys asking this question in the U.S. go all the way back to 1946. Amazingly, the average score for happiness on a 1 to 4 scale, with 4 referring to "very happy" and 1 to "not at all happy," has remained quite stable over time. In 1946 the mean happiness score came in at 3.3 while in 2006 it hit a bit above 3.4. The score drifted downward to near 3.2 in the 1970s and has trended upward very slightly since.[1] The happiness score has remained relatively stable even though our real gross domestic product per person, the value of all the stuff we produce and enjoy, has increased more than 3-fold.[2] In short, we have tripled the amount of material stuff and services we receive, but we on average are no happier for it. For most other affluent western countries, the results of happiness surveys exhibit a comparable pattern.

If we expand our horizon and take a picture of happiness across a range of countries from poor to rich, we get a somewhat different view. Happiness tends to increase across countries up to roughly $15,000 in GDP per capita and then flattens out above that. In short, as a country develops and increases its standard of living, happiness rises, but only up to a maximum threshold level beyond which added average income does little for a country's happiness. As we will soon see, happiness derives less from economic conditions than a range of other factors. At an average output of less than a quarter of its neighbor to the North, one would think that Mexicans would be much less happy than Americans. Surprisingly Mexico's average happiness score lies slightly above that of the U.S.[3] Money must not be everything when it comes to happiness.

Despite constancy in average well being, the richest quarter of all Americans are typically happier than the poorest in the U.S. Money does have its virtues when it comes to happiness within a country just as it does across countries. For the rich in the U.S., 45 percent are very happy and 4 percent are not too happy, while for the poor, 33 percent are very happy and 14 percent are not too happy.[4] A benefit of moving up the income distribution in the U.S. is a gain in happiness. As our country as a whole gets wealthier, we don't gain in overall happiness, but as any one of us increases our income relative to others we personally become happier. The relationship between happiness and income is relative, not absolute. So if you have more money and can buy more stuff than others, you are likely to be happier, but as everyone expands their spending power proportionately along with you, your happiness will remain unchanged. Where you stand in the economic pecking order matters for your happiness.

One might also think that if you buy a new house or a new car you will be permanently happier but happiness research tells us otherwise. The reality seems to be that you get excited at first, especially in anticipation of the acquisition, but eventually you get used to what you own, and your felt happiness settles back down to what it was before. Happiness can be pumped up with new and novel acquisitions, but only temporarily. In short, if our income rises and we buy more stuff, we experience an immediate rush of good feelings, but over time we adapt to our new circumstances. A new fancier cell phone is fun at first, but its novelty eventually wears off. Our happiness returns to a baseline set point. We get used to our new bundle of goods, and to get more pleasure, we will need to increase our purchases yet again.

How do we explain the paradoxical conclusion that *individually* we can become happier by increasing our income and consumption, but *collectively* happiness cannot be raised through such increases for everyone? As all our incomes go up together, we all get a lift in our positive feeling state from our added ability to consume, but it doesn't last. We soon become habituated to our new economic circumstances and our happiness dampens back down to its set point norm. Nonetheless, as particular individuals gain in income and status compared to their peers, their happiness norm increases precisely because of their income or status gain. Being near the bottom of the economic pile in any society carries with it special stresses and feelings of alienation. Just talk to those who have to live in low-income inner city neighborhoods and they will tell you about the anxieties they face in their daily lives. Pulling away economically from such strains by moving up the income distribution will in all likelihood increase felt happiness. Also, for those individuals who gain feelings of superiority by being materially better off than others, their felt happiness will likely increase as they move up the income distribution. Relative well being plays a role in shaping happiness, although the happiness researchers tell us that while the statistical relationship between relative income and happiness is positive it is not especially strong.[5]

Notwithstanding what the Madison Avenue advertising gurus tell us, happiness is largely a non-economic affair. Abject poverty brings misery, but once we reach a secure economic threshold, other factors dominate in shaping our feeling states. Some of us have an inherently sunnier outlook than others, but beyond that the circumstance of our lives matter for our sense of well being, a rather obvious conclusion confirmed by the statistical work of happiness researchers. Our financial situation makes a difference in our happiness, but not as much as one might think. A reduction of our income by a third is much less damaging to happiness than a divorce or separation, never being married, becoming totally unemployed, a significant deterioration in our health, a loss of freedom through government oppression, or a lack of a belief in a higher power. What really matters in our life according to happiness research is our family connections, work, friendship, trust in others, health, personal freedom, and personal values that connect us to the larger world.[6] We are social beings. We want to be in the company of others, and we especially enjoy marriage and having a successful family life. Nothing makes us quite as unhappy as a divorce or other upsets to our family equilibrium.   Second to family disruption, unemployment is especially damaging, not only because of economic loss, but because of the breaking of social ties formed in the workplace.   Health is important to our happiness, although many amazingly adjust to permanent disabilities and still find joy in life.   Whether we feel we can trust those around us in our neighborhood and on the streets we walk affects our happiness as well.   Finally the values we have influence our sense of well being.   Individuals who habitually help others or promote the common good in some way often experience added happiness as a consequence. So do those who feel a connection to something larger than themselves, such as to a religion or some encompassing philosophy of life.   While Nineteenth Century philosopher Frederich Nietzsche claims that "God is dead," those who believe in God and participate actively in a religion are happier than those who don't.   God indeed may be dead, but it is better for one's happiness to believe otherwise.

So far nothing we have said tells us whether any connection exists between felt happiness and either compact urban or spatially expansive suburban living. Happiness studies so far don't directly address the impact of high-density city versus low-density suburban living.   One recent cross-country statistical study finds that neither the proportion of urban population nor population density has any significant affect on average happiness (although it does find that we feel a bit better in moderate climates).[7]   The U.S., Canada, and Australia all have relatively high average happiness and low population densities, but some countries in Europe, such as Denmark and the Netherlands, have both high average happiness and high densities.[8] Density thus appears to lack a relationship to happiness. One can be equally happy living at low density in the suburbs (the Scottsdale's of the world) or at high density in compact cities (the Paris's of the world).

With a little thought, this conclusion stands to reason. Suburbs make the acquisition of material possessions incredibly convenient.   If one's life-project is the accumulation of wealth and possessions, then living in a low-density suburb is an obvious choice to make.   As the Parisian experience makes clear, you don't have to live at low densities to thoroughly enjoy the fruits of the consumer economy. Paris is the birthplace of institutions important to modern consumerism—the department store, luxury goods, and high fashion.   The content of the consumer bundle might alter as urban density goes up—smaller luxury cars rather than large; spacious apartments in multistory buildings instead of detached suburban-style homes; more meals at fancy restaurants and fewer barbecues by the pool—but the pleasure dynamic will remain the same. A new addition to the consumer bundle will cause a surge in pleasure and happiness that will erode away, taking one back to one's underlying happiness benchmark.   If one has money to burn, then additions to felt happiness through consumption increases can be carried out in spatially expansive suburbs or dense central cities.

Many of us choose life projects other than a pure pursuit of consumer goods. We may enjoy an occasional trip to the mall and feel a surge of pleasure from buying a new car, but these activities don't dominate our lives. Our family, our friends, our religious or philosophical beliefs, our opportunities for the creative exercise of personal abilities, or what we do in the world that positively affects others matters more than our economic accomplishments, as happiness research seems to suggest. Whether the way we use space compactly or expansively for most of us may have little to do with these sources of happiness. While it may be true that Americans fled the central city in the 1950s and 1960s—partly out of crime fears and concerns about declining schools—raising development densities in the future and making suburbs more like cities would not alone necessarily increase crime or reduce the quality of schools or otherwise reduce the quality of life. High density European cities, such as Paris or Amsterdam, generally have low crime rates and decent school systems.[9]

Higher densities in truth may improve conditions for realizing certain passions in life. The struggling artist, actor, writer, political activist, or Buddhist visionary can probably find a niche in Paris, or any other large, densely packed city, but probably not in a spatially expansive American suburb. Big, dense cities contain high-rise buildings with cheap rents affordable by those pursuing interesting, but not very high paying, occupations. One needn't own a motor vehicle in a densely packed city, which significantly reduces the cost of daily living. Big, dense cities also have the advantage of size. Diversity of social practice and size go together. The bigger and denser a city, the greater the diversity of its citizens' interests and values and the greater the diversity of its institutions. Esoteric groups, such as those wanting to debate the merits of different Greek philosophers or talk about the French existentialists or American pragmatists, will more likely find a reasonable threshold of interest in the Paris's of the world than in any suburb. Paris is historically famous for its colonies of artists, writers, and public philosophers. This is not to say that smaller towns and cities don't draw creative types, but today Paris or New York or some other large city would probably be the better destination for someone with talent and an idiosyncratic passion for personal expression. Even if one's desire is to be a business entrepreneur, the big, dense, older city has advantages—cheap space, business services ready at hand, a diversely talented workforce for hire, and others with likeminded interests.

Not all of us will be artists or writers, but most of us would have little trouble finding an interesting life while at the same time living compactly. We will give up some of the comforts of suburban living such as spaciousness, the convenience of auto travel, the ready availability of low cost consumer goods in local shopping malls, but we will gain significant advantages as well including an interesting street life, convenient public transit, pleasing public landscapes and urban squares and parks, diverse cultural and social opportunities, a variety of educational institutions, access to a wide range of commercial establishments, and, most of all, urban excitement.

Notes

[1] You can look at happiness trends for 24 countries by going to: Ronald Inglehart et al., *Happiness Trends in 24 Countries, 1946-2000* (World Values Survey, 2008 [cited May 5, 2009]); available from http://www.worldvaluessurvey.org/happinesstrends/.

[2] Bureau of Economic Analysis U.S. Department of Commerce, *Gross Domestic Product (GDP)* (Bureau of Economic Analysis, 2009 [cited May 5, 2009]); available from http://www.bea.gov/national/index.htm#gdp.   The term "real" means that the effects of inflation have been removed from the data. "Real" refers to actual purchasing power.

[3] Ronald Inglehart et al., "Development, Freedom, and Rising Happiness," *Perspectives on Psychological Science* 3, no. 4 (2008); Richard Layard, *Happiness: Lessons from a New Science* (New York: Penguin, 2005).

[4] Layard, *Happiness: Lessons from a New Science.*

[5] Andrew E. Clark, Paul Frijters, and Michael A. Shields, "Relative Income, Happiness, and Utility: An Explanation for the Easterlin Paradox and Other Puzzles," *Journal of Economic Literature* 46, no. 1 (2008); Layard, *Happiness: Lessons from a New Science.*

[6] John F. Helliwell, "How's Life: Combining Individual and National Variables to Explain Subjective Well-Being," *Economic Modeling* 20, no. 2 (2003); Layard, *Happiness: Lessons from a New Science.*

[7] Katrin Rehdanz and Davide Maddison, "Climate and Happiness," *Ecological Economics* 52, no. 1 (2005).

[8] UN Economic Commissions for Europe, *Bulletin of Housing and Building Statistics* (UN Economic Commission for Europe, 2002 [cited May 6, 2009]); available from ttp://www.unece.org/hlm/prgm/hsstat/02pdf/pubH01_02.pdf.

[9] Crime in Europe relative to the U.S. is an insignificant problem. European cities such as Paris lack the high concentrations of poverty found in most U.S. central cities and thus don't experience the kind of central city school problems we have.   For comparative data on crime, see OECD, "OECD Regions at a Glance, 2009," (Paris: OECD, 2009).

Chapter 5
Compact Living as a Source of Green Energy

Recall figures for the amount of space American's consume compared to the French. In the lower 48, we citizens of the U.S. have roughly five football fields available to each of us in total, while the same number for the French is about one and a half football fields. Now most of us live in urban areas and have a spatial experience more limited in scope than inferred by data on the country as a whole. To illustrate what urban reality might look like in France and the U.S., let's compare two cities that are about the same size, Chicago, Illinois and Paris, France. Just as Paris is quintessentially French, Chicago embodies much of what is fundamentally American. Both have comparable populations within their city boundaries and in their larger urbanized areas. A big, obvious difference between the two cities is spatial. Parisians have a tight 50 square meters each within their city limits, but a more liberal 282 square meters each in the urban area as a whole. Inside Chicago's city limits each resident gets 210 square meters, while the comparable figure for the urbanized area as a whole is a substantial 631 square meters (10 percent plus of a football field or nearly 7,000 square feet).[1] Chicagoans clearly live more spatially expansive lives than Parisians.

To lead us into the connection between space and energy, let's move up to the national arenas for France and the U.S. for a moment. Each citizen of France consumes about 200 gigajoules of energy annually, 44 percent less than the typical American.[2] The French on average consume only 31 percent of the energy used by the typical American for transportation. Clearly, the French transportation system with its greater reliance on public transit achieves much higher energy efficiency than the American. In their residential dwellings, the typical French citizen uses 81 percent of the energy consumed by the typical American. This is unsurprising since the French have about 37 square meters (400 square feet) of living space each in their homes, which is about 60 percent of the comparable American amount, 62 square meters.[3] Americans consume more housing space which requires more heating, cooling, and lighting. The French consume only 33 percent of what Americans do on a per capita basis to heat, cool, and light their commercial and public buildings. Gross comparisons of energy efficiency in buildings is a perilous act without accounting for such details as heating and cooling degree day and average building age differences on top of the density of development (we will take up the question of energy consumption and living space in a later chapter). Comparisons of energy efficiency in transportation are not fraught with the same difficulties since climatic differences between cities are largely irrelevant for this task and the French and Americans each have the same transportation technologies available to them. Besides, transportation is where many opportunities for urban energy efficiency improvement can be found.

If we Americans each consumed the same amount of transportation energy as our French friends, we would cut our total energy consumption by

23 percent. We can get a better sense of the story behind this by comparing energy use for getting around Paris and Chicago. The typical resident of urban Paris consumes about 24 gigajoules of energy for transportation, while the typical resident of urban Chicago uses up roughly 56 gigajoules (equivalent to 430 gallons of gasoline), a bit more than twice as much as a Parisian. Interestingly, 96 percent of Paris's transportation energy consumption is private (personal motor vehicles), nearly the same as Chicago's at 98 percent. The big difference between the cities comes in the total amount of travel and the dramatically different split in travel between private and public transportation. In urban Chicago, the typical resident travels 14,000 kilometers (km) per year by private motor vehicle but only 800 km on public transit (1 km=.62 miles). In urban Paris, the typical resident travels 5,000 km by car and 2,000 km on public transit. Simply put, because they live at higher densities and don't need to move around so much, Parisians travel much less than Chicagoans. Parisians also use public transportation more extensively in their travels than Chicagoans, which is much more energy efficient per kilometer than the private motor vehicle. Traveling by the Paris underground is eight times as fuel efficient as navigating the city by auto.

One might be surprised to learn that differences in fuel efficiency between motor vehicles in Paris and Chicago explain very little of the overall difference in per capita energy consumption. European motor vehicles indeed use about 30 percent less gasoline per kilometer than American cars. Europeans buy smaller, more fuel efficient cars mostly because gasoline taxes and prices in Europe are substantially higher than in the U.S. European governments see fuel taxes as a source of general revenues, not as just a means for funding highway projects, and as a way to push fuel prices up to encourage greater energy efficiency. Anyone who has driven in Europe also knows that small is better given the complex of streets of medieval width in most cities. A motor vehicle driven by a Parisian, on average, uses 10 percent less fuel in urban travel per kilometer than one driven by a Chicagoan, not the 30 percent implied by basic vehicle fuel efficiency differences. Because Parisians spend so much time stuck in traffic, slower travel speeds dampen the efficiency gains from owning smaller cars. Parisians consume much less transportation energy than Chicagoans not by driving smaller cars, but by traveling lesser distances and using public transportation more. Living in less space at a high population density means less travel and gives energy efficient public transit a special advantage. In spatially compact Paris, one can easily avoid being stuck in traffic by taking the Metro. [4]

How compact living reduces energy consumption in all sectors of urban economic life can by revealed to us more fully by returning to our own shores and looking at the densest city in the U.S., New York. Only New York approaches the density of Paris in this country—in New York each resident lives on an average of 147 square meters of space in comparison to the 50 square meters available to Parisians. The government of New York City recently took the initiative to undertake an inventory of its carbon emissions, sector-by-sector. Carbon emissions result directly from the burning of fossil fuels, meaning that lower emissions are the mirror reflection of less energy consumption. New Yorkers live at European densities and live in typically smaller dwellings than other Americans. They also avidly use energy efficient public transportation. Europeans love to visit New York, probably because in many ways it doesn't differ from the cities to which they are already accustomed. Annually the average New Yorker emits about 9 tons of carbon emissions divided up by source as follows: dwellings, 2.2; commerce, 2.6, industry, 0.7; public transit, 0.2, and motor vehicles, 1.4, and other transportation, 2.0. The average American emits about 20 tons a year from the following sources: dwellings, 4.1; commerce, 3.5; industry, 6; and total transportation, 6.3. In all categories, New Yorkers emit substantially less carbon than Americans as a whole, and this occurs even though the city suffers hot summers and cold winters, leading to a higher than average demand for heating buildings in the winter and cooling them in the summer. Compactness for dwellings, commerce, and transportation reduces energy consumption and therefore carbon emissions for New Yorkers relative to everyone else. Living in high-rise buildings with less floor space than the American norm saves New Yorkers almost half the energy needs for heating, cooling, and lighting that other Americans face, and results in a bit more than half the carbon emissions of other Americans. Compact living matters for residential energy use. Transportation offers comparable savings. New Yorkers emit 3.6 tons of carbon from transportation each while Americans as a whole release 6.3, not quite twice as much. Mass transit, biking, and walking put a big dent in energy consumption and carbon emissions for New Yorkers. Finally, New York's commercial sector discharges about a ton less per capita than its counterpart in the country as a whole. High rise commercial buildings apparently reap a bit more energy savings than suburban office parks and shopping malls. Industry in New York accounts for much less energy per capita than the country at large, primarily because New York has so little of it. New Yorkers get a bigger portion of their income from the information economy, a sector that is inherently much less energy intensive than industry. Compactness and high density distinguishes New York in all our minds—just think about the New York skyline—and results in substantial carbon admission reductions for New Yorkers relative to the rest of us. New Yorkers, like the French, each consume about half the energy of the typical American.[5]

The greenest and cleanest energy of all is that not consumed. Unconsumed energy takes nothing away from energy supplies and adds nothing to carbon emissions and climate warming. Compact urban living not only possesses internal virtues of its own, but it results in less energy consumption than would otherwise occur under a regime of spatially expansive suburban living. Compact living serves as an important source of truly green energy.

A comparison of spatial and energy consumption patterns in France and the U.S. makes the point about the connection between spatial compactness and energy conservation. Americans live spatially expansive lives (except for New Yorkers) and use more energy for personal transportation and space heating, cooling, and lighting than the French. With things farther apart and greater reliance on the automobile, Americans consume more energy than the French who travel much less by automobile and rely more heavily on energy efficient public transportation. The French typically live in dwellings with less floor space and consequently need less energy for heating, cooling, and lighting than Americans. Like the French, New York City's residents live compactly and use much less energy than the rest of us.

Stated simply, compact urban living requires much less energy consumption than spatially expansive suburban living. For compactness to work, one element is essential—decent, attractive, energy efficient public transit of the variety found in such cities as Toronto, Canada.

Notes

[1] See Chapter 1 for sources.

[2] International Energy Agency, *Key World Energy Statistics: 2008* (International Energy Agency, 2008 [cited]); available from http://www.iea.org/textbase/nppdf/free/2008/key_stats_2008.pdf.

[3] U.S. Bureau of the Census, *The 2009 Statistical Abstract* ([cited]); Walloon Region of Belgium, *Housing Statistics in the European Union 2002* ([cited]).

[4] Newman and Kenworthy, *Sustainability and Cities: Overcoming Automobile Dependency.*

[5] New York City, Mayor's Office of Operations, Office of Long-Term Planning and Sustainability, *Inventory of New York City Greenhouse Gas Emissions* (New York City, 2007 [cited May 7, 2009]); available from http://www.nyc.gov/html/om/pdf/ccp_report041007.pdf.

Chapter 6
Compact Green Urban Transportation

Green Urban Transportation in Toronto, Canada: Our American Future?

The traffic jams on the freeways and outward stretching suburbs in Toronto, Canada would be familiar to most residents of the U.S., but what would be new to many would be an extensive array of pedestrian friendly neighborhoods with a smoothly functioning system of subways, streetcar lines, and buses linking them together and to the downtown. If we American urbanites lived like Torontonians, our urban density would be more than twice what it is currently, and we would still each have on average 240 square meters of land area each to rattle around in. I think most U.S. visitors to Toronto will agree that life there doesn't look a whole lot different on the surface than, say, life in Chicago or Minneapolis, Minnesota. If we indeed lived at Torontonian densities and adopted the city's approaches to getting around, we would also use about half the energy we currently expend on urban transportation (33 gigajoules instead of 64), largely because we would drive our cars by less than half as much. Our urban driving would drop from an average of 16,000 kilometers per year to 7,000, while our travel on public transit would increase from about 500 kilometers per year each to around 2,000. Torontonians own the same sort of cars as Americans, so their ability to save on energy comes not from driving smaller cars, but simply from driving less because of the availability of high quality public transportation and pedestrian and bicyclist friendly urban design. Just living at higher densities in itself cuts back on the amount of driving one would have to do in daily life. On top of all this, Torontonians walk and bike to work at a 33 percent greater rate than urban Americans.[1]

Toronto started down the slippery slope to auto dominant transportation with the Spadina Freeway proposal that would have sliced through downtown and a number of older neighborhoods to the North. Opposition mounted to the Spadina from local neighborhood groups and included such notable figures as Jane Jacobs (*The Death and Life of Great American Cities*) and Marshall McLuhan. The opposition was able to kill the project at the provincial level of government. The Spadina Expressway was to be the lynchpin of a larger expressway system in the Toronto Metro area, but the death of the Spadina popped the balloon of expressway development and initiated a golden era of transit system expansion that continued to the 1990s. The Spadina subway line was built along the route of the proposed freeway, and other subway line extensions were constructed as well. Toronto never tore up its street car lines like many American cities and had constructed the beginnings of a subway system in the 1950s. Today the metro urban area is crisscrossed with a network of subways, street cars, and buses that feed a diesel-powered commuter rail system serving the outer suburbs.[2] Some backsliding on a commitment to public transit occurred in the late 1990s with the cancellation of a subway extension to the airport and cutbacks in planned transit investments, but new projects will provide a rapid transit line to the airport and create a new light rail system to augment the current extensive street car network.[3]

If you have an opportunity to visit Toronto, take a ride on its extensive network of updated trolley cars. You will be pleasantly surprised by how comfortable they are, how smoothly, quickly, and quietly they accelerate, and how fast you get to your destination. The red cars are a delight to ride and their presence adds to the attraction of the city's busy street life. Many of the trolley drivers are interesting themselves, not only giving detailed directions to where you want to go, but imparting tidbits of wisdom or making you laugh.

Light rail, trolleys, and subway lines in Toronto attract high density, multifunctional, pedestrian friendly residential and commercial development. Because renters and buyers pay more for dwellings with close access to rail transit, developers can afford to construct multistory dwellings. Greater foot traffic and residential density near transit stations increases the profitability of restaurants, espresso shops, bookstores, boutiques, and entertainment venues. Residential development with first floor retail and the abundant street life that goes with it creates especially interesting neighborhoods abutting subway stations and light rail and streetcar lines. Rather than seeing its population decline like many American cities, Toronto's central business district, served by an extensive network of subways, trolley cars, and commuter rail lines, added some 20,000 dwellings between 1975 and 1988.[4] If you live in or near downtown Toronto, you can get anywhere you want in the metro area with ease, just as suburban residents have little trouble getting to the city center with it economic and cultural riches.

Toronto feels much like any American city, only with the virtues of high quality public transit and compact living superimposed on it. We Americans are beginning to see the value in an urban place like Toronto. Increasingly we are investing light rail as an alternative to the motor vehicle. Light rail is essentially the modern version of the streetcar system of old, but with larger, modern cars connected in a train that operate on a dedicated off-street corridor, median strip, or street lane. If you have never done it, take a ride on a light rail line if available in your own city or when you visit Denver, Colorado, Portland, Oregon, Charlotte, North Carolina, San Diego, California, and, yes, even auto-dominated Phoenix, Arizona. I think you will soon discover the virtues of riding the light rail—reading a good book en route, people watching, daydreaming, or text-messaging if you are young and modern. On many lines you can take your bike along too.

One would think buses on dedicated bus-ways could do the same job as light rail, only at a much lower cost. With buses, a city can forego the capital cost of laying the track. The trouble is, middle class riders who could otherwise drive simply don't like buses. Much more than buses, light rail attracts the middle class because of its interior spaciousness and seat availability, schedule reliability, ease of transfers to other lines and modes, visual appeal of the stations, the feel of rapid acceleration that comes with electric propulsion, simplicity of the route system, and a sense of permanence emanating from a fixed rail system. Buses that feed a rail system attract riders more readily because people know that the light rail will be a part of their journey.[5]

Critics complain that light rail is doomed to failure in spread-out auto-dependent suburbs. People are just too far apart for there to be enough density to sustain mass transit rider-ship at a level sufficient to reduced auto-use. For most, the walk to the station is too far, and once you are in your car you might as well just go to you final destination as opposed to a park-and-ride lot. Contrary to the critics, light rail, it turns out, has a certain "field of dreams" quality—"build it and they will come." The Englewood Station neighborhood on Denver's light rail offers a perfect example. In the middle of a traffic-laden suburb, high-density, pedestrian friendly building development has sprung up. Near the station, 3-story condominiums and apartments are set on tree-lined blocks with lower-story businesses abutting the sidewalk, including a coffee shop on a key corner with outdoor seating and a large, interesting statute of a lion. The sidewalks are wide and on-the-street parking separates and buffers the traffic from pedestrians. A pleasant green space with public art and a fountain fronts the Englewood Station which is approached by a dramatic, tubular white bridge with a mini-Washington Monument-like obelisk just to the left of its entrance. Seemingly oxymoronic suburban compactness becomes a possibility once the right kind of public transit system is in place, and people in the Englewood neighborhood seem to love it.

Street-Level Urban Design and Getting Around

High quality compact living and good public transit interact. To enjoy compact living, one must be able to get around easily, and the space demands of the motor vehicle makes this too challenging of a transport mode in a high density urban environment. Simply put, cars take up too much space and create too much congestion. Conversely, public transit, especially light rail and subways, thrive in high density settings where transit trip demand will be substantial.

Compact living needs efficient public transit and vice versa. To make compact living and public transit use appealing, streets have to feel comfortable to pedestrians. People in compact cities have to walk the streets to get to public transit stops and most anywhere else. City living and walking go together. The view from the sidewalk should be both stimulating and comforting just as it is around the Englewood Station in Denver or in many Toronto neighborhoods—Chinatown and Greektown are among my favorites. Pedestrian comfort depends heavily on a clear separation from motor vehicle traffic on abutting streets. Wide sidewalks and trees and other vegetation, such as shrubs and flowers in large planters, provide a sense of protection from cars, as do a line of parked cars themselves. Small landscaped plazas with benches or a pocket park always appear inviting to the passerby and may even attract some to linger. Buildings of no more than four or five stories with interesting facades appeal to the pedestrian while tall massive structures are overpowering and alienating. The skyscraper office district in Toronto suffers mightily from the latter problem with its canyon-like pedestrian environments. Walkers appreciate sensual stimuli along a street front including sidewalk cafes or espresso shops, interesting restaurants, the smells emanating from a popular bakery, small public markets with artistically arranged fruit or seafood, bookstores or newsstands, kiosks announcing events, and boutiques and other specialty retailers. Pedestrian comfort and interesting visual stimuli come from attention to such details by city planners such as traffic calming with traffic circles, narrow streets, on-street parking, and strategically placed attractive bollards to keep delivery vans and cars off of sidewalks; street furniture and street-level landscaping; placement of public art, plazas, and fountains; zoning that limits building height, requires buildings to front on sidewalks, and allows for a variety of functions to occur in any given neighbor such as residences, offices, retail outlets, restaurants, and entertainment venues. Above all, we find walking interesting and secure with the presence of large numbers of other people. As Jane Jacobs tells us, this occurs where density is high, blocks are short, and a variety of reasons for being there is present. Cities with successful neighborhoods, such as a Paris, New York, San Francisco, and Toronto, pay attention to these kinds of details.

Getting Around by Bike

Walking and public transit are not the only ways of getting around densely pack urban environments. Portland, Oregon sees itself as the bicycle capital of the world, and it is able to do so in a damp and rainy climate. Despite its 153 days of rain each year, Portland ranks among the top 3 cities in the country for the proportion of workers who commute on a bike.[6] A complex of convenient bike lanes and trails is part of the explanation, but more than anything a culture of biking has evolved in Portland like nowhere else. A huge complex of organizations, bike stores, and other businesses has emerged in the city to support biking.[7] Riding a bike in Portland is almost a social necessity.

Even in Toronto with its frigid winters a large number of people ride their bikes to work. Minneapolis, Minnesota is the top bicycle commuting city in the country despite its extremely cold winter weather.[8] Cities that create systems of bike paths and lanes and provide bike lockups and other forms of storage stimulate the use of bikes for getting around at a substantial savings in energy resources and commuting costs. In European cities, such as Paris and Lyon, France, you can now rent a bike with the flick of a credit card at one of many conveniently located rental stations and simply drop it off at another near your destination. In many cities—Portland is a case in point—buses and light rail cars have bike racks, so one can incorporate public transit in commuting by bike. Again, attention to the simple things by city planners makes the difference.[9]

Costs, Cars, and Public Transit

Biking or walking to work clearly beats the cost of driving a car, but what about the cost of public transit relative to motor vehicles? We know that public transit yields big savings in the amount of energy resources required for getting around, but how do the costs compare for public and private (motor vehicle) transportation? While operating and capital costs for rail and motor vehicles per mile traveled are very close, when we add in social costs, such as those associated with road construction and maintenance, accidents, and pollution, the total cost of auto travel carries a 30 to 40 percent premium over rail transit. In Boston for example, the total cost of a typical suburb-to-city commute runs more than $10 by car while the same figure for rail amounts to about $6.[10] One might complain about subsidies to mass transit—the fare box doesn't cover the full cost of operations for most public transit systems—but cars are heavily subsidized as well.[11] Car owners don't directly pay for road construction funded by property and other non-fuel related taxes nor the costs of pollution and traffic congestion, traffic control and law enforcement, and uninsured damages. In short, everyone who commutes gets some kind of subsidy. The point is, we as a society will pay less of the overall costs per mile traveled if we shift from the automobile to public transit.

Achieving Clean Energy—Compact Living and the Motor Vehicle

Despite the virtues of compact city living, most of us will never entirely forgo the motor vehicle. For some of our activities, cars are just too convenient. This means that getting unhooked from carbon based fuels will require a transformation in the way motor vehicle are powered.

While the path technology takes is never totally predictable, by 2050 cars will probably be completely electric, or else they will be hybrids using biofuels or hydrogen. To grow biofuel feedstock would require shrinkage in the amount of land devoted to agriculture and forest products or natural habitat needed for the survival of nonhuman species. The unpleasant land-use tradeoff we would face in choosing biofuels can be avoided if other options are adopted instead such as electric plug-in cars and hydrogen powered hybrids. Battery capacity constitutes the fundamental technological hurdle for electric cars to give them enough range. Right now the technology is good enough for maybe 25 or 30 miles. This in a high density urban area will be enough for errands and short commutes before a recharge is needed. Once a plug-in network is created, so that one can park and charge, then driving ranges will be extended. Inventing a better battery would resolve the range problem and make electric vehicles the wave of the future. The current most likely candidate for improvement is the lithium-ion battery you now have in your laptop. As you probably know, the battery gets really warm, which is fine for a small-scale use in electronic devises, but not for something as big as your car. The solution if it is to come will be in the arena of new materials. In the meantime, hybrid plug-ins will stretch the efficiency of today's hybrids to 60 miles per gallon, a substantial accomplishment.[12] Of course, for there to be a considerable total saving in fossil fuels consumed, the electricity itself would need to originate from clean energy sources such as wind or solar.

The benefit of a plug-in electric car is the presence already of a distribution system for electricity. Still, if the battery problem is not amenable to an easy solution, hydrogen may be the way to go to get unhooked from fossil fuels. Honda already leases hydrogen powered cars on an experimental basis to some of its customers in Los Angeles where it has set up hydrogen fueling stations, some of which are partially powered by solar energy.[13]   Devising small scale hydrogen production plants using electric power to feed a decentralized distribution system seems more likely than a highly centralized system. Put enough engineers to work, and they will likely figure out how to do this, or how to come up with lightweight powerful new batteries. Either way, given a 40 year time horizon, one can imagine motor vehicles with reasonable operating costs that no longer rely on fossil fuels.[14]   Think about the possibilities. Wind and solar create electrical energy that comes to your house. You may even add to that yourself with some solar panels or a thin cell-solar roof. Electricity powers a reverse fuel cell that produces hydrogen which you store for refueling your own car. You don't even need to stop at the gas station anymore.

In a compact urban world, we will frequently find using high quality mass transit more convenient than driving. If we choose the compact way of life we will use cars less, but we won't totally give them up and they will absorb less energy than currently. Our love affair with the motor vehicle is unlikely to ever entirely die.

On top of efficient, effective transportation, a second prerequisite to leading the good life compactly is high quality, energy efficient buildings. We spend a good chunk of our day in the protective skin of buildings that provide us comfort and protection from the elements. Depending on their construction, these buildings can either be energy sinks or energy savers. To a description of those that save on energy we now turn.

Notes

[1]   Newman and Kenworthy, *Sustainability and Cities: Overcoming Automobile Dependency.*

[2] Ibid.

[3] Metrolinx, *Ontario to Get Started on New Transit Projects* (Metrolinx, 2009 [cited May 7, 2009]); available from http://www.metrolinx.com/en/default.aspx; Toronto Transit Commission, *Projects and Initiatives* (Toronto Transit Commission, 2009 [cited May 7, 2009]); available from http://www3.ttc.ca/About_the_TTC/Projects_and_initiatives/index.jsp.

[4] Newman and Kenworthy, *Sustainability and Cities: Overcoming Automobile Dependency*.

[5] Ibid.

[6] Jennifer Dill and Theresa Carr, "Bicycle Commuting and Facilities in Major U.S. Cities: If You Build Them, Commuters Will Use Them," *Transportation Research Record* 1828 (2003).

[7] BikePortland, *About Bikeportland* (PedalTown Media Inc., 2009 [cited May 8, 2009]); available from http://bikeportland.org/about/.

[8] Dill and Carr, "Bicycle Commuting and Facilities in Major U.S. Cities: If You Build Them, Commuters Will Use Them."

[9] Newman and Kenworthy, *Sustainability and Cities: Overcoming Automobile Dependency*.

[10] Ibid.

[11] Ibid; Sudhakar Raju, "Project NPV, Positive Externalities, Social Cost-Benefit Analysis--the Kansas City Light Rail Project," *Journal of Public Transportation* 11, no. 4.

[12] Andrew Simpson, *Cost-Benefit Analysis of Plug-in Hybrid Electric Vehicle Technology* (U.S. Department of Energy, 2006 [cited May 11, 2009]); available from http://www.nrel.gov/vehiclesandfuels/vsa/pdfs/40485.pdf.

[13] Honda Motor Co., *Hydrogen Station: The Honda FCX* (Honda Motor Company, 2009 [cited May 14, 2009]); available from http://world.honda.com/FuelCell/FCX/station/.

[14] M. Z. Jacobson and W.G. Colella, "Cleaning the Air and Improving Health with Hydrogen Fuel-Cell Vehicles," *Science* 308 (2005). We will have more to say about hydrogen later.

Chapter 7
Achieving Compact, Energy Efficient Urban Buildings

If we lived in perfectly insulated boxes and never entered or left, then the heat would never escape and once we attained our desired temperature, no further energy would be consumed. The size of the box wouldn't matter, apart from the small amount of energy consumed to initially heat it. Unfortunately for energy conservation, we don't live in such a well insulated world. In practice, heat escapes, the more so from bigger boxes with more external surface areas exposed to the elements. Lost heat means more energy consumption to sustain our housing box at a given interior temperature. Insulation is not the only issue. When we come and go heat escapes, and most of our houses leak heat through loosely fitting doors and windows. Heat also escapes through windows themselves, although at a lesser rate with the double-paned, gas-filled, coated energy, conserving variety. So-called low-emissive windows drop the rate of heat loss four-fold. If we move from a large house to a smaller one, we cut out energy consumption, but not quite proportionately. The surface area of a container with half the volume is something more than a half. If you move from a 400 square meter single story house (roughly 4,200 square feet) with 3 meter (10 foot) ceilings to a comparable 200 square meter house (2,100 square feet), you cut your floor space by 50 percent but your house's total exterior surface area by about 42 percent. Still, this would amount to about a 42 percent reduction in heating energy consumption, which is nothing to sneeze at. The kind of building you live in matters as well. If you choose to live in a 16-unit four story apartment building where each apartment has 200 square meters of floor space, you would cut your exterior surface area by 64 percent compared to a 200 square meter detached house and 79 percent compared to a 400 square meter house. The big gain comes because of shared surface areas among apartments. Compact living by itself can lead to huge savings in the amount of energy required by reducing heat lost rates. Smaller is better for energy conservation, but shared exterior surfaces are even better. We don't necessary have to sacrifice the amount of space we live in so long as we are willing to jointly use the land area on which we live with others.

Beyond shrinking the space we live in and sharing the land we live on, we can save energy by attacking heat loss itself and by acquiring new, energy efficient appliances. This is exactly what the U.S. government's weatherization program works at doing for low income homeowners. Weatherizing older homes and apartment buildings leads typically to energy savings of up to 30 percent, according to the Department of Energy's National Weatherization Assistance Program. Born in the 1970s energy crisis, Weatherization Assistance has help 5.6 million low income families improve the energy efficiency of their residences and reduce their home heating, cooling, and electric bills.[1] The most effective measures for saving energy include air sealing (plugging up air leaks), installing attic and wall insulation, replacing old refrigerators with high efficiency units (new ones use about half the energy of older models), turning down water heater settings, and installing programmable thermostats.   These measures to constitute the "low hanging fruit" for energy efficiency gains since heating and cooling absorb about 40 percent of the residential energy consumption pie, hot water another 15 percent, and refrigerators a surprisingly high 9 percent.   Contractors use an innovative blower door that pressurizes a house and reveals air leaks that can easily be plugged with caulking and other measures.   The most dramatic savings in heating and cooling costs also come from blowing insulation into attics and walls.   Although yielding less cost-effective energy savings, adding storm windows or replacing leaky windows with double-pane, low-emissive types improves both heating and cooling efficiency.   Energy savings come fairly cheaply by insulating hot water pipes and putting a "tea cozy" around your hot water heater.   Someday we in this country will go the European route and install "tank-free" water heaters that provide hot water on demand using half the energy we now use keeping a full tank hot all the time.[2]

On top of these comparatively low-tech options at the top of the weatherization list for our federal low-income assistance program, we homeowners can undertake a variety of energy saving measures such as reducing lighting energy use up to 75 percent by replacing our incandescent bulbs with compact fluorescents.   Soon we will be able to use light-emitting diodes (LEDs) instead and save up to 90 percent of the energy we expend on lighting (about 6 percent of the residential energy pie).   Energy savings can also be had by using new front-loading washers which require less hot water than the old top-loading models.   Any new appliance you buy today will use significantly less energy than older models because of federal energy efficiency standards for household appliances—when you buy, check the federal Star Energy Rating system to get the most efficient model available. In the future, "smart appliances" will respond to commands in a larger computer network to power-down when not in use or during the time-of-day when electricity rates are high.   Programmable thermostats are only the beginning in the high-tech management of our heating systems and appliances.   Also, at some point in the future, we may be able to sell surplus solar or other kinds of electrical energy we generate in the home back to our local utility, say when we are not at home and all our power using systems and gadgets are shut down but our solar panels are enjoying a sunny day. While this seems a bit utopian at the moment, much will change by 2050.[3]

Big gains in energy conservation are to be made for those of you who have the privilege of newly constructing a home or some other kind of building.   While the energy efficiency of conventional new construction outperforms older buildings, even bigger gains can be had by following the Leadership in Energy and Environmental Design (LEED) building standards —an average of 30 percent for existing LEED certified buildings.   Founded in 1998, the U.S. Green Building Council established the LEED standards and certification system.[4]   To obtain certification, a building must achieve points based on a lengthy list of environmental building criteria that take into account energy efficiency, pollution emissions, construction techniques, water usage, development density, access to public transit, facilities for bicycle users, reusability of building materials, and indoor environmental quality. LEED awards points for attaining improvements in energy efficiency relative to conventional buildings, building in renewable energy systems such as solar or wind to displace outside energy supplies, and for entering into a long-term contract to buy energy from renewable sources. Builders also get points for choosing a site close to residential areas and basic services, for multistory high density construction, and for a site with close access to subways, light rail lines, or bus systems. While one can quibble about the relative distribution of points to various measures, LEED buildings go a long way toward achieving high levels of energy efficiency and reducing greenhouse gas emissions. LEED standards are also available for housing construction and include requirements that encourage building compactly as well as achieving or exceeding federal Energy Star standards.

LEED certified buildings cost more upfront, as one might expect, partly because architects and builders still fall at the low end of the learning curve for green construction. As the use of LEED expands, this problem will be overcome. Even today, energy and other cost savings, along with productivity improvements from happier employees who work in a more pleasant and comfortable environment, usually justify the increased construction costs. In some cases, building owners even realize upfront cost savings by going green. A 16-story LEED-certified building housing the Oregon Health & Science University uses a variety of measures, including water-chilled beams, rainwater capture for toilets, and solar panels on the south side of the building, to cut the cost of the electrical, mechanical, and plumbing systems by 10 percent.[5]

Buildings absorb about a third of the total energy we consume in this country. Cutting this consumption by 30 percent using existing, off-the-shelf technology seems like a reasonable prospect, one that we could achieve readily in the next couple of decades, and one that would save us money. This would come on top of the huge savings in heating and cooling energy we could save simply by doubling the density at which we live. A doubling of density would also cut our urban transportation energy use almost in half if we take present day Toronto as our benchmark for comparison to U.S. cities.[6] Our target of reducing energy consumption by 30 percent is clearly in reach by adopting a more compact pattern of urban living.

To get unhooked from fossil fuels, stop climate change, and to get off the resulting space subsidy such fuels provide will require more than just conservation, however. We will also need new, green approaches to producing energy, a model of which is offered by nature itself.

Notes

1 U.S. Department of Energy, *Weatherization Assistance Program* (U.S. Department of Energy, 2008 [cited December 6, 2008]); available from http://apps1.eere.energy.gov/weatherization/.

2 Linda G. Berry, Marylyn A. Brown, and Laurence F. Kinney, *Progress Report of the National Weatherization Assistance Program* (Oak Ridge National Laboratory, 1997 [cited December 6, 2008]); available from http://apps1.eere.energy.gov/weatherization/pdfs/con450.pdf; Martin Schweitzer and Joel F. Eisenberg, *Meeting the Challenge: The Prospect of Achieving 30 Percent Energy Savings through the Weatherization Assistance Program* (Oak Ridge National Laboratory, 2002 [cited December 6, 2008]); available from http://weatherization.ornl.gov/pdf/Con-479%20May22-FINAL.pdf.

3 Gwendolyn Bounds, "About the House: Saving Energy on the Cheap," *Wall Street Journal*, October 2, 2008; Yuliva Chernova, "Consumers as Producers: When Homeowners Supply More Energy Than They Need, They Want to Be Paid for It: Not So Fast, Critics Say," *Wall Street Journal*, November 17, 2008.

4 U.S. Green Building Council, *Leed* (U.S. Green Building Council, 2009 [cited May 26, 2009]); available from http://www.usgbc.org/DisplayPage.aspx?CategoryID=19.

5 National Resources Defense Council, *Case Study: The Center for Health and Healing, Oregon Health & Science University* (National Resources Defense Council, 2009 [cited May 26, 2009]); available from http://www.nrdc.org/buildinggreen/casestudies/ohsu.pdf.

6 Newman and Kenworthy, *Sustainability and Cities: Overcoming Automobile Dependency.*

Chapter 8
The Green Energy Revolution: Making the Economic System More like an Ecological System

With perhaps the exception of the geothermal pools you see on vacation at Yellowstone National Park, the natural ecosystems around us run on solar energy. A longleaf pine photosynthesizes carbon-based energy molecules that drive tree growth; a bark beetle munches away on the tree's bark; and a Red-cockaded Woodpecker eats the beetle. In the end, the woodpecker dies and transfers its embodied carbon to bacteria. Life is mainly carbon captured initially by plants and transferred up the food chain to grazers and predators and down through bacteria and other organisms that feed on dead organic matter. All along the way, carbon dioxide is given off until every last carbon molecule taken up in photosynthesis is back in the atmosphere, except of course for those sucked up by the oceans or buried in the earth's crust as fossil fuel or limestone from sea shells. In sum, plants use the light energy of the sun to convert atmospheric carbon dioxide into complex carbohydrates. The cycle is completed when carbohydrates fuel organic metabolism and in the process return carbon dioxide to the atmosphere.

You may not think so off hand, but our economy, like an ecosystem, also largely runs on solar energy. Instead of directly using the sun's energy, we indirectly use it by relying on nature's solar savings bank—fossil fuel reserves. This allows us to avoid consuming the land space that would otherwise be required to convert the sun's rays into a form of energy we can use. In our extraction and burning of fossil fuels, we transfer carbon buried deep in the earth's surface to the atmosphere. This extra carbon in the earth's atmosphere acts like a blanket, keeping in heat energy that would otherwise escape into space, and warms the climate. Eventually, reachable fossil fuel stores will run dry, and this whole process will stop. Before that, if we want to limit climatic warming we will have to forgo using up all the remaining fossil fuel stores in the earth's crust and find our energy supplies elsewhere. The only way we could continue using fossil fuels while stabilizing the climate would be to figure out how to strip out carbon dioxide and inject it deeply underground from whence it came or somehow tie it up chemically, such as in calcium carbonate. Such approaches seem like a pipe-dream and would have no point unless they turn out to be really cheap, something that currently seems unlikely. Our money probably would be better spent on coming up with a permanent renewable replacement for fossil fuels, something we will be forced to do eventually as our reserves run dry. Theoretically, we could replace fossil fuels with nuclear power, but many believe this to be a Faustian bargain that substitutes one kind of problem for another—a huge toxic waste problem in exchange for solving global warming. A simpler more natural option avoids this dilemma altogether—the direct use of energy generated by the sun.

Ecological Energy: The Solar Option

The essential virtues of solar are its simplicity, constancy, flexibility, and environmental friendliness. To put it crudely, when sunlight hits a photovoltaic solar cell, electrons get excited and set off a chain reaction of movement through a wire from one side of the cell to the other. As electrons move through the wire, they can be used to perform work—i.e. run an electric motor or power a light bulb. Two kinds of impurities are added to silicon (n- and p-type) that give them the properties needed for electricity to flow between the two sides of a photovoltaic cell. One impurity adds electrons, creating the n-type semiconductor, and the other adds missing holes for electrons, resulting in the p-type semiconductor. Adding some light to kick extra electrons across the cell from the p- to the n-side sets up a flow of electrons in the opposite direction through a connecting wire, creating an exploitable current.[1]

Year in and year out, a rough average of 6.5 gigajoules (1.8 megawatts) per square meter of energy hits the surface of the U.S. As long as the sun continues to burn, we will have this energy. Solar photovoltaic cells can be put virtually anywhere.[2] A solar energy operation can cover a few square meters or many football field-sized plots. Solar facilities can be concentrated more heavily in the sunnier parts of the country to take special advantage of the greater volume of energy available per unit area, but the sun shines enough almost everywhere to make solar a feasible local source of energy. Utilities can generate solar on a large scale, but individuals can do the same on a small scale. Getting off the grid becomes a possibility with solar. Best of all, solar energy creates no polluting emissions of any kind—most importantly no greenhouse gases.[3]

Solar is not at all problem free. Already, Mohave Desert conservationists complain about planned solar facilities on rare habitats containing threatened species.[4] Solar needs space, especially the kind being proposed for the Mohave which uses large solar mirrors to heat oil that is run through a heat exchanger to generate steam for powering electric turbines. Photovoltaic solar cells offer an alternative to thermal solar, one that uses a similar amount of space per unit energy but not necessarily in such a concentrated fashion.[5] At 15 percent conversion efficiency, each of us today would need about 370 square meters of photovoltaic solar cells to replace our current energy consumption.[6] This roughly equals about a fourth of the land we currently have under intensive development.[7] Some of this is rooftops and other unused surfaces we could cover with solar cells—maybe 100 square meters each. This would leave a need for something like 270 square meters of additional land each in solar panels and perhaps an equal amount for related equipment and transmission systems, or roughly 540 square meters, about a tenth of a football field each or roughly 2 percent of the total land surface in the U.S. (lower 48 states). We already use over half of our land area for intensive development, agriculture, and wood fiber production. Ruggedness and heavy forest cover rules out maybe half of the rest, so the sighting of solar facilities to avoid the takeover of sensitive habitats will be a challenge, but not an insurmountable one. Quite a few wind generators have already been placed on existing farms and idled Great Plains agricultural lands without much disturbance to their productive capacities. We can probably also tuck in quite a few solar panels here and there on developed land without too much disturbance to their present uses. Large scale thermal solar facilities of the kind proposed for the Mohave Desert may in the end not be the right technology because the have to be big and they absorb a substantial amount of water not readily available in sunny climes. In comparison to such large operations, more flexible photovoltaics can be more easily arranged on the landscape in a manner that minimizes damage to the native flora and fauna. Also, through energy conservation and expanding wind energy capacity we can cut down on our land area requirements for solar to 300 square meters as suggested earlier in Chapter 3.

The sun shines every year, but never all day, and on some days in some parts of the country not much at all. Since we use electricity at night and on days when the sun fails to shine enough, storage is essential. Anyone who has looked at all the space in a Toyota Prius hybrid devoted to batteries knows that they currently have their limits for energy storage. We also know that they are likely to improve in time, but probably not enough to store electricity on a really large scale. While plug-in electric cars with battery storage will likely be popular for shorter trips in the future, we will also doubtlessly desire a portable, storable form of energy for longer trips to replace the role that gasoline currently fills. One answer to both small-scale and large-scale energy storage is hydrogen.

In your high school chemistry class you probably undertook an experiment to learn about electrolysis. When electricity is passed through water containing sodium sulfate, hydrogen is produced at one electrode and oxygen at the other. Hydrogen can either be burned as a fuel or used to power an electricity-producing fuel cell, the later being the more efficient and practical option. An essential virtue of hydrogen is its lack of polluting emissions—the only waste product of burning hydrogen is water vapor. To produce electricity, hydrogen and oxygen are fed into a fuel cell at their own separate electrodes inducing a flow of current through an external circuit.

In sum, electricity produced by photovoltaic cells can in turn create hydrogen fuel through electrolysis. The hydrogen can be stored or transported and used in a fuel cell to produce electricity when the sun fails to shine or to power an electric car or other electricity consuming devises. To put it crudely, fuel cell technology can work both ways: run it one direction to produce hydrogen from electricity, and run it in the other to create electricity from hydrogen. Recall that Honda currently leases a number of its hydrogen-powered FCX Clarity models in Los Angeles experimental fueling stations are located, some of which produce hydrogen from electricity generated by solar panels. Honda is also working on a portable home energy system that will use natural gas to produce hydrogen for fueling cars or running a home fuel cell energy system.[8]   Another possibility is a portable home fueling system that produces hydrogen from electricity.

Moving to a hydrogen economy requires honing electrolysis and fuel cell technology and creating an entirely new system of hydrogen production and distribution. Hydrogen cars won't sell well until the fuel is readily available, but a production and distribution system won't be created until a large number of hydrogen powered cars are on the road.   We have the classic "chicken and egg" problem.   The usual concerns about the dangers of hydrogen appear to be misplaced. Old newsreels of the crash and burning of the German blimp, the hydrogen-filled Hindenburg, might lead one to pause in the purchase of a hydrogen powered vehicle, but such fears are overblown. Hydrogen is in practice a safer fuel than either natural gas or gasoline. Most of the Hindenburg passengers survived but may not have in a similar conflagration fueled by natural gas or gasoline.[9]   Experts estimate that the cost for hydrogen to power a fuel-cell vehicle would be comparable to gasoline today given electricity costs of 10 cents per kilowatt hour, a figure that will be achievable using photovoltaic cells manufactured on a large scale as discussed in Chapter 2.[10]   Anytime we do anything in a big way, average costs tend to plunge.   Back in the 1970s, as we already mentioned, the automobile industry complained that placing catalytic converters on cars to control air pollution would render them unaffordable for many people, but this problem never happened because requiring all new cars to have converters drove their unit cost way down.   Such is likely to be the future experience with solar panels, hydrogen production equipment, and fuel cells. A huge virtue of hydrogen technology is its potential for portability.   We don't necessarily have to build a complex system of hydrogen distribution from centralized sources. Hydrogen production from electricity could easily be spread out, even down to the level of our own home.   The energy for doing so can come through the electric grid just as it does today.   The hydrogen "chicken and egg problem" can be short circuited through portability.

Ecological Energy: The Wind Option

As we know from *Don Quixote,* windmills as a source of power for pumping water, grinding grain, or running machinery have been around for a long time, at least since the Ninth Century, but using wind to generate electric power is a comparatively new phenomenon.   Wind, driven by atmospheric air density differences caused by the heat of the sun, possesses most of the virtues of solar as an energy source—pollution free, renewable, and flexible. As long as the wind blows—and in many locations such as on the Great Plains it seldom stops—wind can be used to generate electric power. All that we need is a tower, a blade, and an electric generator. The wind does the rest.

Like solar, the variation in the availability of wind creates a special need for storage. The producing ability of a wind generator increases geometrically with wind speed. Typically, half the energy delivered by the wind occurs when it blows hard during just 15 percent of a generator's operating time, and, as a consequence, actual energy production over a year tends to run at only 20 to 40 percent of the generator's maximum capacity.[11] Wind already competes on cost per kilowatt hour with fossil fuel energy, a key advantage compared to solar. Right now, wind generates less than .5 percent of our electricity, but the U.S. Department of Energy's goal for 2030 is 20 percent, one that they see as conservative.[12] Since 2002, the installed wind generating capacity in this country has increased fivefold. The land footprint for wind energy equipment under the 20 percent scenario would at most cover 2,500 square kilometers, or about 8 square meters for each of us. Wind requires much less land than solar for a comparable amount of electricity produced, although the vertical footprint for wind is of course much greater. Achieving 20 percent of electricity generation with wind by 2030 will cost roughly $2.4 trillion, but it would only be about $43 billion more than would we otherwise spend on equivalent conventional energy production capacity.

The essential constraint on wind generation is location. People love the idea of wind power, but don't want it their backyards. Wind generators are noisy, and to some they are a visual blight (I find them graceful in appearance myself, although I wouldn't want live too close to one). Locating a wind farm in a migratory flyway could threaten already endangered bird populations. Some areas are too remote and rugged for the placement of wind generators, and in many areas the wind doesn't blow enough to make wind energy worthwhile.

Despite these problems, the prospect for exploiting wind energy is huge. The wind potential of much of the Midwest and Great Plains is substantial, and the placement of wind farms there would not take away much from other land uses. The variability of energy from wind can be evened out with hydrogen production that can in turn generate electricity when the wind fails to blow. Farmers already seem happy to have the extra income from wind generators judging from the number of wind farms popping up recently along Interstate 80 in Iowa.

Achieving Clean Energy: Smart Grids

If we shift to solar and wind as our essential energy source, we do have to worry about distribution. Our current national electricity grid, the complex of utility wires and control systems that pushes juice around the country, is a cranky, low tech, inefficient, undependable affair originally cobbled together by neighboring utilities who wanted to sell each other electricity in emergencies. The system has grown to over 300,000 miles of transmission lines connecting some 9,200 generating facilities. The inability to store electricity makes the matching of demand and supply an especially challenging task.   When demand surges, electricity generation has to rise immediately or else the system collapses into a blackout. A heat wave hits the east coast and electricity has to be drawn in from far away or else the supply system breaks down—and this is exactly what happened in the 2003 Northeastern U.S. blackout resulting in some $6 billion in economic losses, trapping people in elevators, and causing tons of food in refrigerators and freezers to spoil. Bottlenecks still exist in the system that can be overcome with a combination of 'smart' management technology, decentralized clean energy production closer to electricity consumers (solar panels on your own roof), and grid capacity expansion.

On top of having to move electricity from one end of the country to the other, we have an emerging need to hook up and redistribute geographically spread-out sources of renewable energy. The Great Plains has an abundance of wind, sun, and space with which to generate an abundance of electricity but not much of a transmission system. Because renewable energy can be generated almost anywhere, the electric grid will need not only to be more extensive, but a whole lot smarter about matching demand and supply. The vision of the future for this task by electrical engineers is something called the "Smart Grid." This amounts to computerizing the entire electric system so that all electricity producing and consuming devises can talk to each other. When demand rises in one part of the system, inessential appliances can be told to shut down temporarily. When the sun is shining and one's solar panels are running full tilt, electricity can be sold back to the utility through a metering system that essentially runs backwards. When demand peaks, the price charge for electricity can be increased, making it worthwhile for some of us to reduce our use. We could conceivably have a wash machine that would wait until night to run when total demand is low. With a system of plug-in electric cars, a smart-grid system will become more essential, where we can get a charge at a convenient location when we need it, and have it charged to our electric bill. What is more important, when our car is sitting in the garage, it could charge up when rates are cheap and sell electricity when they go up. Electric cars and the batteries could in effect become a huge electric storage system, substantially reducing the complexity of electric load management. Add to this numerous fuel cells in cars and homes that could be cranked up on demand using stored hydrogen, and the electric storage problem is largely solved.   The possibilities of increasing the efficiency of electricity use through a smart grid at this point seem almost endless.[13]

Just like the interstate highway system, we might want to consider investing in a publicly coordinated interstate electrical grid, one that can move electricity around nimbly and efficiently. Doing so will cost us, but the economic benefits will be substantial.   To modernize the grid will run roughly $165 billion over the next 20 years, but the cost savings will amount to somewhere between $600 and $800 billion. The smart-grid appears to be a real bargain.[14]

Notes

1 Paul Krugger, *Alternative Energy Resources: The Quest for Sustainable Energy* (Hoboken, NJ: John Wiley & Sons, 2006); Ken Zweibel, *Harnessing Solar Power: The Photovoltaics Challenge* (New York: Plenum Press, 1990).

2 U.S. Department of Energy, *Solar Energy Technologies Program: Multi-Year Program Plan* ([cited]).

3 U.S. Department of Energy, *Solar America Initiative: A Plan for the Integrated Research, Development, and Market Transformation of Solar Energy Technologies* ([cited); U.S. Department of Energy, *Solar Energy Technologies Program: Multi-Year Program Plan* ([cited]).

4 Judith Lewis, "High Noon: As the Climate Warms, Environmentalists Square Off over Big Solar's Claim to the Mojave Desert," *High Country News*, May 4, 2009. Conservationists point to plenty of other desert areas not containing high quality habitats that could be used for solar energy.

5 The Moura photovoltaic power station in Alentejo, Portugal produces roughly 2,400 gigajoules annually of electric energy per hectare of the project land. Nevada Solar One, a solar thermal power plant near Boulder City, Nevada cranks out about 3,000 gigajoules of electric energy per hectare of project land.

6 This assumes that 6.5 gigajoules of solar energy on average hits square meter the U.S. lower forty-eight states annually and a conversion efficiency of 15 percent yielding .975 gigajoules square meter. As already noted, our annual per capita consumption is about 360 gigajoules. See U.S. Department of Energy, *Solar Energy Technologies Program: Multi-Year Program Plan* ([cited).

7 The optimum orientation of solar cells toward the sun generally involves a tilting of the panels. Strictly speaking, this reduces the land area covered by the cells, but tilting creates shade and reduces the usefulness of uncovered land for other purposes. To make life simple, I assume the land impact for a square meter of solar panels is a square meter.

8 Honda Motor Co., *Hydrogen Station: The Honda FCX* ([cited]).

9 Krugger, *Alternative Energy Resources: The Quest for Sustainable Energy;* Zweibel, *Harnessing Solar Power: The Photovoltaics Challenge.*

10 Jacobson and Colella, "Cleaning the Air and Improving Health with Hydrogen Fuel-Cell Vehicles."

[11] Krugger, *Alternative Energy Resources: The Quest for Sustainable Energy.*

[12] U.S. Department of Energy, *20% Wind Energy by 2030: Increasing Wind Energy's Contribution to U.S. Electricity Supply* (U.S. Department of Energy, 2008 [cited December 8, 2008]); available from http://www1.eere.energy.gov/windandhydro/pdfs/41869.pdf.

[13] U.S. Department of Energy and Litos Strategic Communication, *The Smart Grid: An Introduction* (U.S. Department of Energy, 2004 [cited December 15, 2008]); available from http://www.oe.energy.gov/DocumentsandMedia/DOE_SG_Book_Single_Pages.pdf.

[14] Joe Miller, *The Smart Grid—Benefits and Challenges* (U.S. Department of Energy, Office of Electricity Delivery and Energy Reliability, 2008 [cited December 11, 2008]); available from http://www.oe.energy.gov/DocumentsandMedia/SG__Benefits_Challenges_J_Miller.pdf.

Chapter 9
Attaining Green Energy and Spatial Compactness

Achieving Clean Energy: Cap and Trade

Each of us could do quite a bit on our own to shift in the direction of a clean, renewable energy system—move to compact housing, use public transit, bike or walk to work, weatherize, buy energy efficient appliances, hang our laundry to dry, install photovoltaic cells on our homes, purchase renewable energy from our electric utility, and buy a hybrid or other high-mpg motor vehicle. In the end, to solve the global warming problem we as a society will have to shift gears, and this will require political action. Our individual voluntary acts are a good thing, but when all is said and done they will be insufficient in scale to get the energy system to shift off of fossil fuels. We are stuck on fossil fuels, and to move to the clean energy path will require a substantial leap. Once sufficient scale for solar, wind, and hydrogen are achieved along with a big jump in energy efficiency, we will probably end up spending a smaller chunk of our income on energy than we do now. Clean and green energy will be both good for the environment and our pocketbook, but we need to give the energy system a major kick to shift it from the old path to the new. We as individuals need to politically support collective measures that will move our energy system in an environmentally friendly direction. Just as the Highway Trust Fund and FHA backed mortgages set off the mid-20th Century motor vehicle transportation and suburban housing booms, government action can spark a boom in clean energy and compact living.

We already have some useful little kicks on the government books, such as so-called corporate fuel efficiency standards (CAFE) for motor vehicles, energy efficiency standards for appliances, tax credits for investments in energy efficiency and renewable energy such as solar and wind, state level requirements for utilities to supply a target percent of electricity from renewable sources, and federal funding for energy efficient mass transit such as light rail. These all push us in the direction of a clean energy economy, but more can be done. The Obama administration in its early days tightened the CAFE standards from the current fleet-wide 25 miles per gallon (mph) for new cars and light trucks to a 2017 35.5 mph standard.[1]

Economists, who love for things to be transacted in market places because doing so tends to lead to production at low costs, have come up with an approach to reducing greenhouse gas emissions and shifting us to a clean energy that merits our serious attention. The approach calls for declining caps for greenhouse gas emissions and a system of marketable emission allowances, or, in short, "cap and trade." Under this arrangement, to emit a greenhouse gas within the cap, you need emission allowances. If you have more emissions allowances than you can use, you can sell them to others who have less than they want. The cap can be lowered from year-to-year to stabilize greenhouse gases in the atmosphere and ultimately limit the amount of global warming.   A lowering of the cap will reduce the supply of allowances which according to the venerable law of supply and demand will drive up their price.   Since the burning up of fossil fuels causes carbon dioxide to be emitted—the most predominant of the greenhouse gases—use of fossil fuels will require allowances.   Hence, the price of allowances will get cranked into the cost of fossil fuel consumption.   Suppose the price for carbon dioxide allowances is $100 a metric ton (2,205 pounds).   This means that the cost of an allowance used up for burning a gallon of gasoline will be roughly a $1 (when you burn a gallon, about 20 pounds of carbon dioxide goes out the tailpipe).   This would amount to a 33% increase in the price of gasoline to $4 assuming a $3 a pre-allowance price and full passage of costs to consumers.   A coal fired power plant emits about 2.1 pounds per kilowatt hour, which means the price of a kilowatt would increase by $.10, causing the cost of electricity from coal to increase from roughly $.05 to $.15.[2]   This would make solar and wind energy cheaper than coal well before 2030 if the decline in the cost of solar cells follows its projected path (the Department of Energy estimates $.10-.15 per kilowatt hour by 2020).   Remember, if you get your electricity from clean energy sources and if you drive a hydrogen powered car with the fuel produced by wind or solar, you don't need emission allowances.   In practice, you probably would never deal in allowances yourself as a consumer.   Your electric utility or your gasoline wholesaler would have to come up with the allowances, although much of the ultimate cost would be passed on to you the consumer.   Oil and coal producers would also likely take a downward hit to the prices they charge so consumers would bear something less than the full added cost of allowances. Remember that a $100 per metric ton allowance price would not kick in over night.   The Intergovernmental Panel on Climate Change (IPCC) estimates that a global price of this amount, or maybe even less, won't be needed until 2030 to forestall a rise of more than 2 degrees Celsius in the world's average temperature.   The $100 price can be attained by a modest annual tightening of emission caps and small yearly rises in the allowance price permitting a slow, smooth adjustment to higher fossil fuel energy costs.[3]

A fascinating question about emission allowances is this: Who will get the roughly $2 trillion generated globally in 2030 from carbon allowance sales under this system and amounts of a comparable order of magnitude generated in earlier years?   We in the U.S. could be buying some 20 percent of these allowances if we maintain our current cut of the global emissions pie, or $500 billion worth.[4]   The options for initial ownership of such allowances are many as the 2009 cap and trade bill (H.R. 2454) passed by the House of Representatives testifies.   One possibility—the one that the Obama administration favors—is for governments worldwide to own them and auction them off each year.   The resulting revenues could then be returned to the public through tax reductions to help offset rising energy costs, or they could be used to fund government programs such as clean energy projects, energy conservation, and investments in compact urban living.   We will have more to say about such issues shortly when we come to the topic of stimulating compact urban living and later when we talk about public investment and employment creation related to the green energy boom. In any event, emissions allowances generate a huge pool of money that needs to be re-injected back into the economy to keep it ticking along.

The beauty of "cap and trade" for environmentalists is the cap, which puts a limit on greenhouse gas emissions, and for economists it is trade, which puts a cost on those emissions that gets cranked into energy prices. Higher prices to us, the consumers, will cause an alteration in our behavior. We will work harder at cutting our energy consumption to save a buck, and we will shift to cleaner, now relatively less expensive, sources of energy. We will increasingly jump from the fossil fuel to the clean energy path as the price of the former charges upwards. Cap and trade is by no at all "pie in the sky." It is already at work in the European Union and will be in the U.S. when (and if) a "cap and trade bill" passes the Senate.[5]

The Economic Equivalence of Cap and Trade and a Carbon Tax

Debate pops up from time-to-time in the media about the relative virtues of a carbon tax and cap and trade.[6] Some argue for a tax because of its simplicity, while others argue for cap and trade primarily because it is not a tax. In practice, the two approaches are economically equivalent as long as we have accurate projections on the relationship between a carbon tax and resulting emission reductions.

Under cap and trade, as we already know, a cap on emissions is set and marketable emissions allowances are created by the government equal in number to the tons of carbon emission equivalents allowed within the cap. These allowances are then either auctioned off or given away. An emitter of greenhouse gases would be required by law to obtain allowances for each ton of carbon equivalents released into the atmosphere. The interplay of demand and supply for such allowances would establish their actual price.

Under a carbon tax, the government directly sets the price for carbon and the volume of carbon emissions emerges as the result of market forces. A higher tax encourages greater reductions in emissions by stimulating a more substantial shift to clean energy and more energy conservation. Gasoline at 4 dollars a gallon because of a higher carbon tax will lead to more fuel efficient hybrid cars on the road than, say, 3 dollar gas. If the tax equals the carbon allowance price that would otherwise occur under cap and trade, then the two approaches to limiting emissions would be equivalent. Each would yield the same prices for gasoline and other fuels. If the government knew ahead of time the exact response of all carbon emitters, then the tax could be selected to limit emissions to a specified amount (or cap). In its most recent report as we noted earlier, the Intergovernmental Panel on Climate Change (IPCC) suggests that a carbon tax (or price) of roughly $100 per metric ton by 2030 will put us on a path to the limiting average global temperature increase to about a 2 degree Celsius. Either a $100 tax or a cap yielding a $100 carbon price will lead to the same result. Under either regime, the incentives to get unhooked from carbon emitting fuels will be the same. Cap and trade and a carbon tax would be economically equivalent.

The problem is, no one can know ahead of time exactly what the tax should be to obtain a certain limit on emissions. Maybe the IPCC will be right in its prediction that a $100 a ton will bring about the desired amount of emissions reduction, but then again maybe it won't. If the tax turns out to be set at too low a level, emissions will be excessive. Of course the tax could be raised, but this might turn out to be politically challenging. A tax increase would incur the wrath of the fossil fuel lobby and would be tough to pull off. If the tax is initially too high, environmentalists will be happy, but industry would be livid and lobby intensively to push it down, opening up the potential for a downward tax adjustment getting out of hand. Altering a tax once it is set would be politically messy.

The biggest political advantage of cap and trade is that it is not a tax in the ordinary sense of the term. Taxes in this country are politically a tough sell. Cap and trade indeed results in a price being placed on carbon much in the same way a tax would—the right wing critics of cap and trade are right about this—but it is a price, not a tax. The real economic virtue of cap and trade is that we know we are getting a specific cap on emissions. We don't know exactly what we would get from a tax. With caps in place, the political struggle will be done with. Establishing an adjustable tax could be just the beginning of a never-ending battle over its magnitude.

Faustian Bargains: Biofuels and Nuclear Power as Clean Energy Sources

You may be wondering why I haven't said a whole lot about biofuels since these days they seem to be all the rage, especially corn-based ethanol. I haven't said much about nuclear either. As the price of fossil fuel rises because of cap and trade, we can just as easily switch to biofuels or nuclear since they don't emit greenhouse gases. Both are controversial. It's time for me to face the music and deal with them.

One would think that nature would directly be a great source of energy for us humans. The trouble is, plants don't transform enough solar energy per unit area into energy laden compounds to do us modern energy consumers much good. Plants through photosynthesis only fix about 68 percent annually of the total amount of energy in the fossil fuels we consume in this country each year. Each year the amount of energy embodied in crops and forest products we harvest amounts to about 30 percent of the fossil fuel energy we consume. No way can we get very much energy from biofuels.[7] We simply don't have enough land with plants on them to do the job and have anything left over for agriculture and wood fiber production. The other problem is getting much of a positive energy yield from crops produced for biofuels. Some studies of corn-based ethanol production find that more fossil fuel energy goes into producing the corn than comes out after the corn is converted into ethanol. Ethanol survives in the marketplace today because of government subsidies.[8] Now other crops, such as sugar cane, do a better job of creating positive net energy when converted to biofuels, and Brazil, where sugar cane is produced in abundance, squeezes a significant amount of fuel for its motor vehicles from sugar at a reasonable cost. In the end, the big problem for biofuels is that they are a space hog. In the U.S., assuming an optimistic possible production of 100 gigajoules of usable energy per hectare (10,000 square meters), we would produce less than 30 percent of our current energy needs if we devoted 40 percent of our land base (a hectare each) to that task.[9] We will no doubt improve the technology behind biofuels, and they will undoubtedly become a larger part of our energy mix, but they can never be a really big portion of the energy pie.

On October 16, 1973 the Organization of Petroleum Exporting Countries (OPEC) announced a 70 percent increase in the price of crude oil, and the next day Arab countries declared an embargo against the U.S. for its support of Israel in the recently declare Yon Kippur War. The embargo was soon extended to western European countries as well. Like many other European countries, France possesses limited fossil fuel resources and at the time of the 1973 crisis depended heavily on oil imports for generating its electrical power. These events exposed France's special vulnerability because of dependence on foreign sources of energy, and the French government set out to methodically create an electricity supply system based on nuclear energy.

The French love nuclear power, or, at least seem willing to live with its dangers for the energy security that it delivers. Today, France gets 77 percent of its electric power from 59 nuclear power plants scattered around the country and benefits from some of the lowest electricity prices in Europe. France also sells about 12 percent of its electrical energy production to neighboring countries. A byproduct of this commitment to nuclear power is a substantial reduction in greenhouse gas emissions in comparison to countries such as the U.S. that rely mainly on fossil fuels.[10]   French energy consumption per capita amounts to 56 percent of the U.S. figure, but the French per capita CO_2 emissions add up to only 31 percent of the U.S. amount.[11] The French emit less carbon per person than the U.S. because of both a lower per capita energy consumption and greater relative use of nuclear power. The French answer to global warming is both to use less energy and to go nuclear. The French lack uranium stores themselves, but minimize their import needs with a fuel reprocessing program that extracts additional energy from spent nuclear fuel.[12] A side benefit of reprocessing is a reduction of the volume of radioactive waste materials requiring disposal. The essential drawback of reprocessing is the creation of weapons grade nuclear material. The U.S. banned reprocessing in the 1970s because of fears that weapons grade plutonium could be producing using reprocessing technology. Although the ban has been lifted, the U.S. has not taken up reprocessing again. For limiting global warming nuclear power seems like a good deal since its production emits no greenhouse gases.

Nonetheless, many fear the extensive development of nuclear power. Visions of mushroom clouds from nuclear bombs and the horrors of

Hiroshima and Nagasaki are burned into our collective memories. That nuclear power lacks substantial risk is difficult for many of us to swallow despite its generally good safety record in comparison to other human activities such as driving a car. In this country, very few want a nuclear power plant near their community. The French conversely seem happy to have nuclear plants nearby for the economic benefits they generate, although they are less enamored of radioactive waste disposal facilities in their back yard. The big question for many in the U.S. as well as France is whether underground deep geological repositories for spent nuclear fuel, such as Yucca Mountain in Nevada, will be safe from future catastrophic releases of radioactivity. Many experts believe they will, but doubts persist.

Whatever the truth of such fears, I suspect nuclear power is never going to be very popular in this country and will run into significant political opposition, especially around site selections for new plants. We will probably construct enough new plants to sustain our current share of nuclear power at around 20 percent of total electricity generation. In any event, I personally don't think there will be much additional nuclear energy in our future. Even the most sober and favorable studies of nuclear energy describe significant barriers to future expansion. The cost of nuclear energy remains above that for coal and natural gas, although fairly modest carbon emission allowance costs for the later will make nuclear competitive. Despite public fears, new reactors designs reduce accident risks to fairly insignificant levels. The truly serious unresolved problems with nuclear are two: (1) What do we do with the inevitable radioactive wastes that result from the nuclear fuel cycle? (2) How do we prevent the proliferation of weapons grade materials, especially if reprocessing of waste is used to produce fuel? At this point we lack convincing answers to both of these questions.[13] For the moment, nuclear plant construction projects continue to be plagued by cost overruns, causing the costs of a new plants to approach as much as $8 billion each, rendering them uncompetitive with alternative sources of electrical energy.[14]

While my personal attitudes on nuclear safety and proliferation problems are fairly agnostic—I am not really sure whether nuclear energy is evil or not —I don't view a lack of a big nuclear future for us as a serious problem. Nuclear energy is by nature highly centralized and by virtue of its maturity as a source energy faces fairly incremental advances in its technology. On the other hand, solar and wind are highly decentralized and probably close to the beginning of the research learning curve. Almost anyone can get into the business of solar or wind energy supply by putting up some solar panels or a windmill, and solar and wind equipment production is fairly disperse amongst young businesses, most with a strong entrepreneurial orientation. These conditions suggest a fairly rapid advance in the technology down the road for solar and wind caused by a large amount of tinkering in the search of moneymaking breakthroughs. I like the idea of my kids (not me, I am probably to old) someday having a few solar panels or a small wind generator on their roof, a portable hydrogen production plant in their basement, and fuel cells in both their houses and cars. I suspect solar and wind by then will be fully competitive with nuclear power on price, maybe even cheaper if the cost of solving the nuclear nonproliferation and waste problem is factored in. Nuclear energy will by nature end up in the hands of the few and green energy in the hands of the many.[15]

Achieving Clean Energy: Green Utilities

The 1973 oil price shock effects extended well beyond France to energy consumers worldwide. The state of California, and its approach for regulating electric utilities, provides an especially interesting case study of oil shock-induced reforms. Electric utilities traditionally make money by expanding their electrical loads and generating capacities. As regulated beings, they earn a fixed return on any investments they make, and those returns get cranked into the rates for electricity they are allowed to charge. Once the rates are set, utilities can make more money by increasing the volume of electricity sales—this is the economic logic that rules utilities.[16] Utilities lack incentives of any kind to get customers to conserve on electricity consumption. Conservation perversely dents utility profits.

In the eyes of California's utility regulators back in 1973, exploding energy costs called for revolutionary change in the way utilities operate.[17] Consequently, a new regulatory scheme was adopted that'decoupled' a utility's earning power from the volume of its electricity sales and the size of its electrical load. Energy not consumed is the cleanest of all, and California utilities today get economic credit for cutting their load by stimulating energy conservation. They can cut deals with customers to split the cost savings from weatherizing houses or replacing old appliances with energy-efficient models and in the process make an investment return for shareholders. In short, a California utility can make money by doing the opposite of its past behavior, by shrinking the amount of energy it sells rather than expanding it.

if a new world of cap and trade comes to pass, utilities won't be too excited about investing in coal-fired power plants that carry with them huge costs for emission allowances, and California's approach to regulation will look increasingly attractive. To avoid having to buy emissions allowances, utilities will not only be interested in expanding their investment in conservation under "decoupling" schemes, but also in clean energies such as solar and wind that don't require costly emissions allowances. Even here utilities could follow their traditional pattern of large scale investments—big wind farms and huge arrays of solar mirrors running hot water generators— or they could take seriously the California "decoupling" approach to utility regulation which encourages not only conservation but small scale solar and other kinds of energy production by utility customers. In short, a utility could essentially become a load manager routing clean energy between multitudes of sellers and buyers.

The great thing about green energy is that almost anyone can become a producer—a homeowner with solar panels, a farmer with a wind generator, and a stream-side landowner with a small hydro generator—but in order for this to happen, electric utilities have to let meters run backwards. In short, utilities need to buy electricity from all comers. Utilities, perhaps in partnership with the federal government, could establish a clean energy investment bank that would provide loans to utility customers and the utilities themselves to invest in clean energy capacity. The federal government could dangle the incentive of low interest loans from a clean energy investment bank to get utilities to adopt both a strategy of load reduction through energy efficiency gains and the expansion of decentralized wind and solar production. We did this kind of quasi-public financing for mortgages and highways to jump start the suburban housing boom; why not do it for the sake of green energy and compact living as well? Alternatively, utilities could invest their own funds in customer solar panels or wind generators and sell them back the electricity. Instead of owning a few huge coal-fired or nuclear power plants, a utility would own solar panels or windmills scattered all over the place and earn the resulting investment return they generate.[18] These are just a few of the many possibilities for reorienting utilities in the direction of both clean energy production and conservation.

Energy Costs and Spatial Compactness

Today California's per capita electricity consumption lies about 45 percent below the U.S.'s as a whole, attesting to the state's success in energy conservation. Part of this savings can be traced to its astute regulatory reforms, but a good piece can be explained by the higher relative costs of electricity in California over the past thirty years.[19] What one pays for something matters in how much one consumes. Higher energy prices encourage conservation. This is one thing about which economists are right on the money. The lesson of California is that higher prices for fossil fuel energy induced by rising emission allowance prices will be a major motivator for conservation.

Support for the role of high energy costs in conservation comes from Europe. Europeans today pay more for gasoline and consume less than we Americans. But higher prices alone don't explain the full difference in consumption between the Europeans and us. If we used the usual relationship that economists find between gasoline consumption and price in their empirical research to account for the difference between U.S. and European consumption, we would explain no more than about half the difference. The rest is due to the greater compactness of urban life and more extensive use of mass transit in Europe. The point is simple—increases in energy costs are a major inducement to moving to clean energy, but they are probably not enough to get all the clean energy we want. Remember, the cleanest energy of all is that which we don't use, and potential energy savings from compact living along are substantial—as much as half for transportation and housing if we double the density at which we live. To gain both the personal and environmental virtues of compact living in the U.S. will require a concerted public effort to create attractive, high density cities that are easy to get around. High gasoline prices in Europe alone didn't create compact cities. Traditions of high density, pedestrian friendly urban design and efficient public transit set the stage for compact urban development in countries like France.

Achieving Spatial Compactness as a Path to Clean Energy: Urban Growth Boundaries

Increasing the density of urban life will not happen overnight. The basic idea here is to draw lines around existing contiguous urban development and confine future new residential and commercial construction within the resulting lines, or "urban growth boundaries" (UGB), for the next forty years. Europeans seem to limit their outward pace of urban expansion as a matter of course through the ordinary land use planning process. We Americans need to have a concrete restraint to help us kick our spatial expansion habit. As our urban populations grow over the next 40 years, that growth will be largely upwards and only modestly outwards under a system of urban growth boundaries. A projected 50 percent increase in U. S. population plus fixed growth boundaries would boost density by one-third. This in turn would give us at least a 30 percent reduction in per capita urban energy consumption and maybe more if weatherization of older houses and buildings is expanded and if LEED type building standards are followed for new construction and major building rehabs. To get the full energy conservation benefits of compact urban living will require high-efficiency mass transit of the kind already existing in cities like Toronto or Paris. Recall that Toronto is about twice as dense as the typical American city and uses a little more than half as much energy in transportation. Over time, with restricted outward expansion suburbs will gain in connectedness and density and in the process become more city-like and less auto oriented. Suburbs will remain, but they will have a more urban look and feel. Autos will remain as well and need to be accommodated in urban design—our love affair with the motor vehicle will doubtlessly continue albeit with less intensity. Suburbs in a world of urban growth boundaries will in effect become urban towns and villages.

Getting Americans to go on a spatial diet will not be easy. They will need to be rewarded for it, and they can be with beautiful and exciting urban spaces and smoothly functioning public transit systems for getting around. We can't reproduce Paris, but in this country we can apply our own growing conventions of good urban design to create cities that we can love. Two urban design movements, New Urbanism and Smart Growth, offer similar sets of principles for quality urban living. Both call for a variety of transportation options including public transit, bicycles, and walking; mixed land uses; pedestrian-friendly, compact neighborhoods with a range of housing options; distinct urban edges and infill development; a diversity of parks, village greens, community gardens, and natural areas; human scale, compact building design; and architecturally distinctive buildings and spaces focused on a clearly defined urban and community centers. In such a world, one will be in easy walking distance of cafes, grocery stores, small shops, parks, public buildings and spaces and, in some cases, even employment opportunities in local offices and specialized light manufacturing plants. Traveling from one urban town or district to another on public transit will be convenient with compact housing development oriented to transit stations. In some instances, getting from one community to another will be feasible by bike on separate paths through natural corridors along rivers or streams. Both New Urbanism and Smart Growth emphasize the importance of protecting open spaces and natural corridors and incorporating them in overall urban planning and design. Life could be good in a new, more compact urban world.

To realize energy skimping high density urban living will thus require substantial improvements in public transit and street level public amenities as well as and some form of urban growth boundaries. The feds will have a bundle of money from cap and trade to return to the public in order to keep the economy charging forward, and certainly a part of it can be directed to public transit and compact public facility investment (pedestrian friendly streets and squares, bike paths, green space and natural area protection) and to stimulating clean energy through tax credits, weatherization subsidies, and other measures. Before we take up the spending part, let's deal with the more controversial piece, urban growth boundaries (UGBs).

Historically, land use planning in this country has been largely a local affair. To do what you will with you land so long as you don't directly and substantially harm others serves as the fundamental default setting in land use law. Zoning regulations focus mostly on the prevention of nuisance, which is legal language for doing harm to others. Traditionally this was accomplished by separating incompatible land uses such as dirty industries or noisy commercial areas and housing. In an auto oriented world, separation of uses worked—we can drive from one use to another to accomplish our daily tasks—but in a modern pedestrian-friendly urban world, we want mixed uses in near proximity so we can walk around, do our errands, and enjoy the bustle of an interesting street life. Zoning is becoming a more complicated affair and will be driven increasingly by the needs of high quality, pedestrian friendly urban design down the road. Also, to draw a boundary around where urban development can occur requires moving elements of zoning from a local to a regional level. This takes zoning out of the hands of local authorities and limits what people can do with their land on the periphery of urban population concentrations. Messing with people's land use rights, as legitimate as it may be for the benefit of the larger society, can create a political firestorm, as it has recently in Oregon. Before putting our money on urban growth boundaries, we need to sort all this out.

Tom McCall served two terms as Governor of Oregon from 1967 to 1975. McCall gained public attention as a newscaster and commentator for Oregon's first public television station in the 1950s and early 1960s. In 1962 he produced an unusually meaty special on the polluted state of the Willamette River and Oregon's air called "Pollution in Paradise." He leveraged his growing fame into a successful run for Secretary of State and then Governor.   While governor, McCall was instrumental in passing Oregon's famous "bottle bill" requiring that soft drink and beer containers be returnable for a minimal refund value, legislation to cleanup the Willamette River, and a landmark "planning law" that required urban growth boundaries around all of Oregon's cities and towns.[20] Today looking at this record one would hardly guess that McCall was a Republican. He gained notoriety for exclaiming the following about Oregon on national television:

> Come visit us again and again. This is a state of excitement. But for heaven's sake, don't move here to live.

This rhetoric ultimately backfired in future years as Oregon's population growth mushroomed. Worried about "sagebrush subdivisions, coastal condomania and the ravenous rampage of suburbia in the Willamette Valley...," McCall committed himself to passing a law to bring sprawl under control, and, with his passion and ability to turn a phrase, he succeeded. [21]

In response to the planning law, urban growth boundaries are now in place around Portland, Eugene, Corvallis, and other Oregon cities and towns.[22]   Because the planning law requires that enough vacant land for twenty years of forecasted housing development be included within growth boundaries, they ended up being drawn fairly loosely, and Oregon cities have continued to spread outward, although at a slower pace than otherwise. The planning law also requires that urban related public investment be restricted to neighborhoods inside growth boundaries. Portland Metro, the government body in charge of administering the planning law for the city, reviews the positioning of its growth boundary every five years to determine whether the required vacant land inventory provision is satisfied.[23]   Despite relatively modest outward movements of the boundary, the Portland metro area has experienced a boom in residential growth, a fair amount of which has been directed to the redevelopment of inner city neighborhoods. In response to rising land prices, the average lot size for new homes has dropped and the proportion of multifamily housing in the new housing mix has increased. The prices of lots within Portland's growth boundary have risen much more rapidly in recent years than just outside it as one would expect.[24] Owners of farm and forest land beyond growth boundaries face strict limitations in the number of houses they can construct on their property. With few exceptions, to comply with the planning law Oregon local governments have withheld zoning approval for housing development outside growth boundaries, at least until very recently. The passage of Measure 37 in a 2004 referendum upset Oregon's planning law apple cart, as we will now see.

Dorothy English, who died in 2008 at age 95, bought property just outside of Portland Oregon in the 1950s with her husband. The Oregon planning law thwarted her attempt to later subdivide her land for a few houses, and in 2004 she became the primary petitioner and "poster grandmother" for Measure 37, which required compensation to any landowner whose property value was reduced by land use regulations.[25] Dorothy English projected an image of an elderly widow who had for 40 years been rolled over by a land use planning juggernaut that ignored her rights to develop her 22 acres just beyond Portland's urban growth boundary. She and other property rights advocates ran an effective campaign and Measure 37 successfully passed. Dorothy English's estate ultimately won a $1.15 million settlement from Multnomah County under Measure 37.

Ordinarily, if an automobile or defense plant closes in a community or the Federal Reserve pushes mortgage interest rates up, or the housing market crashes because of mortgage lending excesses and the value of property you own drops as a result, no one is obligated to compensate you in any way. Value has been taken from you, but you have no recourse to retrieve it from others. It is written into the constitution that if government takes your land, say for a public road, you have fair and just compensation coming. Historically, this was the one situation where a landowner has legal recourse to retrieve value. Originally, the U.S. Supreme Court stuck to a narrow view of the so-called takings clause, and confined its application to cases where land was physically appropriated by government. This interpretation was expanded to include the idea of a "regulatory taking" in the 1920s and the Court today holds that property owners may have compensation coming where a new regulation totally removes all economic value from a property so long as a nuisance as defined in common law has not occurred. An "economic taking," such as when General Motors closes plants in Detroit, Michigan and property values plummet, some even to zero, doesn't count. Only when a government regulatory action causes property values to go to zero is there a case under the takings doctrine.[26]

Property rights advocates, those who believe in the sanctity of property and the freedom to do with it what you will short of direct harm to others, want to push the takings doctrine even further. They believe that property owners should be compensated for all reductions in property values brought on by government regulatory measures. The citizens of Oregon codified this idea in Measure 37: "If a public entity enacts or enforces a new land use regulation or enforces a land use regulation enacted prior to the effective date of this amendment that restricts the use of private real property or any interest therein and has the effect of reducing the fair market value of the property, or any interest therein, then the owner of the property shall be paid just compensation." For any given parcel, this provision applies to land use regulations passed since acquisition of the property by the current owner (or by a family member) but not before. The provision applies neither to regulatory or legal restrictions on activities recognized as public nuisances according to common law nor to restrictions that protect public health and safety. If legitimate compensation is unpaid two years after it is requested, then the property can be used as the law allowed at the time of acquisition.[27]

On the surface, Proposition 37 seems fair. If government changes the rules of the game, then those who are harmed should be compensated. As a practical matter, Proposition 37 puts significant holes in Oregon's urban growth boundaries by allowing farm and forest land owners outside of growth boundaries who acquired title before 1973 to claim compensation for property value reductions caused by Oregon's 1973 planning law. Since the passage of the law roughly 7,000 claims for compensation equaling $20 billion have been submitted statewide covering about 800,000 acres.[28] Because local governments lack the funds to pay these claims, settlements allow landowners to develop their land according to zoning regulations in force before passage of the planning law.

In Oregon, one ballot measure can trump another. In 2007 the citizens of Oregon passed Measure 49 which limits development arising from Measure 37 claims. Under measure 49, no more than three dwellings can be constructed under any circumstances on parcels of high-value farm and forestland or critical groundwater recharge areas. Nor can industrial or commercial facilities be developed on properties originally zoned before 1973 for dwellings, farms, or forests. Measure 49 plugs many of the holes in Oregon's urban growth boundaries created by Measure 37.[29] Oregon's citizens seem to be speaking with two voices. On the one hand, they want property rights respected—people who want to build another house on their own land ought to be able to do so—but on the other, land use regulations ought to protect the state's natural legacy. In a crude way, Measure 37 and 49 together accomplish both.

The surface fairness of Measure 37 is a little misleading. As any real estate agent will tell you, the essential determinant of land value is location. It's not the actions of the landowner so much as it is the collective decisions of the larger society on where to locate urban activity that fixes land values. As a matter of equity, Oregon could decide to spread the growth in land value associated with urban development around by establishing a transfer of development rights (TDR) program. Under a TDR program, all landowners would receive a certain number of development rights based on the amount of land they own. Development, however, could only take place within urban growth boundaries, but to develop land at higher densities than the allotted amount in those areas, additional rights would have to be acquired from landowners outside growth boundaries. In this way, a farmer owning land where development is not allowed can participate in the growth of urban land values within urban growth boundaries. Under TDR, the growth in value caused by a limited supply of developable land can be spread around rather than going just to landowners who happen to hold land in privileged locations within urban growth boundaries. Politically speaking, TDRs would dampen property owner interest in the movement for takings laws such as Proposition 37. Fairness along with protection of the rural landscape would be the rule under TDR.[30]

In an auto oriented city, urban growth boundaries and rising residential densities would do little more than cause significant congestion absent other essential public actions. A boundary alone will not create a beautiful, pedestrian friendly, easy to navigate urban landscape. In order for this to happen, substantial investments will be required in both public transit and pedestrian-friendly public amenities to draw people out of their cars, onto the streets, and into public spaces. This is the kind of investment the federal government is especially good at funding.   Sticks, such as urban growth boundaries, will not only be needed to achieve urban compactness, but carrots as well.   Since implementing urban growth boundaries requires local government action, the federal government can't mandate such a measure, but it can encourage it.   Federally funded bonus matches could be given for mass transit and urban amenity investments within growth boundaries as an incentive for their adoption.   Instead of, say, a 50 percent federal match for such investments, which is the current norm, the feds could offer an 80 percent match to those cities that possess urban growth boundaries.[31]   One could object to such a heavy federal involvement in local urban development, but recall how the Interstate Highway system arose and the huge role it played in the formation of suburban America.   To create compact, energy efficient, beautiful urban centers and a clean energy economy will require money—a source of funding.   Federal funding historically sparked the creation of our suburbs; poetic justice suggests a similar role for the creation of spatial compactness in our urban areas today.   A target of doubling our urban densities by 2050 through a mix of urban growth boundaries and public investments in urban compactness seems reasonable considering the higher densities that already exist in European (Paris) and Canadian (Toronto and Montreal) cities that we Americans already enjoy visiting.

Cap and Trade as a Source of Clean Energy Funding

Cap and trade not only creates a huge incentive for the adoption of spatial compactness, energy efficiency, and carbon free energy production, but it also offers a substantial source for funding for mass transit and other clean energy projects.[32] To keep temperatures from rising more than a couple of degrees centigrade, the price of CO_2 emissions will need to increase to $100 a metric ton by 2030 according to the Intergovernmental Panel on Climate Change as discussed earlier.[33]   Assuming a steady rise in the emissions price beginning at $15 in 2012, we in the U.S. would be paying a rough grand total for our allowances of $ 3.8 trillion assuming our emissions decline at a steady pace to 4 gigatons over the following 18 years (we currently emit about 7 gigatons a year).[34]   This means that on average roughly $213 billion plus in revenue would come to the government annually assuming it auctions off emission allowances. Some of this money would no doubt be returned to consumers to help offset rising energy costs, especially for low income folks, but a chunk of it could be spent on clean energy tax credits, weatherization, electric-utility regulatory reform, construction of a high tech electrical grid oriented to renewable energy, pedestrian friendly urban amenities, and light rail transit investment.

We currently spend about 10 billion in federal dollars a year on public transit, of which about $1.6 billion goes for capital investment in light rail and subways.[35]   Much of the rest goes for bus and rail car purchases.   In contrast, we spend some $40 billion at the federal level on highways. Increasing spending on light rail investment to, say, $30 billion a year would bring more balance to our transportation spending. This would get us a grand total of roughly 16,000 miles of new light rail lines over 20 years, assuming a 25 percent local match for funding and a $50 million cost per mile. This multiplies the current amount of light rail mileage 16-fold.[36]

In our existing urban landscape, much of the basic public capital required for water supply, sewers, electricity distribution, and streets already exists. Growing upward rather than out will result in a more efficient use of what we already have. The money we would otherwise spend creating this kind of public capital in outward expansion we can redirect to beautifying our streetscapes and making urban life friendlier to pedestrians and bicyclists. The amount of money required for wider sidewalks, more squares and pocket parks, pleasing street furnishings and landscaping, fountains, traffic circles, street markets, bike paths, natural landscape and greenway restorations, and public art would probably not be huge relative to public transit, but its importance cannot be underestimated for making cities truly interesting and pleasing places to live. The attraction of a place like Paris is as much in the street-level details as it is in the city's larger scale public attractions and monuments. New York City now recognizes the importance of street design and recently published a street design manual against which new develop projects will be judged.[37] Increasing density by itself is not enough. People have to be able to get around easily in a compact city and at the same time enjoy doing it. The critics of rail-based transit who say that it fails to get people out of their cars and costs too much will be right if urban street life remains unfriendly and unappealing and if urban densities don't increase enough to support all those things we like about cities—sidewalk cafes, street markets, intimate squares, good bars and restaurants, plenty of great entertainment, good bookstores and libraries, places to play and watch soccer or baseball or basketball, biking and running trails, beautiful parks, wonderful museums, state-of-the art sports stadiums, great shopping of all kinds, and places to simply watch the world go by and contemplate the meaning of life. A portion of emission allowance money devoted to sparking investment in urban amenities would be a great complement to light rail transit expansion and relatively speaking would not cost a huge amount of money. The Europeans don't seem to skimp when it comes to investment in good urban design. Just take a walk around Paris or Lyon and you will see what I mean. You will also notice that the sidewalks in these cities are always alive with people. You don't have to go as far as Paris to see decent urban design. Check out San Francisco's Market Street, Denver's 16th Street Mall, Tempe, Arizona's Mill Avenue, or downtown Portland's Pioneer Courthouse Square.

The virtues of compact living flow not only from decently designed urban spaces, but from high quality urban buildings of the kind that result from the adoption of rigorous design standards of the kind offered by the folks at Leadership in Energy and Environmental Design (LEED). Right now the adoption of environmentally friendly LEED building standards for new commercial construction, building rehabs, and new dwellings is strictly a voluntary affair. Developers of LEED buildings can already take advantage of energy conservation federal tax credits. Builders currently get a $2,000 tax credit for homes that achieve a 50 percent energy savings compared the norm, and $1.80 per square foot tax deduction is available for comparable energy savings in commercial buildings. Homeowners have a huge array of tax credit options available to them for making energy saving improvements to their homes and acquiring energy efficient heating and cooling equipment. Incidentally, significant tax credits are available as well for installing solar panels, wind generators, and fuel cells, or buying plug-in electric, hybrid, or other cutting-edge energy efficient vehicles.[38]   These energy tax credits provide significant incentives, but they are not cost free to the public.[39] The annual reduction in tax revenues for these credits amounts to roughly a billion dollars a year according to the Congressional Budget Office. On the other side of the equation, the tax credit supports a huge amount of clean energy investment.

Other dimensions of the LEED standards apart from heating and cooling efficiency support compact living and energy efficiency. For example, LEED buildings get points for encouraging the use of public transportation by building occupants and for choosing pedestrian friendly locations. A federal tax credit or deduction could be award per square foot to all LEED building developers simply to encourage the use of LEED certification and the range of environmental benefits to the larger public that result.

In a later chapter describing how public investment in clean energy and compact living can help spark an economic boom, we will get more specific about dollar amounts for different kinds of public sector spending. Let's wrap up this chapter with a preview of some of it to gain a sense of the order of magnitude for public sector spending required to create a green compact economy.

If we as society take on this task, the actual allocation of funds to various projects will emerge in practice as a mixed consequence of political pull and detailed quantitative analysis on relative benefits.   I have no way of predicting the ultimate outcome, but I can at least lay out reasonable spending levels on some of the projects we have mentioned so far would move us well along the path to getting unhooked from fossil fuels and creating a compact form of living. So far we have introduced light rail, urban amenities, clean energy tax credits, weatherization, a smart grid, and a clean energy investment bank as good things to spend money on to stimulate a compact, clean energy economy. Federal light rail spending could be productively increased to $30 billion a year as just noted along with another $20 billion for streetscape improvements and urban growth boundary incentives.[40]   Weatherization we will see later could probably efficiently absorb a billion or more[41], and we could easily expand clean energy tax credits of various kinds to $10 billion.[42] We will also see later that smart grid investment will run perhaps $10 billion a year and that the capitalization of a clean energy investment bank would add another $4 billion or so.[43] This all adds up to $75 billion, not a huge amount of money in contrast to the Obama administration's stimulus spending of $737 billion undertaken in 2009 and 2010 to forestall a collapse in the economy.[44]   One could easily imagine funding $75 billion for clean energy from carbon emission allowance sales as we will see later.

Summary

It's time to summarize.   Fossil fuels give us a huge space subsidy, one that we can never replace relying on biotic energy from nature alone. We can take heart nonetheless from the availability of more space efficient forms of clean renewable energy—solar and wind. We can also take heart from huge energy savings we can realize by living more compactly. Think about what life would be like if we adopted the measures suggested so far in these pages. By instituting cap and trade for greenhouse gas emissions and spending $75 billion or so a year on investments in compact living and clean energy, we can move smoothly to a compact, green energy economy without sacrificing our opportunities for obtaining personal happiness. By doubling our urban densities, we cannot only cut our energy consumption and climate-warming emissions substantially, but many of us may find that our lives in a more compact urban landscape become more interesting.   By 2050 instead of consuming 360 gigajoules of energy each, we will likely reduce this to about 250, with the vast bulk of this being produced using solar power and wind. Instead of directly use 1,500 square meters of developed land for each of us, we will have cut the urban portion of that in half (1,100 square meters to 550 by doubling urban densities), reducing the total to about 1,250 square meters including land for solar (300 square meters). [45]

So far we have proposed measures that only marginally shrink the size of our personal land use pyramids. We now know how to go about limiting global warming without putting an obvious dent in our personal well being, but we don't yet have a clear picture on how we can shrink our personal land use pyramids beyond cutting back on our urban densities and the amount of land us city dwellers directly use—the peak area of the pyramid. We have yet to address how we can shrink up our indirect use of land for food and fiber farther down the pyramid to allow more space for the rest of nature. By cutting each of our urban space needs roughly in half, we can come up with enough space in the aggregate to accommodate solar energy production, but not enough to insure that our fellow species on the planet will have enough habitats to survive.[46] Also, in our discussions so far we have hinted at a need to limit climate warming by getting unhooked from fossil fuels without really saying why. This we will now rectify. Finally, we will set out how doing the right thing by stabilizing the global climate and leaving more space for nature will reward us with an economic boom. We will start by considering how we can help out the natural world by shrinking our indirect use of land for food and fiber. We will then be prepared to see how moving to compact living in the broadest sense of the term can set off an economic boom that will bring prosperity to all while saving the global environment.

Notes

[1] John M. Broder, "Obama to Toughen Rules on Emissions and Mileage," *New York Times*, May 19, 2009.

[2] U.S. Department of Energy and Environmental Protection Agency, *Carbon Dioxide Emissions from the Generation of Electric Power in the United States* (U.S. Department of Energy and the Environmental Protection Agency, 2000 [cited December 5, 2008]); available from http:// www.eia.doe.gov/cneaf/electricity/page/co2_report/co2emiss.pdf.

[3] Intergovernmental Panel on Climate Change, *Climate Change 2007: Mitigation of Climate Change* (University of Cambridge Press, 2007 [cited December 3, 2008]); available from http://www.ipcc.ch/ipccreports/ar4-wg3.htm.

[4] This number assumes 20 gigatons of CO_2 equivalent emissions and a price per metric ton of $100. The global 2000 emissions equaled 40 gigatons. Ibid.([cited]).

[5] U. S. Library of Congress, *H.R. 2454: American Clean Energy and Security Act of 2009* (The Library of Congress, 2009 [cited June 17, 2009]); available from http://thomas.loc.gov/cgi-bin/query/z?c111:H.R.2454:.

[6] James Hansen, *The People Vs. Cap-and-Tax* (SolveClimate, 2010 [cited January 14, 2010]); available from http://solveclimate.com/blog/20100113/ people-vs-cap-and-tax? utm_source=feedburner&utm_medium=feed&utm_campaign=Feed%3A +solveclimate%2Fblog+(Solve+Climate%3A+Daily+Climate+News+and +Analysis).

[7] David Pimentel and Marcia H. Pimentel, *Food, Energy, and Society*, Third ed. (Boco Raton, FL: CRC Press, 2008).

[8] David Pimentel and Tad W. Patzek, "Ethanol Production Using Corn, Switchgrass, and Wood; Biodiesel Production Using Soybean and Sunflower," *Natural Resources Research* 14, no. 1 (2005); Pimentel and Pimentel, *Food, Energy, and Society*. There is some disagreement about whether the net energy produced from corn ethanol is positive, but in any case it is very small. For an alternative view see Alexander Farrell et al., "Ethanol Can Contribute to Energy and Environmental Goals," *Science* 311 (2006).

[9] As already report, our current energy consumption is about 360 gigajoules per capita. The most net energy we can expect per hectare is about 100 gigajoules. See Ferguson, "The Logical Foundations of Ecological Footprints."

[10] Steven Erlanger, "French Plans for Energy Reaffirm Nuclear Path," *New York Times*, August 17 2008; World Nuclear Association, *Nuclear Power in France* (World Nuclear Association, 2009 [cited May18, 2009]); available from http://www.world-nuclear.org/info/inf40.htm.

[11] International Energy Agency, *Key World Energy Statistics: 2008* ([cited]).

[12] Erlanger, "French Plans for Energy Reaffirm Nuclear Path."; World Nuclear Association, *Nuclear Power in France* ([cited]).

[13] The folks at MIT believe these problems can be solved. See MIT Energy Initiative, *Update of the MIT 2003 Future of Nuclear Power: An Interdisciplinary Study* (MIT, 2009 [cited May 19, 2009]); available from http://web.mit.edu/nuclearpower/pdf/nuclearpower-update2009.pdf.

[14] James Kanter, "Not So Fast, Nukes: Cost Overruns Plague a New Breed of Reactor," *New York Times*, May 29, 2009.

[15] There are other energy sources I have yet to mention that will fill the zero-carbon emissions bill just as wind and solar, including geothermal, tidal, and low-impact hydroelectric. I haven't brought these up mainly because they will probably not be a huge part of clean energy supply, although they each will play a part. Big hydro projects are a thing of the past because of the ecological problems they cause, but small projects that draw off running water from high velocity streams, run it through a generator, and send it back to the streams from whence it came are a potential source of carbon-free energy.

[16] Joseph Eto, *The Past, Present, and Future of U.S. Utility Demand-Side Management Programs* (Ernest Orlando Lawrence Berkeley National Laboratory, 1996 [cited May 21, 2009]); available from http://www.osti.gov/bridge/servlets/purl/491537-Ttec7Y/webviewable/491537.pdf.

[17] California Public Utility Commission, *California's Decoupling Policy* (California Public Utility Commission, 2009 [cited May 21, 2009]); available from http://www.cpuc.ca.gov/cleanenergy/design/docs/Deccouplinglowres.pdf; Steven Mufson, "In Energy Conservation, Calif. Sees Light," *Washington Post* 2007.

[18] Rebecca Smith, "Lightening the Load: Solar-Energy Advocates Look for Innovative Ways to Reduce the Upfront Installation Costs," *Wall Street Journal*, October 6, 2008.

[19] Cynthia Mitchell, "Stabilizing California's Demand: The Real Reasons Behind the State's Energy Savings," *Public Utilities Fortnightly*, March 2009.

[20] Oregon State Archives, *Governor Tom McCall's Administration: Biographical Note* (Oregon State Archives, 2009 [cited May 26, 2009]); available from http://arcweb.sos.state.or.us/governors/McCall/ mccallbiography.htm; William G. Robbins, *People, Politics, and the Environmental since 1945: Pollution in Paradise* (Oregon Historical Society, 2002 [cited May 26, 2009]); available from http://www.ohs.org/education/ oregonhistory/narratives/subtopic.cfm?subtopic_ID=173.

[21] William G. Robbins, *Landscapes of Conflict: The Oregon Story, 1940-2000* (Seattle: University of Washington, 2004).

[22] Tom Daniels and Deborah Bowers, *Holding Our Ground: Protecting America's Farmland* (Washington D.C.: Island Press, 1999).

[23] Metro, *Urban Growth Boundary* (Metro Regional Government, 2009 [cited June 8, 2009]); available from http://www.oregonmetro.gov/index.cfm/ go/by.web/id=277.

[24] Justin Phillipps and Eban Goodstein, "Growth Management and Housing Prices: The Case of Portland, Oregon," *Contemporary Economic Policy* 18 (2000).

[25] Eric Mortenson, *Court Orders Multnomah County to Pay $1.15 Million to Dorothy English Estate* (The Oregonian, 2009 [cited May 27, 2009]); available from http://www.oregonlive.com/environment/index.ssf/2009/04/ court_reverses_multnomah_count.html.

[26] Eric T. Freyfogle, *The Land We Share: Private Property and the Common Good* (Washington D.C.: Island Press / Shearwater Books, 2003).

[27] Oregon Department of Land Conservation and Development, *Dlcd Measure 37* (Oregon Department of Land Conservation and Development, 2008 [cited May 27, 2009]); available from http://www.oregon.gov/LCD/ MEASURE37/legal_information.shtml#top.

[28] Institute of Portland Metropolitan Studies, *Measure 37 Database* (Portland State University, Institute of Portland Metropolitan Studies, 2007 [cited May 27, 2009]); available from http://www.pdx.edu/ims/measure-37-database#regioncounty; Oregon Department of Land Conservation and Development, *DLCD Measure 37: Summary of Claims* (Oregon Department of Land Conservation and Development, 2007 [cited May 27, 2009]); available from http://www.oregon.gov/LCD/MEASURE37/ summaries_of_claims.shtml.

[29] Oregon Department of Land Conservation and Development, *Measure 49 Guide* (Oregon Department of Land Conservation and Development, 2008 [cited May 27, 2009]); available from http://www.oregon.gov/LCD/ MEASURE49/docs/general/m49_guide.pdf. New claims for property value losses caused by regulation can be made under Measure 49, but such claims are restricted to certain kinds of regulations, the property value loss must be clearly documented with appraisals, and added development of residential dwellings is limited to the amount of the property value loss. On farm and forestland, such compensating developments are restricted in acreage and must be clustered to reduce the negative affect on the land's basic use. Commercial and industrial development is prohibited on land originally zoned as residential or high-value farm or forestland.

[30] Daniels and Bowers, *Holding Our Ground: Protecting America's Farmland.*

[31] The match for federal highway projects usually amounts to 90 percent. See Susan Pantell, *Tipping the Playing Field: How America's Federal Funding Policy Heavily Favors Roads over Transit* (Light Rail Now, 2009 [cited June 8, 2009]); available from http://www.lightrailnow.org/features/ f_lrt_2009-05a.htm.

[32] A tax on carbon emissions and their equivalents were adopted instead, it would provide an equivalent stream of revenues.

[33] Intergovernmental Panel on Climate Change, *Climate Change 2007: Mitigation of Climate Change* ([cited]).

[34] The emission allowance schedule used is based on HR 2454, the "American Clean Energy and Security Act of 2009" and the Congressional Budget Office cost estimates for this bill. See U. S. Library of Congress, *H.R. 2454: American Clean Energy and Security Act of 2009* ([cited]); U.S. Congressional Budget Office, *Congressional Budget Office Cost Estimate: H.R. 2454 American Clean Energy and Security Act of 2009* (U.S. Congressional Budget Office, 2009 [cited June 17, 2009]); available from http://www.cbo.gov/ftpdocs/102xx/doc10262/hr2454.pdf.

[35] U.S. Department of Transportation, *U.S. Department of Transportation Fiscal Year 2009 Budget in Brief* (U.S. Department of Transportation, 2008 [cited December 6, 2008]); available from http://www.dot.gov/bib2009/htm/ FTA.html.

36   Federal Transit Administration U.S. Department of Transportation, *Analysis of Capital Costs and Their Effect on Operating Costs* (U.S. Department of Transportation, 2005 [cited December 6, 2008]); available from p://www.utrc2.org/research/assets/107/utrc-2005-fta1.pdf; Research and Innovative Technology Administration U.S. Department of Transportation, *Pocket Guide to Transportation 2007* (U.S. Department of Transportation, 2007 [cited December 6, 2008]); available from http://www.bts.gov/publications/pocket_guide_to_transportation/2007/.

37 David W. Chen, "In the Future, the City's Streets Are to Behave," *New York Times*, May 20, 2009.

38 Energy Star Program U.S. Department of Energy, *Federal Tax Credits for Energy Efficiency* (U.S. Department of Energy, 2008 [cited December 8, 2008]); available from http://www.energystar.gov/index.cfm?c=products.pr_tax_credits#s3.

39 U.S. Congressional Budge Office, *Estimated Changes in Direct Spending and Revenues under H.R. 5351, the Renewable Energy and Energy Conservation Tax Act of 2008* (U.S. Congressional Budget Office, 2008 [cited December 9, 2008]); available from http://www.cbo.gov/ftpdocs/90xx/doc9001/hr5351.pdf.

40 In the $737 billion 2009 stimulus bill, the Obama administration plans to spend an added 9.3 billion on inner-city high speed rail and an additional $8.4 billion on public transit. Highways and bridges will get 27.5 billion. Farhana Hossain et al., *New York Times* (New York Times, June 7, 2009 [cited June 8, 2009]); available from http://projects.nytimes.com/44th_president/stimulus.

41 As a part of the 2009 stimulus package, the Obama administration plans to spend upwards of $5 billion on weatherization in a year. Ibid.([cited]).

42 Energy tax incentives in the stimulus bill will be increased by $14 billion and the smart grid will get $10.9 billion. Ibid.([cited]).

43 The stimulus bill has $11 billion in it for smart grid. For an estimate of spending need for a smart grid, see Miller, *The Smart Grid--Benefits and Challenges* ([cited].. The stimulus bill includes $6 billion for an innovative energy loan guarantee program. Hossain et al., *New York Times* ([cited).

44 Hossain et al., *New York Times* ([cited]).

45   USDA Natural Resources Conservation Service, "2001 Annual NRI: Urbanization and Development of Rural Land." The land requirement for solar is explained in Chapter 3.

[46] About 78 percent of our developed land occurs within urban area boundaries. Ibid. This means doubling our urban density would cut the amount of developed land each of us uses in urban areas from 78x1,400=1,092 square meters to roughly 550 square meters. To accommodate solar we already suggested a need for about 300 square meters.

Chapter 10
Saving Nature Through Compact Living

Arizona today is among the fastest growing states in the country.[1] The bulk of that growth is concentrated in a huge swath of Sonoran desert landscape stretching from the northwestern suburbs of Phoenix to the southern edge of Tucson, Arizona. As cities such as Phoenix, Scottsdale, and Tucson have expanded in recent years, the surrounding Sonoran Desert has receded, resulting in threats to some of the desert's rarest species. One of these is the Cactus Ferruginous Pygmy-Owl.

Pygmy-Owls

The reddish-brown cactus pygmy-owl is so small that it will fit in the palm of your hand. The owl lives in woodpecker-carved cavities of tall softwood trees and columnar cacti, especially the saguaro, and likes a patchy landscape with a mixture of dense scrub and open areas where it can find its lunch. The pygmy owl's menu includes birds, lizards, insects, and small mammals. Despite its diminutive stature, the owl is a ferocious predator, and will attack robin-sized birds twice its size. Wherever it lives, the pygmy-owl terrorizes birdlife. The owl calls for its mate from perches on tall tree branches or the entrance to its cavity and likes the presence of fairly tall trees for their shade, protection from predators, and perch sites for spotting prey. The owl seems to require the presence of low shrubs around its cavity, probably for the protection of its fledglings when they first venture outside the nest from hawks and other predators. At one time, the pygmy-owl lived along rivers throughout much of the Sonoran Desert where its ideal habitat requirements were best met and where historically its presence was commonly noted. The decline of Arizona's riparian woodlands at the hands of woodcutting, agriculture, overgrazing, water projects, and urban development led to a substantial reduction in pygmy-owl populations. The few remaining Arizona owls were forced to retreat from riparian habitats to desertscrub with saguaro for nest cavities near washes. A pair of owls in Arizona will defend an area of up to 4 hectares, although they will use a much larger amount of land than that outside the breeding season, as much as 100 hectares. Today, Arizona populations of the owl are concentrated in the Tucson area.[2]

Pygmy-owls, like human beings, need space to live in, but space of a very specific kind. The type of space they need has shrunk so much that very few owls remain in Arizona. In recent years, the number of documented pygmy-owls in Arizona has ranged from about 20 to 80. In the simplest possible terms, the human invasion of pygmy-owl space means fewer pygmy-owls.

The remaining prime occupied habitat for pygmy-owls occurs in Pima County, which includes Tucson, and covers a total area of 24 million hectares. Unfortunately for the owl, Pima County is near the top of the list for U.S. county growth rates.   Development in the County consumes anywhere from 1,800 to 2,600 hectares (a hectare is a bit less than two football fields) of desert a year to accommodate population growth ranging from 15,000 to 30,000. Development removes saguaros cacti needed as nesting and perching sites and the shrubby vegetation required for fledglings. Owls also fall prey to foraging house cats and suffer mortality at the hands of increase motor vehicle traffic. Development alters drainage patterns, often increasing water flows damaging to desertscrub vegetation favored by owls. Ironically, vegetation growth associated with planting of ornamentals and watering in low-density residential areas appears to be attracting pygmy-owls, but naturalists fear that these areas act as population sinks or black holes where owls can't survive human-connected depredations (i.e. house cats and vehicle collisions).[3]

To retain pygmy-owl populations in the Tucson area, desert landscapes will have to be set aside for the owl's exclusive use. In short, if we human beings care at all about their continued survival, pygmy-owls have their own ecological footprint that requires respect. If we lack such a concern, then their footprint doesn't much matter, unless we want to protect their habitat for other reasons.   The existence of the U.S. Endangered Species Act suggests at least some regard on our part for nonhuman species.

The U.S. Fish and Wildlife Service listed the pygmy-owl as endangered under provisions of the Endangered Species Act in 1997 (although it was taken off the list in 2006 despite opposition to this move by scientists). In response both to the listing and a larger desire to address the impacts of rapid growth on the area's Sonoran Desert landscape, the Pima County Board of Supervisors initiated a science-based planning process oriented to the protection of natural, cultural, and historical land-based resources. The process resulted in the Sonoran Desert Conservation Plan. The purpose of the Plan is not to bring growth to a halt, but to direct it away from key natural, historical, and biological resources and to keep ranchers in business. The plan will guide land use decisions and the spending of public money on open space conservation. A key element of the plan is the conservation of critical habitat and biological corridors with an eye to protecting 55 vulnerable species, including our friend the pygmy-owl. The basic idea behind the plan is to conserve a number of species simultaneously by protecting large chunks of habitat. The plan includes more than 2.5 million acres (1 million hectares) as biological core habitats and important riparian areas, of which a little over 200,000 acres (80,000 hectares) is in private hands.   Through zoning regulations and other measures, the goals of the plan include protecting 80 percent of core habitat (113,000 acres) and 95 percent of riparian areas (37,000 acres) on private lands.[4]

The plan puts money where its mouth is. In 2004 the citizens of Pima County approved a $174 million open space bond issue for the acquisition and preservation of critical habitat. About 100,000 acres of key habitats have been protected using bond funds so far through acquisitions and other actions.   Nonhuman species need space; the citizens of Pima County have opened their pocketbooks to insure that the pygmy-owls of the world and other desert plant and animal species will have some. Again, the strategy directs development away from key natural habitats by buying up or otherwise protecting land from human intrusion.[5]

Life is far from perfect. Anyone who has ever driven around Tucson knows that it is low density, spread out, and strongly auto oriented. Still, Tucson residents have expressed a willingness to spend at least some of their tax money on the protection of desert habitat, perhaps because open space is a highly desired amenity that enhances property values, or perhaps out of concern for the well being of threatened desert species. Whatever their motives, the residents of Tucson seem willing to protect at least some natural landscapes from human development.

Henslow's Sparrow

Compared to the pygmy-owl, Henslow's Sparrow is pretty nondescript with its light brown body with black and white streaks and an olive face and neck. To non-birders, they look similar to any other sparrow. Like the pygmy-owl, at 11-13 centimeters (4-5 inches) in length, you could easily hold it in your hand. The Henslow's Sparrow originally occupied the coastal marshes along the eastern seaboard and the tall grass prairies of the central U.S. Today both habitats are shadows of their former selves and the sparrow has moved into large fields with tall, dense grass, a thick litter layer, standing dead vegetation, and an absence of trees and shrubs. Even this kind of habitat has shrunken in abundance as urban development has encroached into farmland, and farmers expand row crop planting and hay production. As a consequence, the sparrow appears on the Audubon Society's watch list and is a threatened species for states such as Wisconsin.[6]

The Henslow is hard to see because it prefers to stay on the ground, running from its enemies through tall grass rather than flying. Since the sparrow constructs its nest in grass litter just above the ground, it becomes easy prey for house cats in urbanizing landscapes, especially near field edges. The sparrow forages in the grass, feeding primarily on beetles and spiders, and sometimes adds seeds to its diet. The sparrow is a songbird, which sings mainly at dawn, and migrates to the South in winter. In its summer haunts, the sparrow needs space. U.S. populations of Henslow's Sparrow have decline since 1966 by 68 percent or more, primarily because of habitat loss. In Illinois, one study finds that the sparrows avoid habitat patches of less than 100 hectares. Each breeding pair appears to need about a hectare, and they sometime occur in colonies, but a pair will frequently be found apart from others. In short, breeding Henslow's just don't like small grassland patches.[7] They also don't seem to like patches very close to houses constructed on ridgetops.[8]

The rolling hills just to the west of Madison, Wisconsin are prime habitat for the Henslow's Sparrow. The soil is often too thin and rocky or too steep for row crops and is left in grass for pasture or fallow in return for government payments through the USDA Conservation Reserve Program. Landowners receive a government payment for leaving such lands planted in grass. Developers tempt farmers to sell their lands for housing subdivisions at prices above the land's agricultural value to feed the spreading of Madison's urban population. Such development poses a clear danger to the perpetuation of the Henslow's Sparrow in southwestern Wisconsin, and local conservation organizations are attempting to draw a line in the sand using various land protection measures to contain the outward spread of Madison's human footprint.[9]

Sage Grouse

The male sage-grouse announces the coming of spring in the high mountain prairies of the Rocky Mountain west with an unreserved display of its puffed up white breast, dual air sacs, and circular array of brown and white tail feathers and a loud and haunting, gurgling song that carries for quite a way over flat prairie landscape. The sage-grouse's hope in this display is to attract females for mating. The display occurs on leks in open areas with good acoustics near sagebrush habitat, and it is competitive. Only the most eye-catching and sonorous of the displaying males wins the attentions of the females. For this reason, mating is polygamous with one male impregnating a number of females. Sage-grouse are good sized (2-7 pounds), chicken-like birds with a black belly and brown to gray body and wings with some black striping.

After mating, the females disperse to areas with fairly tall sage brush where they set up their nests beneath the taller shrubs and lay four to seven eggs. On departing the nest, chicks feed on new-growth, succulent grasses and insects. As the heat of the summer comes on, grasses dry out and the sage-grouse move to riparian areas or wet meadows with nearby sage brush for cover. Here they can continue to feed until fall. In late fall and early winter, broods of grouse migrate to valley-bottom or flatland fields of sagebrush. Here they feed on the sagebrush itself and dig burrows in the snow for cover when it gets deep.[10]

The Gunnison Grouse has recently been declared a separate species from what was formerly called the Greater Sage-Grouse, now referred to as simply the Sage Grouse. The Gunnison Grouse is smaller than the Sage Grouse and differs from the later in terms of certain behaviors, physical features, and genes. The Sage Grouse in general faces stresses from human activities, but the Gunnison Grouse is even worse off because of its comparatively small population, most of which is concentrated in the Gunnison Basin in central Colorado. The World Conservation Union and the Audubon Society have both declared the Gunnison Grouse to be an endangered species, although the U.S. Fish and Wildlife Service has yet to list the species under the Endangered Species Act. In any event, the Gunnison Grouse appears to be in trouble. Somewhere around 2,500 grouse reside in the basin including 500 breeding males. More than this may be needed over the long haul to avoid inbreeding depression and the threat of extinction.

In the Gunnison Basin today, grouse range over 240,000 hectares of sage brush habitat, using roughly 100 hectares each. About a third of this is privately owned, and about 45 percent of the 2003 active leks occurred on private property. Conservation agreements protect approximately 11,000 hectares of grouse habitat on private lands. The existing range in the basin can probably support an average population of 3,000, enough experts say to avoid extinction.

To survive in the long run, the Gunnison Grouse needs space of a certain kind. The grouse require sagebrush that includes the right kind of open areas for leks as well as riparian areas or wet meadows in the summer. The beauty of the Gunnison Basin and its proximity to popular skiing, mountain biking, and hiking areas is not a blessing for the Gunnison Grouse. Housing development in the basin is rapidly invading grouse habitat. This adds to historical habitat losses from clearing sagebrush to make room for hay fields and pasture. On top of this, Grouse habitat on public lands is chopped up by backcountry roads increasingly popular with mountain bikers, motor cycle riders, and retirees on all-terrain vehicles. Charging around the prairie on a warm summer day in an incredibly scenic landscape for many is irresistible. Unfortunately, Gunnison Grouse easily spook from such human intrusions and pull back from habitat and leks near roads. In the long run, this will mean fewer grouse. Despite inherent vulnerabilities to predators from their inability to fly more than a few meters, Gunnison Grouse have managed to survive in evolutionary time, but human invasions of their habitat create even more challenging problems for them to which they cannot easily adapt.[11]

The Sage Grouse, Henslow's Sparrow, and pygmy-owl face clear and present dangers from the outward march of suburban and rural development into their respective habitats. Numerous species of all kinds in this country —plants, birds, mammals, reptiles, invertebrates—must contend with habitats receding because of an ever expanding human spatial footprint. The biggest single threat to nonhuman plant and animal species today is habitat loss.[12] Plants and animals, just like us humans, need space. As we expand our own land use pyramid, space for much of the rest of nature shrinks. Going on a spatial diet and constraining outward urban and rural housing expansion will not only help reduce our greenhouse gas emissions and do the other good things we have already described, it will do a favor for the rest of nature as well. Urban growth boundaries around Tucson, Arizona, Madison, Wisconsin, and Gunnison, Colorado would help protect key threatened species from future extinction. Similar stories can no doubt be found for other localities as well.

Threatened Species and Habitat Gaps

To survive, most native plant and animal species require habitat free of any substantial human encroachments. A sizable amount of relatively natural habitat in this country lies within landscapes protected from significant human disturbance, but much does not.[13]   Many species find their most desired habitats outside of protected landscapes and face threats from expanded human occupancy and use of such areas.   Again, as the human imprint on the earth's surface expands, nature's space forcibly contracts. Gaps in protected spaces for a variety of plant and animal species unfortunately exist, and the first step in figuring out what to about it is something called "gap analysis" which seeks to identify "gaps" in protected habitats for vegetation types and species vulnerable to further human intrusions and harms.

The U.S. Geological Survey oversees gap analysis, but much of the work is done at a state or regional level by scientists with special knowledge of local landscapes. The essential goal is to produce detailed digital maps using remote sensing that show land ownership and conservation status, the coverage of actual vegetation by plant community type, and the predicted distribution of vertebrate species based on habitat suitability. This first step discovers where the gaps occur in habitats needing protection. The maps also can be combined to determine where plant community types and vertebrate species are poorly represented on protected lands. Gap analysis relies heavily on remote sensing to determine the distribution of vegetation and then uses vegetation and other information to predict vertebrate species distribution.   Nothing beats on the ground surveys for determining where plants and animals occur, but such surveys on a large scale would be prohibitively expensive.[14]

Let's use California to see how gap analysis works and how it can help us understand human affects nature's space.   Gap analysis divides the landscape up into four categories that define the level of protection. Status 1 lands have permanent protection from conversion of natural land cover to human uses and a legally mandated management plan with the goal of protecting native plant and animal species from local extinction.   Status 2 lands are protected from the conversion of natural cover, but have a slightly weaker management mandate that allows for some habitat degradation. Status 1 and 2 lands are usually under public ownership, but some are controlled by nonprofit conservation organizations such as the Nature Conservancy. Status 3 lands are afforded some protections from the natural vegetation conversion, but can be used for natural resource extraction, such as logging, grazing, oil and gas production, and some forms of mining. These are mostly federally owned lands where compliance with the provisions of the Endangered Species Act is required. Finally, Status 4 lands are largely privately owned and lack any substantial legal protection from conversion of natural habitat to intensive human uses. In California, about 18 percent of the state's lands fall in category 1 and 2, and another 30 percent in category 3 for a total of 48 percent, a substantial amount by any standard. On the face of it, California appears to do quite a good job in protecting its natural habitats, but to get a more accurate assessment we need to dig a little further.

California is especially blessed with a high degree of plant and animal species diversity, both because of its size and landscape variability. In the evolutionary scheme of things, species adapt to their own special habitat niches which will be found in greater numbers in big landscapes with extensive environmental diversity. From California's south to north one goes from the Mohave Desert to snowy, mountainous landscapes symbolized by Mount Shasta. From the state's west to east one moves from a stunning and biologically rich coastline, up over the western slopes of the heavily forested Sierra Nevada Mountains, into high elevation desert country. Such an unusual geography and big differences in climate make for plenty of possible habitat niches for a wide variety of flora and fauna. California is also the most populous state in the union with some of the most substantial threats to is native plants and animals caused by expansive human uses of the state's landscape. Californians love their low density suburbs nestled into beautiful hills along the coast and inland mountain ranges. The state is both a national leader in biodiversity, with 455 vertebrate species and 194 plant community types covered by its gap study, and in federally endangered or threatened plant and animal species—130 animals including invertebrates and 179 plants. To be fair, part of the reason the state has so many threatened and endangered species is because of its extensive landscape diversity that creates such a variety of niches for its plant and animal. More species occur in California than any other single state. Of course, without human invasions and disturbances of nature's habitats, threats to the continued survival of native plants and animals would be minimal. California's huge human population (36 million plus) spreads out over privately owned lands, crowding out and disturbing numerous native plants and animal species.[15]

While California protects more land from development than most states, this still isn't enough to avoid threats to the diversity of the state's biological riches. The largest pieces of protected landscapes occur in the Sierra Nevada Mountains and the Mohave Desert in the southern part of the state. Of all the families of animals in the state, reptiles enjoy the greatest degree of protection, primarily because so much desert habitat is preserved from disturbance and change. Unfortunately, other animals, such as amphibians and birds, lack the security they need from human landscape development and disturbance. In many instances such species suffer because the critical plant communities they occupy, such as coastal and Great Basin scrub, prairie grasslands, riparian forests, hardwood oak woodlands, and old-growth conifer forests, are insufficiently protected from human encroachment. These plant community types and the animal species they support unfortunately are found exactly where we humans love to live—on the coast, in the open valley bottoms and the foothills, and near water and mountains.

When we develop lands for intensive human use of any kind, the first thing we do is put in roads. Roads carve up large chunks of habitat and reduce its suitability for occupancy by native species. Many animals will not go near roads, especially large predators such as wolves and grizzly bears, and many face death from motor vehicles, particularly birds, small mammals, and amphibians as well as large mammals such as deer. Roads not only reduce usable habitat, but subdivide it into pieces that may not be big enough to support populations of some species, especially larger animals that need more space to survive. In California, roughly 30 percent of Status 4 lands (privately owned) is negatively affected by roads as is 15 percent of Status 3 lands (mainly lands under management by the U.S. Forest Service and the Bureau of Land Management). Fortunately for the natural world, status 1 and 2 lands preclude road development. While gap analysis tells us that Status 3 lands amount to about 30 percent of the California landscape, a good portion of that land is unusable as habitat for many species because of the presence of roads.[16]

Simply put, California is amongst the best situated of the lower 48 states to protect its native plants and animals but yet has quite a ways to go to fully accomplish the job. Other states, where land development is more extensive and land protection less prevalent, face a more difficult challenge. Placing growth boundaries around our large urban areas as well as our rural communities would put a substantial constraint on further human invasions of natural habitats. Compact living in this way can play a critical role in protecting nature's riches from further human-induced degradation. This would be an important side-benefit from each of us limiting our both our direct and indirect spatial footprint on the earth's environment.

To place California's landscape protection efforts in perspective, let's compare them to the country as a whole. For the 48-states, status 1 and 2 lands amount to approximately 7 percent of the total (based on an analysis of the 35 states that have completed their gap studies).[17] In per capita terms, this amounts to 1,750 square meters for each of us, or a bit less than a third of a football field. The national figure for status 3 lands equals 23 percent of the total, or 5,750 square meters per capita, about a football field. Because California has so much of its landscape in public ownership, it does much better for Status 1, 2, and 3 lands at 48 percent than the U.S. (lower 48 states) at 30 percent (or about 7,500 square meters for each of us). Remember, these protected lands lie outside our own personal land use pyramid on landscapes that are still naturally vegetated and not subject to intensive human use, the total of which equals 12,100 square meters per capita in the lower 48 states. Of our naturally vegetated areas, 62 percent bear some level of protection (Status 1, 2, or 3) from substantial human incursions, but the rest doesn't, and a huge chunk of this land lies in western states, such as California, where federal ownership of land is much more prevalent. While we have protected quite a bit of land in total, its relative distribution is lacking in balance across the landscape.[18] Some habitat types are quite well protected but many are not.

Sadly, the species extinction cow is out of the barn for many plant and animal species around the world. If we protect remaining habitats, we might be able to at least shut the door before more escape, but we will not recover those species who are threatened by habitats already well on the way to disappearing because of an ever-expanding human spatial footprint. Putting boundaries around urban areas won't get us back the habitat we have already lost and won't reverse the harm to landscapes already heavily disturbed by roads and other human intrusions.

The point of all this is simple; our work is cut out for us if we want to protect those species suffering a shortage of habitat cause by our own ever-expanding land use pyramid. Containing further expansion of that pyramid is important for protecting nature's space, but we will need to do more. In short, we will have to give back to nature some of our own exploited spaces.

Notes

[1] U.S. Census Bureau, *Population Projections* (U.S. Census Bureau, 2008 [cited December 8, 2008]); available from http://www.census.gov/population/www/projections/usinterimproj/.

[2] Center for Biological Diversity and Defenders of Wildlife, *Petition to List the Cactus Ferruginous Pygmy Owl as a Threatened or Endangered Species under the Endangered Species Act* (Center for Biological Diversity, 2007 [cited May 28, 2009]); available from http://www.biologicaldiversity.org/species/birds/cactus_ferruginous_pygmy_owl/pdfs/petition-to-list-cactus-ferruginous-pygmy-owl-03-2007.pdf; R. Roy Johnson et al., "Cactus Ferruginous Pygmy-Owl in Arizona, 1872-1971," *Southwestern Naturalist* 48, no. 3 (2003).

[3] Center for Biological Diversity and Wildlife, *Petition to List the Cactus Ferruginous Pygmy Owl as a Threatened or Endangered Species under the Endangered Species Act* ([cited); Chuck Huckelberry, "The Sonoran Desert Conservation Plan," *Endangered Species Bulletin* 27, no. 2 (2002).

[4] Pima County, "Pima-County Multi-Species Conservation Plan," (Tucson, AZ: Pima County, 2006).

[5] Coalition for Sonoran Desert Protection, *Open Space Bond Acquisitions* (Coalition for Sonoran Desert Protection, 2006 [cited May 28, 2009]); available from http://www.sonorandesert.org/learning-more/open-space-bond-acquisitions.

[6] James R. Herkert, "Status and Habitat Selection of the Henslow's Sparrow in Illinois," *Willson Bulletin* 106, no. 1 (1994); Lori Pruitt, "Henslow's Sparrow: Status Assessment," (Bloomington, IN: U.S. Fish and Wildlife Service, 1996).

[7] Herkert, "Status and Habitat Selection of the Henslow's Sparrow in Illinois."

[8] David W. Sample and Michael J. Mossman, "Managing Habitat for Grassland Birds: A Guide for Wisconsin," (Madison, WI: Wisconsin Department of Natural Resources, 1997).

[9] Douglas E. Booth, *Land Trusts and Biodiversity* (Milwaukee, WI: Driftless Conservation Books, 2007).

[10] Gunnison Basin Gunnison Sage-Grouse Local Working Group, *Gunnison Sage Grouse Conservation Plan: Gunnison Basin, Colorado* (Colorado Division of Wildlife, 1997 [cited May 29, 2009]); available from http://wildlife.state.co.us/NR/rdonlyres/30FDBAF5-1C11-48F9-A797-9827CA6181CF/0/GunnisonSageGrouseLocalPlan_GunnisonBasin.pdf; Gunnison Sage-Grouse Rangewide Steering Committee, *Gunnison Sage-Grouse Rangewide Conservation Plan* (Colorado Division of Wildlife, 2005 [cited May 29, 2009]); available from http://wildlife.state.co.us/WildlifeSpecies/SpeciesOfConcern/Birds/GunnisonConsPlan.htm.

[11] Gunnison Sage-Grouse Local Working Group, *Gunnison Sage Grouse Conservation Plan: Gunnison Basin, Colorado* ([cited]); Gunnison Sage-Grouse Rangewide Steering Committee, *Gunnison Sage-Grouse Rangewide Conservation Plan* ([cited]).

[12] Wilcove et al., "Rebuilding the Ark: Toward a More Effective Endangered Species Act for Private Land."

[13] Scott et al., "Nature Reserves: Do They Capture the Full Range of America's Biological Diversity?"; Wilcove et al., "Rebuilding the Ark: Toward a More Effective Endangered Species Act for Private Land."

[14] U.S. Geological Survey, *About the Gap Analysis Program* (U.S. Geological Survey, National Biological Information Infrastructure, 2009 [cited May 29, 2009]); available from http://gapanalysis.nbii.gov/portal/server.pt?open=512&objID=1482&PageID=5113&cached=true&mode=2&userID=2.

[15] U.S. Geological Survey, *A Gap Analysis of California* (U.S. Geological Survey, 1998 [cited May 29, 2009]); available from http://gapanalysis.nbii.gov/portal/server.pt?open=512&objID=1483&PageID=5125&cached=true&mode=2&userID=2.

[16] Ibid.([cited]).

[17] Complete gap analysis studies can be found at U.S. Geological Survey, *About the Gap Analysis Program* ([cited]). My own calculations for status 1, 2, and 3 land area for the lower 48 are based on the 35 state gap analysis studies completed as of June 2008. I extrapolated the figures for these 35 states to the lower 48 as a whole to come up with my estimates.

[18] Scott et al., "Nature Reserves: Do They Capture the Full Range of America's Biological Diversity?."; Wilcove et al., "Rebuilding the Ark: Toward a More Effective Endangered Species Act for Private Land."

Chapter 11
The Ecology of Grass and Compact Green Cuisine

By late summer, settlers moving across Illinois or Iowa in the 1850s would find themselves in a sea of grass, sometimes reaching as much as nine feet in height. At first, in choosing their homesteads settlers passed over the prairie for the more familiar woodlands located near rivers, but farmers soon discovered the incredible organic richness of the thick prairie sod. Once the challenge of breaking the sod up was overcome with new, larger steel-bladed plows, settlers swarmed to the prairies much like the locust that sometimes infested them. Today the boundaries of the old tallgrass prairie largely define the spatial extent of our modern corn and soybean agricultural economy. Less than one percent of the original prairie remains in small remnants, most confined to areas too rocky to plow. These remaining remnants suffer potential extinction for lack of the fire needed to fend of the invasion of woodland species. Without fire, forests would have marched across the tallgrass landscape, and the environment early settlers found would have been entirely different. Because of the virtual disappearance of the tallgrass ecosystem, grassland birds such as the Prairie Chicken, Sandhill Crane, and Baird's and Henslow's Sparrow are among the most threatened in the central U.S. Prairie invertebrates, such as the beautiful regal fritillary butterfly, and a number of wildflower species, such as the prairie white-fringed orchid, Mead's milkweed, and prairie bush clover, face endangerment as well. These along with hundreds of other species have been replaced mostly by corn and soybeans.[1]

The Wonders of Corn

No one describes the wonders of corn more incisively than Michael Pollan, author of the bestselling *Omnivore's Dilemma*.[2] You can't see it, but in the grocery store, corn is everywhere—in steaks, pork chops, chicken, eggs, dairy products, soda, beer, margarine, baked goods, and on and on. You will find it at the drugstore as well—in toothpaste, cosmetics, disposable diapers, and vitamins. Corn finds its way into trash bags, cleaners, joint compound, wallboard, linoleum, fiberglass, and biodegradable water cups at my neighborhood espresso shop. You can't easily escape the reach of corn.

Corn has prospered as a species in human hands because of its versatility. Among the grasses, corn produces more seeds per plant than any other, and through plant breeding these seeds have been enlarged and filled with an abundance of starches, proteins, and oils. Even in the pioneer days corn had a multitude of uses such as the essential ingredient for brewing beer and distilling whiskey, feed for growing hogs, winter silage for livestock, fuel for stoves, grain for flour, and a toilet paper substitute for the outhouse. No wonder we humans have become so adept at helping corn along on its road to evolutionary success.

Corn's triumph as a plant is mirrored in U.S. production statistics. Each year we produce 9 to 11 billion bushels using roughly 30 of the 120 million plus hectares under row crop cultivation.[3] This amounts to about 35 bushels for each of us requiring 1,000 plus square meters of cropland (a fifth of a football field). Corn clearly takes up much space. Corn production also absorbs a huge amount of energy, about 31 gigajoules per hectare,[4] equivalent roughly to the amount of energy in 230 gallons of gasoline. This means each of us on average consumes an equivalent to about 24 gallons of gasoline a year as corn. In short, corn hogs both space and energy, and in the process adds to greenhouse gas emissions.

Of all the corn produced in the U.S. about 47 percent goes for animal feed consumed mainly in feedlots or, more technically, confined animal feeding operations (CAFOs). The later term covers not only feedlots for beef, but crowded chicken houses and hog barns. Another 26 percent or so ends up in the production of ethanol, although this amount took a nosedive recently because of the recession beginning in 2008. The rest goes into a variety of products including high fructose corn syrup (our favorite sweetener for soft drinks and many other foods), dextrose and sucrose, corn starch, cereals, and our favorite alcoholic drinks.[5]

Corn to Grass

We could now easily bring up some of the health horror stories associated with corn and the environmental problems corn causes. There wouldn't be much point in doing this if we couldn't replace corn with something else. So let's turn the sequence around and talk about the possibility of plowing under about half our corn fields and turning them back to grass. On this grass we can feed beef, restore some tallgrass prairie, help out grassland birds, sequester some carbon, and create a slug of rural jobs. In the process we can dump corn-based ethanol production, which absorbs more fossil fuel energy than it creates, and do some favors for the environment.

Settlers, and later scientists, marveled at the depth of black, unplowed, carbon rich, organic prairie sod. Accumulating evidence suggests that this soil built up over time to such depths in part because of grazing. Perennial prairie grasses periodically shed portions of their carbon-filled roots, adding to the soil's organic matter, and episodic, intense grazing by bison and ungulates historically accelerated root-shedding and re-growth. After grazing, plants redirect energy from roots to shoots and allow some of their root biomass to die off. Clipping off the top of grasses by grazers jump-starts plant productivity by cutting back on self-shading and resetting grass height to its level of most rapid growth. Plant biomass increases below ground by even more than above once the shoots recover. With accelerated root growth and periodic shedding induced by grazing, deep, dark, carbon rich prairie soils built up over the centuries.[6]

Rich organic soil sequesters carbon, and busting the prairie sod and exposing it to air caused much carbon in the soil to be released back into the atmosphere by setting off the breakdown of organic matter at the hands of oxygen-using, CO_2 emitting microbes in the soil. Putting a permanent grass cover on previously plowed landscapes curtails such carbon releases and restarts the process of carbon accumulation in the soils, and carefully managed grazing accelerates the carbon accumulation process.   The conversion of cultivated land to grass can result in as much as a metric ton of carbon accumulation on each hectare (slightly less than two football fields) per year.   Studies in the U.S. suggest that improved pasture management alone on a hectare of land can lead to an average added annual carbon accumulation of about half a metric ton.[7] If carbon offsets are priced at $100 a metric ton, farmers could earn an extra $50-100 a hectare (or $20-40 an acre) for pasture agriculture.[8] This of course assumes a system where carbon offsets can be created by sequestering carbon and then sold to greenhouse gas emitters who could use them in place of emission allowances under a cap and trade system (we will have more to say on this approach at the end of the next chapter). Since, the profit from $3 a bushel corn adds up to about $250 a hectare ($100 an acre), up to 40 percent of the profit from corn can be alternatively earned by letting the grass grow and be clipped from time-to-time by grazing animals.[9]

The beauty of intensive pasture management is that you need neither a huge amount of land nor a huge amount of equipment to make a living. Joel Salatin, a pioneer in pasture management and one of Michael Pollen's heroes, describes in simple terms how one can do so on a 100 acres (40 hectares) of Midwestern grain farmland by putting it into grass.   According to Salatin, one could buy 200 calves at 500 pounds each in the spring for roughly $80,000, put 260 pounds on each by grazing them over the summer, and sell them in the fall for $114,000. After taking of $4,000 for fencing, water line, mineral and vitamin supplements, and fuel, we have $30,000 left, which is a whole lot more than the $10,000 you could earn from corn. Add to this the $2,000-$4,000 from carbon sequestration, and one is up to at least $32,000, which is not bad for a summer's work of moving cattle around each day from paddock to paddock and the electric fending you would need to keep them eating in the right spot. The income is probably underestimated here because of the premium price one can get for grass-fed beef, but more on that shortly.[10]

The secret to pasture farming is in the timing. Once grass is sheared off by grazing, the plant sheds some roots, adding to soil fertility and carbon stores, and devotes its energy to re-growing the above ground shoot. During "the blaze of growth," photosynthesis drives the increase in both shoots and roots, and only after completion of this phase should cows be put back on a pasture. Cows should be continuously grazed, but moved from paddock to paddock making sure they clip off only a first bite. An electric fence is repositioned after each move to make sure the cows stay where they belong. According to Salatin, he spends no more than thirty minutes a day moving the cows around.[11]   This leaves plenty of time for complementary farm enterprises to bolster income further. Check out one of Salatin's books for ideas about additional ways to earn income on a pasture operation, or Michael Pollan's discussion of Polyface Farm in *Omnivore's Dilemma*. Don't miss the one about the mobile chicken coops that can be moved around in the wake of the cows to perform a pasture cleanup as well as to grow some free-range chickens much in demand in the market for organics meats these days.

Of course for every corn farm we plow up, we lose the corn we need to support feedlot beef. A forty hectare farm (nearly 100 acres) can produce 15,000 bushels of corn or alternatively 52,000 pounds of beef under Salatin's intensive pasture system. Since 15,000 bushels of corn weighs in at 840,000 pounds, and since feedlots convert 8 pounds of corn into about a pound of beef, we would be giving up 105,000 pounds of feedlot for 52,000 pounds of grass-fed beef. So if we got rid of the feedlot system and switched to pasture beef, we would need to cut our consumption in half or else double the amount of land devoted to feeding beef cattle. If we give up corn-based in favor of pasture-fed beef, we will save roughly 13 percent of the corn we produce.[12] We can save another 26 percent or so by getting rid of corn-based ethanol production.[13] We could easily double the amount of land devoted to feeding beef cattle by converting 13 of the 26 percent of corn lands now used for ethanol into beef pasture. In short, we don't need to give up any beef at all, and we would have 13 percent of corn lands left over that could be devoted to something else, such as tallgrass prairie restoration or grassland bird habitat, but more on that shortly. Finally we could save another 5 percent or so of corn lands by shifting to grass-based dairy farming for a grand total reduction in corn production and acreage of 44 percent. Let's talk first about why we want to dump corn-based ethanol. Then we will take up the feasibility of switching to grass-based dairy.

The problem with corn-based ethanol is simple—the total production system from the corn itself to its fermentation and refining into ethanol absorbs more energy than it produces. Fermentation takes place in a mix of corn and water to produce a solution containing 8 percent ethanol. This liquid then needs be heated to evaporate off and capture the ethanol. A hectare's worth of corn requires about 31 gigajoules of fossil fuel energy to grow, 30 percent of which is taken up for nitrogen fertilizer alone. Another 49 gigajoules gets used up in the fermentation and refining process, and the result is about 2,900 liters (1,100 gallons) of ethanol containing roughly 62 gigajoules of energy. About 80 gigajoules goes into the process, but only 62 come out—29 percent more energy is absorbed than produced. Unsurprisingly, the government needs to subsidize the process to keep it profitable to the tune of $3 a gallon including the normal subsidy for the corn itself. In short, ethanol production under present-day technologies makes little sense either energetically or economically. Corn-based ethanol is a waste of fossil fuel resources and would not otherwise be produced were it not heavily subsidized.[14] Carbon emissions would decline if we simply used fossil fuel directly instead of converting it into ethanol.[15]

Rural landscapes dominated by corn and soybean farms, such as those in the state of Iowa, have experienced an emptying out of population in recent decades as the optimal farm size has increased over time. The essential economic virtue of this phenomenon is the realization of what economists refer to as economies of scale. As the size of the typical farm grows, average operating costs per farm decline.[16]   Today row crop farming is a capital intensive business requiring huge investments in capital equipment, the costs of which need to be spread over many units of output. Converting corn to grass and taking beef production out of the feedlot and putting it back into the pasture returns farming to a more labor intensive business based less on big capital investments and more on a deep knowledge of grass ecology. In the process, efficiencies get transferred from fossil fuel consuming big machinery, to intensive pasture management based on human capital as opposed to the physical kind.   As more experience is gained in pasture management, nothing precludes a rise in grass-based beef productivity. Research shows that pasture grass has the potential to create a huge amount of plant-based energy.[17]   It's a matter of figuring out how to capture it through efficient use of pastures.

The dairy business today experience's the same kind of trends facing corn and soybean agriculture—the number of dairy farms is shrinking while the average size of dairy herds is increasing. The Wisconsin countryside epitomizes the rural landscape we know and love—red barns, corn silos, cows grazing in pastures, and small towns dotting the landscape. While this vision still holds true in much of the state, it may not in the future given current trends. Since 1960, Wisconsin has lost more than 80 percent of its dairy farms even though dairy production increased by about 20 percent. As time marches on, each dairy farm gets bigger and each cow puts out more milk.[18]

The growth of organic dairy, rooted in intensive pasture management, may be the savior of the traditional farm landscape in Wisconsin and elsewhere. While cows are often seen in pastures, corn remains the essential feed in the dairy industry and dairy operations are starting to look like feedlots inside of big milking sheds.   It doesn't have to be this way. Converting corn fields to pasture and adopting intensive pasture management allows dairy farmers to make a decent living with anywhere from 75 to 100 cows on from 100 to 300 acres. The amount of land required per cow is in truth a bit less for pasture-based than for conventional corn-based dairy operations, although conventional milk output per cow is a bit more than for pasture cows.   The real difference between the two is in the structure of operating costs.   Conventional dairies require much larger upfront investments in equipment and much greater expenditures on fertilizers and pesticides because of their dependence on row cropping for corn.   Grass-based dairies don't need all the machinery required for growing corn and as a consequence have much lower fixed costs to worry about than conventional operations. Lower fixed costs means less of a need for growing big to spread costs over more units of output. Cows magically harvest their own feed and spread their own fertilizer on a pasture-based dairy operation, something that has to be done with energy-demanding machinery for corn-based operations. Because they get more exercise, spend less time feeding on grains, and crank out somewhat less milk, grass-fed cows are healthier, require fewer veterinary visits, and produce more milk over their lifespan than their corn-fed compatriots. All this drives down costs and increases the annual net income earned per cow for pasture operations in comparison to corn, meaning that pasture-based can earn a decent income with smaller herds than corn-based dairies. The efficiencies of harvesting grass with cows offset the scale economies of harvesting fossil fuel intensive corn with energy sucking equipment, feeding it to the cows, and then using still more a fuel-demanding equipment to spread the manure on row crops. Since land requirements for producing an equivalent amount of milk from pasture as from corn are roughly the same (less land per cow for pasture than corn offsets the somewhat less milk productivity per year), converting corn to pasture in dairy shouldn't have much affect on total output.[19]

The Environmental Virtues of Grass

Now that we know corn production can be cut by 44 percent if we deem it the right thing to do, it's time to explain why we should. Remember, the beauty of doing it is that we loose nothing. We get rid of uneconomic and environmentally unfriendly ethanol, and by replacing feed corn and ethanol lands with pasture, we can still raise the same amount of beef cattle and dairy cows.

First, converting corn to pasture will cut down on carbon emissions and absorb some of the carbon already in the atmosphere. Second, doing so will cut back on something called the "dead zone" in the Gulf of Mexico. Third, we can probably save grassland birds from extinction and expand tallgrass prairie habitat giving a variety of threatened species a shot at survival. And finally, we will all end up being healthier eating grass-fed beef, and we can treat ourselves to a more interesting and tastier beef-based cuisine. Let's begin by reviewing the reduction in carbon emissions forthcoming by switching from corn to pasture.

Corn production adds to greenhouse gas emissions in a variety of ways. First, corn uses a huge amount of fossil fuel energy, 31 gigajoules a hectare. Burning fossil fuels creates carbon dioxide emissions. Second, the process of producing corn and the fertilizer that goes into corn adds to greenhouse gas emissions through the breakdown of humus in expose soil and nitrous oxide emissions from both fertilizer production and the application of fertilizer to corn fields. Nitrous oxide is greenhouse gas that is more potent than carbon dioxide per unit weight. Third, for corn transformed into ethanol, the distilling and refining process itself absorbs a substantial amount of energy (49 gigajoules for a hectare of corn) and creates significant volumes of carbon dioxide emissions. Tad Patzek, a scientist at UC Berkeley, has crunched the numbers and come up with the total carbon dioxide equivalent emissions associated with producing and transforming a hectare of corn into ethanol and estimates that in the process roughly 9 metric tons worth. This turns out to be about 3 metric tons more than if we simply burned an equivalent amount of gasoline.[20] So by converting a hectare of ethanol corn land to pasture we can save 3 metric tons of emissions, and we can inject roughly another ton into the soil for a total of 4 metric tons. This would sum up to a total of about 32 million metric tons of CO_2 emissions reduction (4 tons times the 8 million hectares converted to pasture). Add to this another 5 million tons CO_2 injected into the soil on feed corn lands converted to pasture (1 ton times 5 million hectares converted) and we are up to 37 million metric tons CO_2 reduction. It doesn't end there. We still need to account for the CO_2 (equivalent) reduction from the fossil fuel energy saved and nitrous oxide emissions avoided by not producing the feed corn. This amounts to roughly another 4 metric tons per hectare and brings our grand total reduction in CO_2 to 57 million metric tons by converting beef and dairy feed corn and ethanol corn lands to pasture grass.[21] This equals almost 1 percent of our current emissions or roughly 400 pounds for each of us. A percentage point here and a percentage point there, and soon we are talking real emissions reductions.

Now for the "dead zone," an area of up to 20,000 square kilometers that forms off the mouth of the Mississippi River in the Gulf of Mexico each summer. Here the bottom waters become "hypoxic," a condition formally defined to occur when dissolved oxygen in water falls below 2 milligrams per liter of water. Without enough oxygen, fish and other organisms suffocate if they don't move away in time. The condition results from an excessive injection of nutrients, such as nitrogen and phosphorus, into the Gulf waters from the Mississippi River. These nutrients stimulate algae blooms in the Gulf, and as the algae sink and die, their remains come under attack by microorganisms that decompose the dead organic matter and in the process suck up dissolved oxygen. The famous gulf shrimp, an essential ingredient of New Orleans' cuisine, cannot survive in these waters. The nutrients that feed the dead zone largely originate in the farm fields of the Midwest where heavy application of fertilizers enrich the runoff that ultimately ends up in the Mississippi. Corn is heavily implicated because it is the Midwest's primary row crop and a huge amount of nitrogen fertilizer is applied to corn lands. Increased nitrogen inflows into the Gulf appear to be the primary cause of dead zone emergence and expansion over the last fifty years.[22] Switching half the corn lands to grass will staunch substantial flows of nitrogen to the Gulf and should help shrink the dead zone which is so harmful to local biodiversity. Less corn in the Midwest will be a significant benefit for nature in the Gulf of Mexico.

Grass will be a benefit for nature in the Midwest as well, particularly for grassland birds. Grassland birds, as one would expect, need grass, and it doesn't matter too much what kind. In the spring and early summer, grassland birds require grass that is tall enough to nest in and extensive enough for protection from nest raids by raccoons and crows and infestations of nest parasites, such as Brown-Headed Cowbirds. A nest parasite tricks other species into raising its young by laying eggs in their nests. Grassland birds face this problem only if they have little choice but to nest in small fields near edges where cowbirds can easily spot them. In short, grassland birds like big fields lacking in nearby perches for predators or parasites, such as trees or buildings. Hayfields can fit the bill as well if, of course, farmers restrain themselves from mowing until after grassland bird nesting is done. With a conversion of corn to pasture farming and the accompanying need for hay as winter feed, grassland birds will have a greater shot at survival.[23]

Even better, converting corn to grass will open up opportunities for restoring tallgrass prairie. Remember, we won't need all the corn land we convert to grass for beef. We will have 10 percent left over (about 3 million hectares) that could be restored to native forbs (wildflowers) and grasses. The restoration of an ecosystem almost driven to extinction has never been attempted before. To bring back the tallgrass prairie is a huge challenge and this is not the place to set out the details of such an effort. The richest tallgrass landscape types long ago fell to the plow. Nonetheless, prairie sod remains in rocky areas too rough to cultivate. Conservation groups already target many of these areas, such as the Flint Hills in Kansas, for protection and restoration.[24] Restoring these areas to natural prairie will require shifting them away from managed pasture to a less intensive, more natural grazing regime. Natural prairie requires infrequent, intense grazing to flourish, not the repeated, closely managed grazing of pasture farming. Bison ranging over large areas on their own do a better job than cattle in maintaining natural prairie. Natural prairie also flourishes in the presence of fire, something that could be reintroduced to a landscape free of pasture farming. The idea is simple—shift pasture off of remaining prairie sod to newly planted grass on old corn-lands. Old prairie sod often pops back quickly to natural prairie through burning to eliminate exotic plants that compete with native species. Fire releases remnant, suppressed, fire-adapted prairie plants still existing in the sod.

The tragedy of tallgrass prairie decline is that the richest of the plant community types on the deepest soils fell first (the so-called wet and mesic prairie types) and most completely to the plow because they occupied the best land. To repeat, most of the remaining tallgrass remnants occur on rocky, thin-soiled uplands unsuitable for cultivation. To bring back the prairie with its full array of plant community types will require replanting. While restoring prairies on previously cultivated landscapes is a tough challenge, recent experience by researchers supports its feasibility.[25] The most productive pastures seem to be those that contain a diversity of native grass species, an idea that stands to reason since those species have stood the test of biological time by adaptation to local conditions.[26] One route to highly productive pastures may be through prairie grass restoration.

Incentives for Shifting to Grass

After reading about the wonders and profitability of intensive pasture management, farmers will unlikely run right out and start plowing under their corn. Nor are they going to rush out and protect grassland bird nests in their hay fields, restore prairie sod to a natural condition, or plant grass on their corn fields and buy a herd of cattle. Farmers stick to the familiar unless given clear incentives to do otherwise. Only then they will change there ways.

The best example of this responsiveness is the Conservation Reserve Program, or CRP. The initial purpose of the program at the time of its creation in 1985 was to take highly erodible cropland out of production and retard topsoil erosion. Later the program placed more emphasis on wildlife habitat increases and water quality improvements from sedimentation reductions. Under the CRP, the U.S. Department of Agriculture signed contracts with participating landowners who removed eligible cropland from production for 10-15 years and planted it in grass or other vegetative cover in return for an annual rental payment and half the cost of establishing permanent cover. The average rental payment since 1985 equaled $50 an acre ($125 a hectare), and the amount of land currently enrolled is around 34 million acres (14 million hectares).[27] Clearly, farmers will substantially alter the use of their lands when given the right incentives.

So how do we get farmers to shift from corn to intensive pasture management and prairie restoration? One option is to extend CRP to include corn land conversion to pasture, grassland bird habitat, and tallgrass prairie. On top of this, farmers could sell carbon emission offsets based on soil carbon increases as well as make money from beef production using intensive pasture management and other complementary farm enterprises of the kind Joel Salatin employs on his Polyface Farm. To encourage grassland bird and prairie habitat conservation, a premium annual rental could be paid for such efforts much as it is in the current Conservation Reserve Enhancement Program (CREP) established in 1997 for environmentally sensitive lands. All this could make shifting to pasture and protecting habitats much more profitable than continuing to grow corn. Instead of needing thousands of acres to earn a living, farmers could do well on 200-300 acres. The countryside in Iowa, Illinois, and elsewhere would refill with farm families, igniting a rural economic resurgence. The fossil fuel requirement for farming would drop dramatically as would greenhouse gas emissions. Fertilizer laden runoff would virtually disappear and the dead zone in the Gulf of Mexico would shrink. What could be better?

Grass and Human Health

There is one other truly important benefit from replacing corn with grass —a healthier beef supply. Not only would our cuisine be more compact in the sense that it would absorb less fossil fuel energy and require less land in environmentally damaging corn production, but it would be better for us. Let's explain.

When you go in for your physical exam, your doctor tests your blood for cholesterol and he tells you about the virtues of the good kind (HDL) and the horrors of bad (LDL). The later plugs up our arteries while the former helps keep our blood flowing. The bad increases our risk for heart attacks and strokes while the good reduces it. For starters grass-fed beef contains much less saturated fat than corn-fed. Corn feeding causes a cow to add weight rapidly, an economic benefit, but more of that gain goes to fat than it would for an equivalent gain in a grass-fed cow. Equally as important is the composition of fat in corn-versus grass-fed beef. Omega-3 fats come from plant leafs and algae while Omega-6 comes from seeds—i.e. corn. Omega-3 keeps the blood flowing and reduces inflammation while Omega-6 does the opposite. Since Omega-3 fats occur at especially high concentrations in fish, your doctor will suggest fish and fish oil supplements to increase the amount of your good cholesterol. In corn-fed cows the ratio of Omega-6 to Omega-3 is very high, while in grass-fed it is very low. Like fish, grass-fed beef is really good for your vascular health. Cows evolved on grass—they are ruminants with the equipment to break down the tough cellulose found in grass. If cows fed on corn were not butchered within a few months of their arrival at the feedlot, they would eventually die from enlarged livers and other corn-induced health problems. Corn is not good for the cows, and corn-fed beef is not good for us. If you want to increase your good cholesterol, you don't have to eat increasingly rare fish species suffering from overexploitation. Instead, pick up some grass-fed beef next time you go to your natural foods store.[28]

Compact Cuisine

There is another way we could make our cuisine more compact and reduce our space demands, leaving more for nature—eat less meat. What is the world's most tasty cuisine? Now I know we in this country easily rise to anger in the face of what we see as French arrogance, but we have to admit the French really know how to cook and enjoy great meals, and they do so without putting on very much weight. The U.S. suffers from an obesity rate of about 31 percent, while only 9 percent of the French are too fat. How do the French manage to eat so well and stay skinny? A big part of the answer is portion size. The French simply eat smaller portions, especially meat. While the French eat slightly more pork per capita than us, they consume only half as much chicken and 60 percent as much beef. The French consume annually 90 kilograms (196 pounds) of meat per capita, while we Americans take in roughly 125 kilograms (275 pounds).[29] We could enjoy life just as much as the French and be healthier by cutting our meat consumption by a fourth, reaping the environmental rewards of less land in corn and other animal feeds (such as soybeans). Since we devote roughly 28 percent of our corn lands to feed for pork and poultry, eating 25 percent less meat would cut acres in corn by another 7 percent (on top of the 44 percent reduction already proposed). By doing so, we would further cut CO_2 equivalent annual emissions by 10 million metric tons and open up another 2 million hectares plus a fourth of our beef pastures for other uses such as prairie restoration, free range chicken and hog production, and maybe even solar electricity generation. Such a move to a compact green cuisine would result in a more compact human use of the landscape.

In her provocative little book, *French Women Don't Get Fat*, Mireille Guiliano charmingly explains the virtues of what I would call a compact cuisine.[30]   French women eat chocolate, drink good wine, and love the pleasures of preparing, talking about, and enjoying great meals. Yet they manage to keep their slender figures from youth through old age. Compact eating leads to a shapely, compact body. Coming from the Midwest where high-volume eating is endemic, on my first trip to France, the first big difference to jump out at me was the dramatic contrast in body shape between Americans and the French. Yet it is the French who are known for great cuisine—incredible food stands out as a key reason why we all love to visit Paris.

How do the French manage to keep their weight in check even though they eat such wonderful food? In essence, for the French less is more. They enjoy a variety of foods, but consume each kind in moderation. They savor each bite and enjoy fully what they taste, but don't take too many bites. They eat at meal time, but don't snack in between; they walk all the time, and take the stairs whenever they can; and they orient their social life around the preparation and enjoyment of meals. In short, the lesson of the French is simple: enjoy the pleasures of life, but don't let them take over and run you. On a daily basis, the French spend more than twice the time eating meals at home than the Americans and they have refrained from letting that time shrink as it has in the U.S. and elsewhere in Europe.[31] The lesson I think is this: devote time to the simple pleasures and one can enjoy life more and become healthier in the bargain.

Notes

[1] Stephen Packard and Cornelia F. Mutel, eds., *The Tallgrass Restoration Handbook: For Prairies, Savannas, and Woodlands* (Washington D.C.: Island Press, 1997); The Nature Conservancy, "Ecoregional Planning in the Northern Tallgrass Prairie Ecoregion," (Minneapolis, MN: The Nature Conservancy, Midwest Regional Office, 1998).

[2] Pollan, *Omnivore's Dilemma: A Natural History of Four Meals*.

[3] U.S. Bureau of the Census, *The 2007 Statistical Abstract* ([cited]).

[4] Pimentel and Pimentel, *Food, Energy, and Society*.

[5] These figures are based on and average of annual data for 2006-2008. USDA Economic Research Service, *Feedgrains Database: Yearbook Tables* (USDA Economic Research Service, 2008 [cited November 20, 2008]); available from http://www.ers.usda.gov/Data/FeedGrains/FeedYearbook.aspx.

[6]Douglas A. Frank, Michelle M. Kuns, and Daniel R. Guido, "Consumer Control of Grassland Plant Production," *Ecology* 83, no. 3 (2002).

[7] Richard T. Conant, Keith Pustian, and Edward Elliott, "Grassland Management and Conversion into Grassland: Effects on Soil Carbon," *Ecological Applications* 11, no. 2 (2001).

[8] The 2009 clean energy "cap and trade" bill includes provision for the purchase of carbon offsets from farm owners. U. S. Library of Congress, *H.R. 2454: American Clean Energy and Security Act of 2009* ([cited]).

[9] Pimentel and Pimentel, *Food, Energy, and Society;* Joel Salatin, *You Can Farm: The Entrepreneur's Guide to Start and Succeed in a Farm Enterprise* (Swoop, VA: Polyface, Inc, 1998).

[10] Salatin, *You Can Farm: The Entrepreneur's Guide to Start and Succeed in a Farm Enterprise*, 237-39.

[11] Joel Salatin, *Salad Bar Beef* (Swoope, VA: Polyface, Inc., 1995).

[12] USDA Economic Research Service, *Feedgrains Database: Yearbook Tables* ([cited]).

[13] U.S. Bureau of the Census, *The 2009 Statistical Abstract* ([cited); USDA Economic Research Service, *Feedgrains Database: Yearbook Tables* ([cited]).

[14] Pimentel and Pimentel, *Food, Energy, and Society*.

[15] Tad W. Patzek, *Thermodynamics of the Corn-Ethanol Biofuel Cycle* (University of California, Berkeley, Department of Civil and Environmental Engineering, 2006 [cited November 21, 2008]); available from http://petroleum.berkeley.edu/papers/patzek/CRPS416-Patzek-Web.pdf.

[16] John Anderlik, *Rural Depopulation: What Does It Mean for the Future Economic Health of Rural Areas and the Community Banks That Support Them?* (FDIC, 2006 [cited January 13, 2009]); available from http://www.chicagofed.org/community development/files/07 2006 rural depopulation.pdf.

[17] The classic work on this issue is Andre Voisin, *Grass Productivity* (Washington D.C.: Island Press, 1989).

[18] Bradford L. Barham, Jeremy Foltz, and Ursula Aldana, "Expansion, Modernization, and Specialization in the Wisconsin Dairy Industry," in *Research Summary* (Madison, WI: Program of Agricultural Technology Studies, University of Wisconsin, Madison, 2005); Program of Agricultural Technology Studies, *Economic Indicators of Wisconsin's Dairy Industry* (Program on Agricultural Technology Studies, University of Wisconsin, Madison, 2002 [cited November 25, 2005]); available from http://www.pats.wisc.edu/daigra10.html.

[19] Tim Johnson, "The Economics of Grass-Based Dairy," in *Livestock Business Guide, Appropriate Technology Transfer for Rural Areas* (Fayetteville, AR: National Sustainable Agriculture Information Service, 2002); Program of Agricultural Technology Studies, *Economic Indicators of Wisconsin's Dairy Industry* ([cited).

[20] Patzek, *Thermodynamics of the Corn-Ethanol Biofuel Cycle* ([cited]).

[21] One of the environmental disadvantages of grass-fed cows is their higher rate of methane flatulence in comparison to their feedlot brethren—about three times as much. The global warming potential of methane is about 23 times that of carbon dioxide, meaning that methane is dangerous stuff when it comes to climate change. A cow gives off more gas eating tougher to digest grass than corn, but this doesn't mean that feedlots do better in terms of their total greenhouse gas emissions—they emit huge amounts of ammonia and methane from their manure ponds. Switching from feedlot to grass-fed beef will on net reduce methane emissions as far as I can tell from the research. A grass-fed heifer on rotational-grazing will give off about 65 grams of methane per cow day, but a feedlot dairy cow gives off at least 330 grams a day, taking into account manure pond and other emissions from wastes. See the following articles for the relevant data: H. Alan DeRamus et al., "Methane Emissions of Beef Cattle on Forages: Efficiency of Grazing Management Systems," *Journal of Environmental Quality* 32 (2003); L.A. Harper et al., "Direct Measurements of Methane from Grazing and Feedlot Cattle," *Journal of Animal Science* 77, no. 6 (1999); A.B. Leytem, D.L. Bjorneberg, and R.S. Duncan, *Emissions of Ammonia and Methane from Concentrated Dairy Production Facilities in Southern Idaho* (2009 [cited November 2, 2009]); available from http://adsa.asas.org/meetings/2009/abstracts/0146.PDF.

[22] Nancy N. Rabalais, R. Eugene Turner, and Donald Scavia, "Beyond Science into Policy: Gulf of Mexico Hypoxia and the Mississippi River," *BioScience* 52, no. 2 (2002).

[23] Sample and Mossman, "Managing Habitat for Grassland Birds: A Guide for Wisconsin."

[24] For a good summary of prairie conservation see Fred B. Samson and Fritz L. Knopf, eds., *Prairie Conservation: Preserving North America's Most Endangered Ecosystem* (Washington D.C.: Island Press, 1996).

[25] Packard and Mutel, eds., *The Tallgrass Restoration Handbook: For Prairies, Savannas, and Woodlands*.

[26] Salatin, *Salad Bar Beef*, 42-46.

[27] Patrick Sullivan et al., "The Conservation Reserve Program: Economic Implications for Rural America," in *Agricultural Economic Report Number 834* (Washington D.C.: USDA, Economic Research Service, 2004).

[28] Pollan, *Omnivore's Dilemma: A Natural History of Four Meals*, 72-84, 266-69; Salatin, *Salad Bar Beef*, 24-28.

[29] NationMaster.com, *Health Statistics: Obesity (Most Recent) by Country* (NationMaster.com, 2008 [cited November 20, 2008]); available from http://www.nationmaster.com/graph/hea_obe-health-obesity; U.S. Bureau of the Census, *Per Capita Consumption of Meat and Poultry, by Country* (U.S. Bureau of the Census, 2000 [cited November 20, 2008]); available from http://www.allcountries.org/uscensus/1370_per_capita_consumption_of_meat_and.html.

[30] Mireille Guiliano, *French Women Don't Get Fat* (New York: Vintage Books, 2007).

[31] Alan Warde et al., "Changes in the Practice of Eating: A Comparative Analysis of Time-Use," *Acta Sociologica* 50, no. 4 (2007).

Chapter 12
Letting Forests Grow Old: Saving Biodiversity and Absorbing Carbon Through Compact Green Forestry

Settlers arriving at the end of the Oregon Trail in the 1840s and 1850s quickly filled up the Willamette Valley, a grassland that had been kept free of trees because of fires set by Indians to attract game to fresh grasses for easy hunting. Much of the rest of western Oregon and Washington were covered with thick forests of huge trees at which settlers and lumberjacks alike marveled, some as much as 10 feet in diameter and 400 feet in height. Settlers wanted agricultural land not trees, but forests were all that was left. They tried the laborious process of clearing away the trees, but were usually rewarded with cropland of little value. Some were able to supplement their income by selling timber to markets in nearby emerging urban centers, such as Portland and Seattle. In the end, the Donation Land Act of 1850 that allowed a settler to claim 320 acres, or 640 acres for a married couple, failed to create a Jeffersonian paradise of small yeoman farmers in the Pacific Northwest.

The only way to make real money at this point in the history of the Northwest was to harvest timber, mill it into lumber, and ship it off to the booming gold fields of California, and this is what the early lumber barons did. Rather than the family farm, the basis of the region's economy became the lumber camp with its army of lumberjacks, the mill, and the port for loading and shipping lumber. Later with the arrival of the railroad, and a new class of timber barons such as Frederick Weyerhaeuser, the orientation of the market shifted to feeding the booming urban markets of the East. Within a century, the vast old-growth forests were reduced to a shadow of their former selves.[1]

Saving Old-Growth Forests and Absorbing Carbon

Foresters of the old school viewed old-growth as something to be cut down. Mature Douglas-fir forests contain a huge amount of biomass, more on a per hectare basis than any other plant species in the world. Mild, wet winters and warm, dry summers provide ideal conditions for a conifer—a tree that doesn't loose its leaves in the winter—to accumulate a huge amount of woody material. The tree can photosynthesize the sun's energy year around. Douglas fir will live up to 750 years, obtaining a height of up to 100 meters (300 plus feet) and a diameter of 2 meters (6 plus feet) or more. Once a Douglas-fir crashes to the floor from old age, chances are it won't be replaced by one of its own kind because its seedlings don't survive in the deep shade of old-growth forests. More than likely a shade tolerant tree, such as the western hemlock, will pop up into the canopy and replace the Douglas-fir. If a forest is struck by a massive blow-down, or better yet a fire, then Douglas-fir seedlings will emerge in the open sun and grow rapidly, creating a thick forest that will eventually prune itself with a few large trees surviving.

The trouble with an old-growth Douglas fir from a forester's perspective is its failure to add woody biomass once it reaches maturity. Forests, like people (fast food addicts excepted), grow in their youth but stop adding biomass in old age. A mature tree gains branch growth in its sunny upper canopy, but sheds branches in its shady lower reaches. After roughly a hundred years of age, the net addition to woody material in a Douglas fir slows dramatically. While an old-growth Douglas-fir forest (200 plus years of age) contains a huge amount of living biomass, it doesn't add any. Conversely a young Douglas-fir forest adds biomass at an exceptionally high rate. The economic logic of forest exploitation in such circumstances is simple—clear-cut remaining old-growth, replant it with seedlings, let it grow 75-100 years, and cut it again. This amounts to converting a natural forest to a plantation. Forestry becomes tree farming.

Today foresters recognize the ecological virtues of old-growth ignored by the older logic of exploitation. The pioneering research of Jerry Franklin, a forestry professor, and his colleagues established the ecological significance of Pacific Northwest old-growth forests.[2] Old-growth forests possess special biological features lacking in their younger counterparts starting with really big trees that perform a host of ecological functions and provide habitat for a multitude of species. By intercepting fogs and mists in their huge canopies, old-growth forests add substantially to local terrestrial water supplies. Lichens love to hang from the upper branches of the canopy, suck up still more moisture, and fix nitrogen that adds to the nutrient base of the forest as a whole. The same canopies take on an irregular shape that causes spotty light flows to the forest floor and a patchiness and diversity to understory vegetation. An absence of much light at all beneath densely packed young stands of Douglas fir excludes understory vegetation in such forests and reduces biodiversity. Age in forests reduces growth but supports much greater species diversity than youth. Large old trees with their big tall trunks and diverse climate niches, beginning with the cool, quiet, damp forest floor and ending at the top with crowns often broken up from exposure to the elements, provide all sorts of potential homes for a variety of species. The irregularities of the crown attracts rare nesting Spotted Owls and perches for Bald Eagles watching nearby waterways for prey. An abundance of insects find their home on and in the bark of big, old trees and serve as a source of food for a variety of birds and mammals, including bats that feed on flying insects above the crown. As many as 1,500 species of invertebrate insects can be found in, on, and around a large, old-growth Douglas fir.

The special role that big trees play in old-growth forests don't end with tree death. Large, dead snags become feeding grounds for all sorts of bacteria, fungi, and insects. Most important of all, snags become the home of cavity-excavating birds such as the Pileated Woodpecker and other birds that move in after woodpeckers move on. Once the snags come crashing down, they still have work to do as habitat for a variety of organisms. Fallen logs turn out to be an important nursery for tree seedlings that have trouble competing with ground-layer plants, and provide a path into open areas for small mammals that eat fungi and inject spore laden feces near seedlings. The spores grow to become fungi which form a symbiotic relationship with new tree roots and help accelerate reforestation.

Some snags end up falling into streams to the benefit of juvenile salmon who hang out in the resulting pools, waiting for prey to float by. Adult salmon roam the Pacific in search of food until the time for reproducing arrives. They then return to the forest stream of their birth, and find a gravel bed where the females can lay their eggs and the males fertilize them. Adults with their energy spent from the long and perilous trip die and add what remains of their biomass to the local forest ecosystem. The cycle is completed once the juvenile salmon head out to sea.

In the ordinary timber harvesting cycle, the biological riches that old-growth forests support are lost to the economic desire for the vigor of youth. Income from creating woody biomass achieves a maximum by keep forests in a young, high-growth state. Conservationists have responded by advocating for the placement of old growth in a protected status, such as designated wilderness, to keep it out of the hands of the forest products industry.[3] The trouble with this solution is the insufficient amount of forests around the country that contain big, old trees. If we care about preventing species that depend on old growth from heading down the path to extinction, we could use more old-growth forests. This can be accomplished by simply letting some of our young forests grow old. In the age of global warming, an attractive benefit of doing so is carbon sequestration. As young forests grow old, they add carbon rich biomass to tree trunks, branches, and roots, and accumulate carbon in forest floor litter (broken branches, downed trees, dead needles), snags, and soil.

Let's now consider how to pull off letting forests age more and accumulate carbon while extracting from them a reasonable flow of wood fiber for human use.

The Forest Stewardship Council (FSC) was founded in 1994 by a broad array of environmental groups, forest products industry interests, and others to improve forest management practices globally and bring into reality the notion of environmentally sustainable forestry. The FSC pursues this ambitious goal by certifying forests around the world as being managed in an "ecologically, socially, and economically exemplary" fashion. The products of these forests can then by sold as FSC certified to customers who desire environmentally friendly products and are willing to pay for them.[4] The ultimate benefit for forest landowners is the receipt of a price premium for certified harvested wood.[5] The LEED building certification process we discussed earlier awards points to developers who use FSC approved forest products in their buildings.

A list of core principles drives the certification process and includes compliance with all valid local laws and international agreements; assurance of clear tenure rights; protection of the rights and interests of local community members, workers, and indigenous peoples; efficient delivery of a wide range of economic, social, and environmental benefits from forests; and the protection and enhancement of biological diversity and ecological functioning in forests. The FSC has developed customized standards that fit local forest conditions around the world, including a set that applies to the old-growth forest of the Pacific Northwest. These particular standards call for not only the protection existing old growth, but its long-term expansion by letting some timber stands age and take on old-growth characteristics. To get certification, a Pacific Northwest forest landowner must keep a specified portion of trees under management in old growth or in stands that will become old growth. The essential idea behind certification is to encourage the human use of forests, but to accomplish such use in a manner that is at once ecologically sustainable and protective of all native forest species. This does not mean that big, old trees would all be put away in a natural museum and never harvested. It simply means that the amount of old-growth in the aggregate will be brought up to a level that will conserve total forest-based biological riches over the long haul. Big, old trees with their fine grain woods can be harvested, but only if they get replaced by growing other big, old trees.[6]

FSC certification around the world now includes roughly 100 million hectares—an amazing accomplishment in such a short time, but more needs to be done. One path to increasing certified forests in the U.S. and elsewhere is to combine the whole certification process with marketable carbon emission allowance offsets. FSC-certified forest landowners could sell carbon emission allowance offsets created by simply letting their forests age and accumulated carbon-laden biomass. To participate in carbon allowance markets in this fashion, forests would have to be certified by the FSC or other equivalent organizations, and would be monitored not for just forest management practices, but also for carbon accumulation. Payment for accumulating carbon would require certification.

Forests suck up carbon by simply growing, but how much? The current average for all our forests is about 3.2 tons per hectare (1.3 tons per acre) and sums up to roughly 1,000 million metric tons a year.[7] Forests clearly possess a substantial ability to absorb carbon. How much added carbon dioxide can be soaked up by forests in a year on top of what's already being done? This of course depends on the rewards available for doing so. A recent study suggests that the ability sell carbon allowances at $100 per ton for sequestration would yield roughly an added 500 million metric tons of CO_2 reduction annually from privately owned forests, or about 8 percent of our current fossil fuel related emissions.[8] This could be accomplished by planting more trees, increasing the amount of time between harvests, and forest management practices that reduce carbon emissions from plant matter breakdown.

Harvesting of commercial Douglas-fir forests in the Pacific Northwest occurs roughly on a 60-year cycle. At harvest, a forest is clearcut and either replanted or allowed to grow back through natural reseeding. Carbon storage in the vegetation, the woody debris on the ground, and the soils just before harvest equals nearly a million metric tons CO_2 per hectare for a typical 60-year old forest. In contrast, a representative old-growth Douglas-fir forest (250 years plus) stores nearly 2.3 million metric tons CO_2 per hectare, more than twice as much as its younger counterpart. A clearcut harvest removes carbon from the forest in the cut trees and accelerates the breakdown of carbon-rich debris on the forest floor. In the milling process, a significant portion of the harvested wood ends up as waste or being burned for fuel, causing the embodied carbon to find its way back into the atmosphere fairly quickly. Roughly 45 percent of the woody-carbon ends up being stored in building materials and other products.[9]

The future of newly cut Douglas-fir forest can take two paths. One is to treat it like a tree farm and replant and cut trees every 60 years. The other is to let the forest grow old. After 250 years, an old-growth forest will have stored about 2.3 million metric tons CO_2 per hectare, but the comparable tree farm will only have stored about 70 percent of that assuming generously a permanent 45 percent wood products storage rate for harvested carbon. In short, allowing forests to age will significantly accelerate carbon sequestration. While the additions of harvestable wood may slow fairly quickly in the aging process, because big, old trees are always shedding branches that decompose slowly, carbon stores continue to accumulate well into very old age for a Douglas-fir forest.[10]

Whether a forest certification program combined with marketable carbon allowance offsets would increase or decrease total wood fiber production cannot be easily predicted. If a forest landowner received credit for the CO_2 permanently embodied both in harvested wood (40-45 percent) and the forest itself, harvests could go up if a landowner plants more land to trees because of the added income from carbon offsets.[11] On the other hand, if landowners are required to devote more land to old growth for certification and adopt longer periods between timber harvests to accumulate more carbon, then harvests could drop, even if the total amount of land devoted to forests expands. This drop could be mitigated somewhat by selectively harvesting old-growth trees through low-impact methods using horses to drag trees out of the woods or lifting them out with helicopters. Since trees would grow back in gaps and harvested carbon would be partially embodies in wood products, the net affect on total carbon accumulation could be positive because of such harvests. Moderate selective harvesting can be undertaken without substantially altering the old-growth structure of a forest and its functionality as habitat. Still, moderate old-growth harvesting would not likely produce the volume of wood that could be produced from a comparable land base of 60-year rotation tree farms.

Forest productivity statistics suggest the presence of a fair amount of wiggle room for expanding harvests from younger forests to compensate for old-growth protection. Publicly owned timberland unreserved for habitat protection or any other purposes constitutes about 29 percent of all land in the U.S. potentially usable for timber harvesting. On this land, only about 20 percent of the total annual growth is harvested annually at present. After World War II, the public forests came under intense harvesting pressure to provide raw material for the housing boom. In recent years, the same forests have been in a recovery mode. Clearly there is plenty of room for harvest expansion on public lands in the future even if more old growth is protected. Non-industrial forests, those owned by individuals who don't process wood for living, compose about 58 percent of the timberland in the U.S. and currently remove about 75 percent of their annual growth. Even with additional old growth protection, there is some room for sustainable expansion in harvests on these lands. Industrial forests, mostly tree plantations with young, planted, fast growing trees, currently harvest about 105 percent of annual growth.[12] Plantation forests indirectly play a role in the protection of their natural counterparts by reducing harvesting pressure on the latter. Certification allows for plantation forestry so long as it is done in an environmentally sound manner and a portion of the certified land is sustained in natural forests including old growth. Plantations look a bit like row crop agriculture, but they do have a role to play in protecting forest ecosystems and if managed right they can accumulate carbon.

Irrespective of whether wood-fiber supply expands or contracts because of forest certification, demand for housing related wood products will shrink if we adopt a true compact living strategy of the kind described in earlier in chapters. Why? If we increase the share of multifamily housing in the total mix, the amount of building material required per house will decline. Remember in a four unit townhouse, each housing unit shares two of its walls with others. The amount of building material for walls can be cut roughly in half. Similarly in apartment buildings, walls are shared. The point is simple—urban high-density housing uses less material per unit of floor space than the low-density, detached, suburban kind. Also, high density living will favor older cities where many solid older buildings can be recycle for housing, saving on virgin materials. The stimulation of LEED-certified construction with tax credits and LEED points for recycled building materials should also reduce the demand for virgin lumber. Forest certification and carbon sequestration could put a dent in the supply of virgin wood fiber, but compact living will dampen demand as well, keeping lumber prices from shooting up too far.

Moving the domestic supply of wood fiber in an environmentally friendly direction will tend to push up the demand for less costly, uncertified imports. This would amount to transferring bad forestry practices in this country to the rest of the world, something we want to avoid given the degree to which ecologically rich forests overseas stand threatened by exploitation. Requiring the certification of imported wood products in one fell swoop avoids this problem and gives good forest management a global boost.

Along with compact living, compact energy, and compact cuisine, we can have compact forestry in the sense that we leave more of the forest to nature itself and make use of the rest in a manner friendly to biological diversity. At the same time, we can absorb some extra carbon and diminish the extent of global warming. Compact living will make compact forestry more economically feasible than otherwise by reducing our demand for wood fiber.

Environmentalists versus Ecologists on Carbon Offsets—a Path to Reconciliation

Environmentalists (Greenpeace and Friends of the Earth staffers in particular) harbor deep suspicions about the idea of carbon offsets as part of a system of emissions allowance trading. Under such a scheme as we know, an electric utility that burns coal would be required to acquire allowances to cover its CO_2 emissions.[13] In each year the government would auction off or give away allowances equal to a fixed and declining annual cap. If offsets were allowed, then a utility could substitute offsets for allowances. Offsets would be created by a certified source that carries out some action causing a reduction of atmospheric carbon. Offsets are a potential problem because their creators might get credit for greenhouse gas reductions they don't really undertake. An example would be a landowner who initially reduced carbon stored in wood fiber through timber harvests but then later gets offset credits for sequestering carbon in newly planted trees. A utility that acquired such offsets and substitutes them for allowances would in effect defeat the goal of a shrinking emissions cap by continuing to emit carbon without in truth offsetting through real additions to stored carbon.

To the consternation of wary environmentalists, conservation ecologists find the idea of offsets appealing because certain landscapes, such as grasslands and forests, accumulate carbon and offsets would provide landowners a way to earn income for conserving their property instead of exploiting it. The point is simple—two environmental problems can be killed with one stone through offsets—carbon can be sequestered and natural habitats protected. On top of habitat protection, rural communities would benefit from economic reinvigoration by doing the work of carbon sequestration. Converting corn lands to grass, sequestering carbon, and raising grass-fed beef through intensive pasture management would do much to create employment in declining farm communities. Similarly, undertaking the work of forest restoration needed to let forests grow old and accumulate carbon could create significant amounts of rural employment in timber-dependent communities in the western U.S. (more on both these issue in the next chapter).

Let me comment on two possible options that could be followed in cap and trade legislation that would go some way toward reconciling environmentalists and ecologists. The first insures a scrupulous external certification for offset projects and the second places offsets outside the existing cap.

The experience with forest certification by the FSC suggests that a rigorous approach to verifying carbon sequestration is distinctly possible. By all appearances, the American Clean Energy and Security Act (the 2009 cap and trade bill passed by the House) as written establishes a thorough review process for insuring the legitimacy of offset credits that can be used in lieu of emission allowances. The standards used in this process will be overseen by an Offsets Integrity Advisory Board. The process requires an accredited third party verification to assure that applicants for offsets have truly sequestered additional carbon equivalents in the amount claimed. Because the greatest opportunities for offsets occur in the world's forests and because of its extensive experience in forest certification, the Forest Stewardship Council can and should play a major role in the verification of offsets both domestically and internationally. Given the FSC's stellar reputation, critics would be assured that offsets are real and not faked in any way. The standards established for international deforestation reduction offsets in the cap and trade bill read exactly like those followed by the FSC in its current certification work including the "following of widely accepted, environmentally sustainable forest management practices," the restoration of "native forest species and ecosystems," and "due regard to the rights and interests of local communities, indigenous peoples, forest-dependent communities, and vulnerable social groups." Achieving multiple environmental and social goals at the same time we sequester significant amounts of carbon seems like too good a deal to pass up. The devil is in the details of this approach, but then again it always is no matter what one does.

Another more radical option is to remove offsets from the cap and fund them with allowance auction revenues. The House cap and trade legislation would allow for up to 2 billion tons of carbon equivalent offsets annually to be used instead of government issued allowances to satisfy emission requirements under the cap. As the cap shrinks from its peak of 5.4 billion tons of carbon equivalents in 2016 down to roughly 1 billion tons in 2050 and beyond, offsets will loom larger as a proportion of the cap. Instead of such a heavy dependence on offsets, the legislation could be rewritten so that the cap is fully satisfied by allowances and that a portion of emission allowance auction revenues is allocated to offset purchases, perhaps a fifth. If the existing annual caps in the House bill became law and legitimate offsets were funded from allowance revenues, the volume of greenhouse gases entering the atmosphere would shrink at a more rapid rate than otherwise while gaining the ecological and social benefits of an offsets program. This approach would also assure attainment of the cap irrespective of the actual performance of offsets projects, alleviating the concerns of wary environmentalists.

Notes

[1] Douglas E. Booth, *Valuing Nature: The Decline and Preservation of Old-Growth Forests* (Lanham: Rowman and Littlefield, 1994).

[2] J. F. Franklin et al., " Ecological Characteristics of Old-Growth Douglas-Fir Forests," in *GTR, PNW-8* (Portland, OR: 1981).

[3]   Booth, *Valuing Nature: The Decline and Preservation of Old-Growth Forests.*

[4] Forest Stewardship Council, *Some History* (Forest Stewardship Council, 2008 [cited November 28, 2008]); available from http://www.fsc.org/history.html.

[5] Francisco X. Aguilar and Richard P. Vlosky, "Consumer Willingness to Pay Price Premiums for Environmentally Certified Wood Products in the U.S," *Forest Policy and Economics* 9, no. 8 (2007); Yuan Yuan and Ivan Eastin, "Forest Certification and Its Influence on the Forest Products Industry in China," in *Working Paper 110* (Seattle: Center for International Trade in Forest Products, University of Washington, 2007). The price premium in the U.S. amounts to about 6 percent. A premium greater than 11 percent appears to be needed to earn an above normal profit margin.

[6] Forest Stewardship Council, *Revised Final Pacific Coast (USA) Regional Forest Stewardship Standard* (Forest Stewardship Council, 2005 [cited November 29, 2008]); available from http://www.fscus.org/images/documents/2006_standards/pcwg_9.0_NTC.pdf.

[7] Kenneth E. Skog and Geraldine A. Nicholson, *Carbon Sequestration in Wood and Paper Products* (USDA Forest Service, 2000 [cited December 1, 2008]); available from http://www.fpl.fs.fed.us/documnts/pdf2000/skog00b.pdf; Smith et al., "Forest Resources of the United States, 2002."

[8] Robert N. Stavins and Kenneth R. Richards, *The Cost of U.S. Forest-Based Carbon Sequestration* (Pew Center on Global Climate Change, 2005 [cited December 1, 2008]); available from http://www.pewclimate.org/docUploads/Sequest_Final.pdf. The 2009 clean "cap and trade" bill includes provisions for carbon offset purchases from landowners who sequester carbon in forests. U. S. Library of Congress, *H.R. 2454: American Clean Energy and Security Act of 2009* ([cited).

[9] Mark E. Harmon, William K. Ferrell, and Jerry F. Franklin, "Effects on Carbon Storage of Conversion of Old-Growth to Young Forests," *Science* 247 (1990).

[10] Ibid.

[11] Again, 60 million tons CO_2 gets embodied in wood and paper products based on 1990 data, but 85 million tons goes up in smoke from burning wood and paper and in CO_2 emissions from the breakdown of wood and paper in landfills.   Some of this occurs as methane that is converted into CO_2 equivalents for this calculation.   Wood fiber use in effect fosters each year a flow of 530 million tons CO_2, of which 40 percent or so (220 million tons) gets bound up in wood-fiber products and 60 percent (310 million tons) finds its way into the atmosphere.   These figures fluctuate over time because of changes in housing construction and the demand for paper and other wood-fiber products.

[12] Smith et al., "Forest Resources of the United States, 2002."

[13] Stacy Morford, *Friends of the Earth: Why It's Suicide to Base Our Future on Offsets* (SolveClimate, 2009 [cited January 14, 2010]); available from http://solveclimate.com/blog/20090910/friends-earth-why-its-suicide-base-our-future-offsets.

Chapter 13
Expanding Employment and Reducing Poverty Through a Green Investment Boom

Turning to compact green living and freeing ourselves from the environmental tyranny of fossil fuels will set off an investment boom of a new kind—a good boom that will help solve both social and environmental problems such as inner city and rural unemployment, the physical decline of central cities, shortages of decent public transit, the consumption of unhealthy food, global warming, runoff water pollution, and declining biodiversity. This good boom will come about because of investments in renewable sources of energy such as solar and wind, energy conservation (the cleanest energy of all), urban compact housing, energy efficient public transit, pedestrian friendly urban amenities and commercial activity, grass-based agriculture, and environmentally friendly forest management practices. Unlike the economic boom of the 1990s, a good boom will be less oriented to current consumption and more to investment in the future, less inclined to the consumption of imports and more to the production of domestic goods, and less focused on the accumulation of debt and more on using our energy and spatial surroundings more efficiently. The good boom will create new urban and rural employment and diminish both urban and rural poverty.

A Future Green Investment Boom

So how can all the measures suggested in the pages of this book work as a package to foster a good boom? This is the most challenging of the questions posed here so far. We will begin by first reviewing essential vehicles for moving to a compact and green economy: cap and trade, green energy and LEED tax credits, clean energy investment incentives for utilities, urban growth boundaries, a grass-based Conservation Reserve Program, and forest certification. The first of these, cap and trade, also constitutes a key source of financing for public sector green investments. Estimating the amount of revenue cap and trade carbon allowance auctions can generate for such investments will serve as a point of departure for our second step—coming up with ball park numbers for public sector green investment spending and for the resulting amount of employment created. The greatest boon of all for the economy will flow from diverting our current spending on foreign oil to a domestic clean energy industry. This we will need to explain. Finally, we will want to describe the type of jobs likely to be created by the good green boom, and show how such jobs will help alleviate urban and rural poverty. Let's get started.

The most important of the incentives to change our fossil fuel energy consuming ways will be "cap and trade." This means simply that a declining cap will be placed on carbon emissions and their equivalents, and to emit a metric ton within the cap will require an allowance. This is exactly the approach set out by Congress in the 2009 American Clean Energy and Security Act, H.R. 2454.[1] If this bill or one like it were to become law, the federal government would require emitters of carbon and distributors of carbon-containing fuels, such as gasoline, diesel oil, or natural gas, to possess emission allowances. The government would both auction off allowances and give some away initially to energy users to dampen their initial costs of compliance with caps.[2] Utilities burning coal for instance would need carbon allowances for all CO_2 emissions that rise from their smoke stacks, a bit more than a third of our greenhouse emissions;[3] gasoline and diesel wholesaler selling its products to retailers would have to have allowances for all CO_2 ultimately emitted from motor vehicle exhaust pipes, about 28 percent of all greenhouse emissions;[4] and methane emitting landfills would require CO_2 equivalent allowances for their emissions.[5]

Global CO_2 equivalent emissions of greenhouse gases as of 2004 amounted to 46 gigatons (billions of metric tons) of which the U.S. emitted 7 gigatons. If nothing is done, the global total is predicted to rise to 57 gigatons by 2030 and will continue to grow after that. The global average temperature could ultimately rise by as much as 10 degrees centigrade if this occurs. To keep temperature increases within 2 degrees Celcius, emissions need to be cut more than 40 percent by 2030 and driven to near zero by 2050. To accomplish this, the price of carbon emission allowances under a global cap and trade system will rise to approximately $100 a metric ton by 2030. We will assume cap and trade is instituted in both the U.S. and globally for the sake of discussion. We will also assume optimistically that the approach taken to greenhouse gas reductions is rigorous enough to limit warming to 2 degrees centigrade. The House Bill (H.R. 2454) comes very close to the kind of limits needed globally to reach this goal by reducing emissions to 58 percent of 2005 levels in 2030 and 17 percent in 2050. From this point to zero emissions will not be very far. So let's accept that shrinking greenhouse gas allowances on a global scale will reduce emissions at least 40 percent by 2030 and that as a consequence the carbon allowance price will rise to approximately $100 per metric ton as the Intergovernmental Panel on Climate Change (IPCC) projects.[6]

The H.R. 2454 caps begin in 2012 and are tightened steadily through 2030. This means that the carbon allowance price will rise steadily as the supply of emission allowances shrink. One of our key interests here is to calculate the amount of revenue generated by carbon emission allowances to insure that adequate funding will be available for greenhouse gas reducing public sector incentives and investments. Let's assume simply that the allowance price begins at $15 a metric ton initially in 2012 and rises steadily over 20 years to $100 and that emissions decline to 4 gigatons by 2030 as the allowance cap shrinks. The total value of allowances for 18 years under these assumptions is $3.8 trillion or an average per year of $213 billion.[7] If an equivalent carbon tax scheme were implemented instead of cap and trade, the revenue stream would be exactly the same. Remember, a carbon tax set at the right level is economically equivalent to cap and trade.

To put these projected carbon emission allowance prices in more understandable terms, the allowance cost for a gallon of gasoline would amount to about 15 cents in 2012 and not quite a dollar in 2030. This projection assumes that gasoline allowance costs will be fully passed on to consumers, something that is unlikely to occur since competition and reduced demand pressure suppliers to reduce the net price they receive after they pay for allowances. In short, allowance costs will be split between consumers and producers. For electricity generated from coal, the added cost per kilowatt hour in 2012 for emission allowances would be about one and a half cents and would rise in 2030 to around ten cents.[8] Since most of us currently pay somewhere around a dime per kilowatt hour for electricity at retail, if coal-fired utilities fully pass on the cost of carbon allowances, their electricity prices will double by 2030. Coal by then will not look very attractive as an energy source. The U.S. Department of Energy projects that the retail cost of electricity generated from solar cells should drop to 10-15 cents per kilowatt hour because of scale economies and technological advances and will consequently be 5-10 cents cheaper than electricity from coal in 20 years.[9] Coal-fired power plants will shut down in favor of solar and wind generated electricity.

Of course the federal government could spend a larger or smaller amount on public sector green investments than the revenue generated from auctioning off carbon emissions allowances by engaging in deficit spending in the first case or returning revenues to the public through tax reductions in the second. We will assume that between now and 2050 we don't want to add to the federal deficit, and for this reason added spending will ultimately need to be financed from carbon emission allowance auctions.

So where should the spending go? The compact living and clean energy spending options we summarized earlier include light rail transit and urban streetscape amenities, tax credits for clean energy and LEED-certified buildings and FSC-certified lumber, low income home weatherization, a clean energy investment bank, a refurbished renewable-friendly electricity grid, and a grass-based Conservation Reserve Program (CRP). Lets review the proposed annual spending for clean energy and compact living set out at the end of Chapter 10: light rail, $30 billion; urban streetscape investment and urban growth boundaries, $20 billion; weatherization, $1 billion; clean energy tax credits, $10 billion; clean energy investment bank, $4 billion; and smart grid, $10 billion. The grass-based CRP proposed in Chapter 11 would cost roughly $2 billion a year at $125 a hectare for a conversion of half our current land in corn to grass. This brings total added clean energy and compact living spending to $77 billion a year.

One can quibble over the amount of money and how it should be spent. Numerous options I haven't mentioned could easily be added to this list, including basic clean energy research (some of which the U.S. department of Energy is already funding), clean energy and smart-grid demonstration projects, clean energy retrofits of public buildings, and direct public sector investment in clean energy production capacity. The central point I want to make here is simple—there exist plenty of productive options for spending in the $75-100 billion a year range on compact living and clean, green energy.

Let's suppose that added public sector spending on clean energy and compact living ends up amounting to $100 billion a year through 2030 and explore its likely affect on employment presuming that spending is funded from "cap and trade" emission allowance sales revenues. The Obama Administration stimulus bill of 2009 added $78 billion in new spending for clean energy and rail transportation projects, and the House cap and trade bill (H.R. 2454) allocates to clean energy projects allowance revenues to the tune of $14 billion a year on average.[10]   To imagine a $100 billion of such spending annually is not at all out of the question in given the fairly substantial start the Obama administration has already made. Through 2030, the bulk of the allowances in the cap and trade bill will go to fossil fuel users to offset the burden of shifting to a clean energy path. After 2030, such provisions in the bill expire and the allowance auction revenues from 2030 to 2050 will be available for deficit reduction or government programs. At $100 price for allowances, the total revenues in 2030-2050 will amount to roughly $4.4 trillion, most of which is unallocated right now.[11]   Assuming something equivalent to the House 2009 cap and trade bill is ultimately signed into law, over the full period to 2050 the total market value of emissions allowances would equal about $8.2 trillion (an average of $215 billion annually).   This would be more than enough to fund fuel user transition relief and other measures currently in the bill as well as $1.8 trillion in clean energy projects at $100 billion a year for 18 years. On top of this, plenty would be left over for reducing the government debt. The idea is simple.   Boost spending on clean energy right away by $100 billion a year, but pay for it after 2030 from carbon allowance sales.

In a world where everyone who desires to is working, spending on clean energy projects would not add substantially to employment, but would move it around between occupations and locations.   Given significant unemployment, an added $100 billion in expenditures annually will substantially boost the number of workers who have jobs.   The kind of spending we are outlining here would tend to flow toward compact urban areas and central cities and to rural areas that shift to grass-based farming, renewable energy production, and sustainable forestry. We will address some of the details of this flow and the kinds of employment it creates later, but for now let's focus on the total number of jobs likely to be added by "cap and trade" financed spending.

Let's face it. Because of our current economic difficulties (now referred to as the "Great Recession"), our economy is going to be much less than fully employed for some time. If we add to the economy's overall demand for goods with increased government spending, their supply will rise to the occasion and the unemployed will find new jobs. This is simple Keynesian macroeconomics. For a long time, this kind of economic thinking fell out of fashion, but in an economic crisis, economists tend to return to the wisdom of Keynes: in a deep economic downturn spend your way out. [12]   If the federal and state governments spend more on constructing and equipping light rail transit systems for instance, more people become employed as a direct result, and those individuals will have more income to spend. The initial round of spending on construction will find its way into mostly local pockets, and expenditures on rolling stock will flow to those localities where it is manufactured. Some of this spending might leak out of the economy through imports, but probably not much.[13]   The added income earned by U.S. residents will go to consumer spending, savings, and the payment of income of taxes.   The consumer portion will further stimulate U.S. productive activity, employment, and incomes, although again some will leak out of the economy through imports. Economists refer to such additions to spending on top of the initial amount as a multiplier effect, meaning that the original expenditure ($100 billion) will ultimately get magnified in the aggregate economy by some multiple.

A recent study jointly sponsored by the Political Research Institute and the Center for American Progress sets out exactly the kind of spending approach I have in mind and finds through input-output analysis that an additional $100 billion in annual expenditures on green energy projects will create approximately 2 million jobs once the economic multiplier process dust settles.[14]   The spending targets envisioned in the study include retrofitting buildings to improve energy efficiency, expanding mass transit and freight rail, constructing 'smart' electrical grid transmission systems, and investing in wind power, solar power, and next-generation biofuels.   The input-output approach used in the study carefully accounts for the direct, indirect, and induced effects of the new spending on employment. The direct effects include the construction, service, and manufacturing jobs created for light rail and the other projects; the indirect effects add on the jobs created in industries that supply the materials, equipment, and services needed by those doing the upfront work on the funded projects; and the induced effects take account of the jobs created as a consequence of the consumer spending generated by those who gain employment and incomes directly and indirectly from the new government spending. In short, the $100 billion will result in spending beyond this initiating jolt to the economy, and ultimately 2 million jobs will be created, or more than 1 percent of the current labor force. This would for instance reduce an 8 percent unemployment rate down to 7 percent, or roughly a 13 percent reduction of the amount of unemployment, not a trivial amount.

One could argue that added personal expenditures on energy due to carbon emission allowance costs will drag consumption down and offset any employment creation from investments in green energy and compact living. Emission allowance costs function like a tax, and economists have long argued that tax increases pull spending power out of the economy. This is the case of course only if tax revenue is not re-injected back into the economy. The cap and trade bill accomplishes just such a re-injection. From 2012 to 2030, the bill requires that most of the value of carbon allowances be returned to the public. Since such a return will be unrelated to recipient expenditures on energy, it will not dampen the conservation effects of a relative rise in fossil fuel energy prices. Think about you own circumstances. If the price of gasoline rises, you initially don't have much choice in what to do. You will have to devote more of you income to paying for gasoline because it will be tough to reduce your driving much. Eventually, to cut your transportation costs you may car pool to work part of the week, combine shopping trips, use public transit more, haul out your bike for running errands, and maybe even replace your gas guzzler with a car that gets more miles to the gallon. Just because you get a tax rebate from the government funded by carbon allowances won't cause you to change these economizing behaviors very much. You will of course be happy to get some of the spending power back that you lost from rising energy costs. To sum up, carbon allowance payments will be a wash for macroeconomic activity if they are re-injected back into the economy.

Each of us currently spends roughly $3,800 a year directly and indirectly for the energy that we consume on an annual basis.[15] In 40 years when we have unhooked ourselves from fossil fuels and rely mostly on sun and wind, we will probably be spending about $4,300 a year in today's dollars.[16] The extra energy spending ($500 a year) shouldn't be a special burden on us because we are likely to be making more money in the future because of our ability to produce more stuff from less labor. From the early days of the industrial revolution on, the creation of new, more efficient technologies has brought us continuous advances in labor productivity.

The way we spend our energy dollars does matter for the economy, and focusing such spending on clean energy will fortunately bring a substantial permanent increase to employment beyond the effects of public sector spending as we will now explain.

Shifting from fossil fuels to domestic clean energy will give a big boost to overall economic activity by redirecting spending flows away from imported oil and toward a new domestic clean energy industry. We each spend about $1,100 of our energy dollars on imported petroleum for a grand total of roughly $331 billions.[17] This money ends up largely in the hands of the big, wealthy oil producers around the world who don't buy very many of the goods that we make. The Saudis, who control a substantial chunk of global oil reserves, only spend around $7 billion a year on imports from the U.S. while we buy more than $28 billion in fossil fuel energy from them.[18] Just to be conservative, let's suppose that redirecting $331 billion in spending on foreign oil to our own clean energy industry boosts expenditures on our domestic goods by 75 percent of that amount, or $250 billion a year, with the other 25 percent accounting for a reduction in our exports to oil producers caused by their declining oil sales.[19] This redirection of spending to our domestic economy will mean a permanent addition of 5 million jobs.[20] Rather than our money flowing outward into the hands of the Saudi rulers, it will go to solar panel production-line workers and installers and wind energy fabricators and mechanics. On top of that our trade deficit, which in recent years has been on the rise, will shrink by a substantial amount reducing the buildup of money we owe beyond our borders. With a trade deficit, we buy more from our friends overseas than we sell to them, meaning that we have to borrow the difference. In short, we end up borrowing big money from the Saudis and others who sell us oil.

Let's summarize our estimated additions to employment stimulated by a shift to clean energy. If the federal government spends an added $100 billion annually through 2030 on clean energy, we will see employment increase by 2 million jobs. From 2012 through 2050, employment will rise by 5 million jobs as we get unhooked from foreign oil. After 2030, the added 2 million in clean energy employment will disappear because of federal clean energy spending cuts, and employment will be further dampened from paying back the clean energy portion of the federal debt. Such employment reductions will be offset partially or wholly by an increase of jobs induced by the creation of a new domestic clean energy industry and elimination of our dependence on foreign oil. From 2050 on, a net addition of 5 million jobs will be fully realized once we are unhooked from foreign oil and have paid off the clean energy debt. In essence, the oil sheiks of the world will be footing much of the bill for our transition to a clean energy economy. Clean energy is not a free lunch for them, but it is essentially one for us in the sense that we will be putting people to work who would otherwise be standing in the unemployment lines and seeing their potential for productive labor going to waste.

These numbers underestimate the ultimate boost that going green will give to the U.S. economy. A conservative economist by the name of Joseph Schumpeter lived at about the same time as the more famous John Maynard Keynes who revolutionized economic thinking about using the tools of government to get the world economy out of the 1930s Great Depression. Overshadowed by the Keynesian revolution, Schumpeter nonetheless created a new and fruitful way of thinking about the economy he called "creative destruction."[21] Rather than a growing economy being akin to an expanding balloon with all sectors increasing at the same pace, he saw growth exploding forth due to new revolutionary forms of economic activity coming to fruition, displacing the old and obsolete. Chaos, change, and intense competition provide the dynamic elements for the capitalism Schumpeter envisions. New ideas and new technologies bring forth investment-driven booms that feed the creation of new and novel forms of economic activity. These new forms not only push aside the old, but they become the engines of economic progress. The clean energy-compact green revolution, pushed forward by strategic government action, will set off a new wave of creative-destruction and a cycle of private sector investment activity that will act as an engine of growth propelling the economy forward if everything we have said so far in these pages is a rough approximation of future reality. Huge amounts of investment spending will take place in a diversity of economic arenas including clean energy technologies, energy conservation, solar and wind energy production capacity, compact urban housing and commercial buildings, hybrid and plug-in electric vehicles, and sustainable wood fiber production and recycling capacity.   The concrete outcome for aggregate incomes and employment cannot easily be predicted and we will not try, but it is likely to be substantial, much more than the added 5 million jobs per year we have accounted for so far.   If nothing more than the positive effects from increased government spending and the substituting of domestic clean energy for fossil fuel imports occur (5 million jobs per year), the shift to clean energy and compact living is worth it for the economy as a whole, not to speak of the intrinsic virtues of both environmental improvement and compact living. A little bit of Schumpeterian chaos can be a good thing.[22]

The kinds and locations of jobs created because of a shift to a green compact economy matter as much as the total addition of such jobs. Central cities, rural areas, and the old industrial belt suffer higher rates of unemployment and poverty than much of the rest of the country. A green compact economy will create added employment opportunities in just these areas and in a range of occupations requiring a variety of skill levels. Jobs will be created for highly trained software or electrical engineers as well as entry-level building insulation workers and solar thin panel roofers. While new occupations will emerge, such as "windsmiths" to operate and maintain wind turbines and solar panel installers who have to know both carpentry and solar technology, most occupations will involve the kinds of skills already present in our society—electricians, heating and air conditioning installers, welders, laborers, sheet metal workers, machinists, transit workers, civil engineers, architects, building inspectors, energy auditors, machinery assemblers, window installers, materials engineers, meteorologists (to site wind farms), truck drivers (to move equipment into place), and a the vast array of occupations that it takes to run a business such as managers, marketers, lawyers, accountants, and the information technology experts (these folks are indispensable in almost any endeavor these days).[23] Weatherizing and retrofitting older buildings will occur mainly in older cities including low-income communities and will create numerous local jobs. Light rail transit construction will by its nature be centered on relatively dense urban settings and create employment opportunities for both those who live in low-income and middle class neighborhoods. The need will be both for heavy lifting as well as heavy thinking to create pedestrian friendly, energy efficient urban environments with comfortable and speedy public transit systems. The big advantage of these jobs is that they are relatively well paying, and for the most part they can't be shipped overseas.   To weatherize a building, put up a wind farm, install a solar panel, construct a light rail line, or put up a LEED-certified building requires local labor.

The Midwest industrial- and farm-belt, turns out to be a likely location for a major piece of the green energy economic pie. Toledo, Ohio, a city that in the past depended heavily on auto-industry related employment, already has reapplied its auto glass making skills to the production of solar panels. Pilkington, a huge glass maker, recently started a solar division that is currently experiencing a 40 percent annual surge in sales growth. Stepping up to the renewable energy plate, the University of Toledo now has 15 faculty research solar technologies. The U.S. has been slow off the starting line in wind energy with most of the dominant wind turbine producers having a European background. Nonetheless, the Midwest turns out to be a great location for wind turbine assembly. Acciona, a Spanish wind turbine producer, recently located a turbine plant in old West Branch, Iowa hydraulic pump factory. Iowa and the Great Plains may well turn out to be the Saudi Arabia of the wind farm industry with its relentless wind which sometimes drove settlers mad in the past.[24]

Turbines are not the only kind of green energy equipment manufacturing attracted to Iowa farm country. Newton, Iowa thought its days of prosperity were gone once the Maytag plant that employed 1,800 and paid upwards of $20 an hour closed in 2007. The arrival of TPI Composites and a new factory producing the huge fiberglass blades that power wind generators saved the day. Across the street in the old Maytag plant another manufacturer has set up production of the concrete towers for mounting the huge turbines. TPI promises to eventually employ 500 and is paying around $13 an hour—less than Maytag, but not bad in a community where living costs are fairly low. The local community college now holds classes in blade construction to improve TPI-employee skills. With the huge projected growth in wind energy, Newton's future should be assured.[25] Turbines and the blades to propel them are huge and costly to ship giving local producers, such as those in West Branch and Newton, a special advantage.

Towns in the rural midwest suffer not just from rust belt industrial decline but have to contend with a long-term trend of corn belt depopulation caused by the inexorable increase in the size of farms and decline in the demand for farm labor. In Iowa between 1950 and 2000 the size of the typical farm increased from just over 160 acres to 350 acres and the number of farms dropped from 206,000 to 90,000.[26] Persistent improvements in labor saving technology and capital intensity drive the increase in farm size. To support the large, hugely efficient row crop farm machinery used today in the corn belt, farms need to be really big, and they can be operated by very few individuals. The inevitable result of bigger farmers and less need for labor is rural population decline. In the wake of depopulation, towns that depend on selling to farmers shrink in scope and number, the young and the brightest move away, and the old and the poor are left behind.[27] Farm equipment suppliers increase in size but shrink in number, grain terminals are fewer and farther apart, and farmers travel farther on a Saturday to get to town, and increasingly they shop at Walmart, not the local downtown retailer.

Sun and wind may be a saving grace for the economy of the corn belt, and maybe even more for the Great Plains which is suffering an even higher rate of rural depopulation. With plenty of both, wind and solar energy will likely be an economic boon to these two regions. A movement to grass-based agriculture could be even more of a boon. Instead of a 400 or 500 acre corn farm, a family can prosper on a 100-200 acre grass farm with meat as the final product. Keeping cattle on the farm and intensively managing them (i.e. moving them around from pasture to pasture to keep them from taking more than one bite in one spot) will likely be a better deal for farmers than spending their life in a hermetically sealed tractor raising corn and shipping it off to feedlots. Doing this will also be a better deal for the economic health of rural areas—smaller farms will mean more farmers, more people, and more and bigger towns. More rural economic opportunities will keep more of the young and brightest on the farms and alleviate rural unemployment and poverty. The corn belt and the Great Plains could see an economic boom based on green energy and a grass-based agricultural economy. A Conservation Reserve Program that transforms row crops to grass will not only create healthier meat, increase the amount of carbon stored in the soil, reduce water pollution and the dead zone in the Gulf of Mexico, and restore the ecological health of the prairie, it will also give the rural economy a boost and bring back a smaller-scale agriculture. One could easily imagine the average size for farms in Iowa declining to 200 acres and the number of farms increasing from 90,000 to more than 150,000.

The Great Plains and midwest are not alone in suffering rural population losses. Forest communities, such as Forks, Washington and Oakridge, Oregon, fell victim to a dramatic decline in harvests from the national forests in the 1990s caused in part by a court case that put 24 million acres of old-growth forests off-limits to timber harvesting to protect the endangered Spotted Owl. In 1994 the Clinton administration put into place the Northwest Forest Plan to bring a balance between timber harvesting and ecosystem protection. About 30,000 Forest Plan-area lumber industry jobs disappeared in the 1990s, roughly a third due to harvest declines from public lands and the rest mostly because of employment-reducing technological changes. The last lumber mill in Oakridge shut its doors in the early 1990s, the town's population is shrinking, and board-ups of Oakridge commercial buildings are common. Some residents commute 35 miles to Eugene, Oregon for work, but nothing has sprung up in town or nearby to replace the lost lumber industry jobs. Not all timber rural timber communities in Oregon and Washington have suffered economic decline. A number of towns along the I-5 corridor, stretching from central Oregon up to Seattle, Washington, have attracted new, high technology industries to replace lost forest products jobs. Larger towns, such as Eugene and Springfield, Oregon, with good transportation connections and solid education institutions, proved resilient in the face of job losses.[28]

One answer to job losses in rural forest communities is forest certification combined with marketable carbon offset emission allowance creation. The idea is to combine the environmental virtues of forest certification as we discussed earlier with atmospheric greenhouse gas reduction and in the process make some money on both publicly and privately owned forests throughout the country. Let's focus on the Pacific Northwest national forests to illustrate how all this would work.

Over the last quarter century an epic struggle has taken place between environmentalists and forest communities in the Pacific Northwest over the use to which the vast expanses of the public forests are to be put. Forest communities pushed hard to keep their timber related jobs while environmentalists fought to protect the rapidly diminishing stands of old growth needed for the survival of threatened species such as the Spotted Owl.

Certification public forests appears to be an answer to these conflicting interests. Through certification, local communities can be assured of employment in forest related industries having a special environmental edge in the market place, and environmentalists will know that forests are managed according to ecologically sound principles. Taking the idea to heart, the U.S. Forest Service has been conducting experiments with certification. Although results have been generally positive, acceptable forest practices were found to be impeded by excessive buildups of overstocked and undersized trees that can cause stand-destroying wildfires and by a backlog of road maintenance and closure projects. The Forest Service has long recognized the need for this kind of work and has responded recently by issuing stewardship contracts in some localities. Stewardship work of this type creates local employment directly in the woods as well as indirectly through harvests of small-diameter trees useful as raw material for wood products enterprises or as feedstock for biofuel producers. The essential problem facing the Forest Service is the absence of a source of funding for stewardship. Combining certification on the national forests with carbon emission offset sales would solve the funding problem. Stewardship could in effect become a cash cow by accelerating forest growth through thinning and other management practice that would sequester more carbon and expand allowance sales. In short, managing certified forests is a labor intensive undertaking that will generate local employment and help reverse economic decline and growing poverty in small rural communities. Not only will stewardship be labor using, but the selective harvesting that certification requires will be as well. Certification and carbon sequestration will be a good deal for both the ecological health of the forests and the economic health of local communities.[29]

Peak Oil, Climate, and Compact Living

Recent global and national political events suggest a fairly high probability that government efforts to restrict greenhouse gas emissions could turn out to be modest at best. After the chaos at Copenhagen and struggles over cap and trade in the U.S. Senate, optimism about tackling global warming head on seems to be waning. What if next to nothing of substance is done to unhook us globally from fossil fuels as our primary source of energy? If this were the case, then climate will ultimately warm by anywhere from 5 to 6 degrees Celsius according to the Intergovernmental Panel on Climate Change (IPCC). If "peak oil" theory turns out to be true, beyond about 2040 we will be on the downward slope of fossil fuel supplies in the face of continuing global growth in energy demand. This will mean accelerating increases in the price of energy and a huge income transfer from the world as a whole to the already wealthy owners of fossil fuel reserves.

As energy prices increase because of growing fossil fuel scarcity, we will ultimately be forced to shift to green energy and a compact form of life as described in previous pages, but only after we have been shaken down by Arab oil sheiks for trillions of dollars. We can avoid this and give a huge boost to our domestic economy by unhooking ourselves from the tyranny of fossil fuels sooner rather than later. Doing nothing to move to clean energy now is a collectively brainless thing to do, not only because of the consequences for climate change, but because of immediate harm to our own narrow economic self-interest. Let me now explain.

The IPCC in its latest report, "Climate Change 2007" sets out a range of scenarios for addressing global warming.[30] The most aggressive strategy calls for reducing global emissions 50 to 85 percent below 2000 levels by 2050. If we are able to do so, warming will be limited to 2-2.4 degrees Celsius. Under the least aggressive strategy emissions could grow to as much as 140 percent of 2000 levels by 2050, and the climate could ultimately warm as much as 6 degrees Celsius (11 degrees or so Fahrenheit). Under the most aggressive strategy, a carbon equivalent emission allowance price somewhere near $100 per metric ton range will be required by 2030 to dampen emissions sufficiently to hold climate change in check, while under the least aggressive the carbon price will need to be no more than $20. A concrete commitment by the U.S. to unhook itself from fossil fuels by 2050 would do the world a huge good turn by getting the ball rolling on climate stabilization.

Although good turns are morally uplifting, we can instead look to our own immediate self-interest as justification for moving quickly as possible to a clean energy, carbon emission-free economy. For starters, we will have little choice but to make this move eventually according to the idea of 'peak oil.' The logic of peak oil is impeccable. The earth's crust necessarily contains a finite amount of fossil fuel deposits; with exploitation of these deposits, at some point in historical time the rate of feasible production will reach its maximum and begin a slide downward. The essential question for us is when? This idea was controversial for many years after being introduced in the 1950s by Shell Oil petroleum geologist, M. King Hubbert, who argued that worldwide peak oil would be reached by the year 2000.[31] While that prediction proved inaccurate, today experts agree that the global peak will arrive by 2040. This is the central conclusion of a 2007 U.S. General Accounting Office study on the need for a public response to the inevitability of peak oil.[32] With continued rapid growth in energy demand, the economic effect of declining oil production is not hard to predict— accelerating petroleum prices. Imported crude oil prices facing the U.S. between 2008 and 2035 are already projected by the U.S. Department of Energy to grow by 1 percent a year above the annual rate of inflation. As the production peak is reached, this rate of price growth will undoubtedly accelerate without a concerted movement to get unhooked from fossil fuels. Shifting to natural gas and coal will be a partial but temporary solution to a scarcity in crude petroleum.[33] A global peak in both natural gas and coal production will not be far behind oil according to the experts. Simply put, beyond 2040, rising fossil fuel prices will force us to shift to alternative energy sources even if we do nothing beforehand to limit greenhouse gas emissions by reducing fossil fuel consumption.

The obvious question to ask is this: why not unhook ourselves from fossil fuels and turn to compact living sooner rather than later? As of 2006 we were spending $330 billion on petroleum imports annually. The Department of Energy projects a rough stability in the volume of these imports through 2035 but rising real petroleum import prices (inflation adjusted) to the tune of 1 percent a year.[34] If these trends prevail beyond 2035, then by 2050 we will be spending more than $500 billion a year on petroleum imports in today's dollars. Over the entire period from 2006 through 2050 our import spending will amount to a bit more than $18 trillion. Perhaps 25 percent of this figure[35] will return to our shores as U.S. export purchases leaving some 14 trillion in the hands of oil sheiks and others to be disposed of elsewhere. In short, our spending on energy currently benefits relatively well-to-do owners of petroleum reserves outside the U.S.

Fortunately for us, this need not be the case. Instead of a huge income transfer to wealthy foreigners lucky enough to own oil reserves, we could instead direct that income to our own citizens in return for the creation of clean energy. In the end, after such a transition our average household energy bill in today's dollars will increase only modestly, if at all (as we just noted). Remember, about 5 million jobs will be permanently created because of a shift to clean energy, many of which will be well paying and located in economically stressed central cities and rural areas. In short, instead of adding to the wealth and power of Arab sheiks and oil-supported dictators, we could create a domestic clean energy economy that brings growing economic prosperity for many of our fellow citizens and increasing economic security for everyone.

Notes

[1] U. S. Library of Congress, *H.R. 2454: American Clean Energy and Security Act of 2009* ([cited]). At this writing, a similar bill, *S. 1733: The American Power Act*, is bogged down in the Senate as of this writing. See U.S. Library of Congress, *S. 1733: The American Power Act* (The Library of Congress, 2010 [cited June 15, 2010]); available from http://thomas.loc.gov/cgi-bin/query/z?c111:S.1733:.

[2] This is the stated justification for including such giveaways in the bill, but the real reason for doing so probably was the political hope of obtaining fossil fuel user acquiescence to cap and trade.

3 Energy Information Administration U.S. Department of Energy, *Emissions of Greenhouse Gases Report* (U.S. Department of Energy, Energy Information Administration, 2008 [cited June 3, 2009]); available from http://www.eia.doe.gov/oiaf/1605/ggrpt/index.html.

4 Ibid.([cited]).

5 Carbon dioxide equivalency is the amount of CO_2 that would have the same global warming potential measured over a specific period of time (usually 100 years) as a given volume of another greenhouse gas such as methane. A metric ton of methane has 23 times the global warming potential as a metric ton of CO_2. A metric ton of nitrous oxide has a global warming potential 296 times that of carbon dioxide. Energy Information Administration U.S. Department of Energy, *Units for Measuring Greenhouse Gases* (U.S. Department of Energy, 2003 [cited December 10, 2008]); available from http://www.eia.doe.gov/oiaf/1605/archive/gg03rpt/summary/special_topics.html.

6 Intergovernmental Panel on Climate Change, *Climate Change 2007: Mitigation of Climate Change* ([cited]). This report is the source of all the data on climate change used here. No one knows for sure what the relationship between the emissions prices and reductions will be with any precision. The IPCC reports likely ranges for this relationship. The Congressional Budget Office (CBO) in its projections of costs for H.R. 2454 predicts a price equal to $26 a metric ton in 2019. If we project CBO's rate of price growth to 2030, the predicted carbon allowance cost would be $55 a metric ton to reduce emissions by 42 percent from the 2005 level. CBO's allowance price predictions seem low in comparison to those made by others, even in some of their own reports. See Mark Lasky, *The Economic Costs of Reducing Emissions of Greenhouse Gases: A Survey of Economic Models* (U.S. Congressional Budget Office, 2003 [cited); available from http://www.cbo.gov/ftpdocs/41xx/doc4198/2003-3.pdf; U.S. Congressional Budget Office, *Congressional Budget Office Cost Estimate: H.R. 2454 American Clean Energy and Security Act of 2009* ([cited]).

[7] The 2009 clean energy bill, H.R. 2454, sets out a schedule emission allowances that will reduce U.S. emissions to 58 percent of the 2005 level by 2030. This schedule should reduce emissions to around 4 gigatons from 7 gigatons currently for the U.S. Consequently, I adopt this schedule for my calculations here. The Congressional Budget Office (CBO) predicts an allowance price of $26 by 2019 and apparently about $55 by 2030 if one projects the same rate of growth after 2019 as before in CBO's data. This figure is much lower than the international price need to reduce global emissions by a comparable amount as reported by the Intergovernmental Panel on Climate Change (IPCC). Consequently, I will stick to the probable $100 per metric ton required to reduce emissions by as much as 42 percent by 2030. See Intergovernmental Panel on Climate Change, *Climate Change 2007: Mitigation of Climate Change* ([cited); U.S. Congressional Budget Office, *Congressional Budget Office Cost Estimate: H.R. 2454 American Clean Energy and Security Act of 2009* ([cited). In its cap and trade accounting, the CBO assumes that allowances distributed free to fuel users are first sold and the revenue from the sale then allocated to users. This convention is followed in calculations here.

[8] Burning a gallon of gasoline causes about 20 pounds of CO_2 to be emitted. Each kilowatt hour of electricity generated using coal leads to approximately 2 pounds of CO_2 emissions according to the Department of Energy. See U.S. Department of Energy and Environmental Protection Agency, *Carbon Dioxide Emissions from the Generation of Electric Power in the United States* ([cited]).

[9] U.S. Department of Energy, *Solar America Initiative: A Plan for the Integrated Research, Development, and Market Transformation of Solar Energy Technologies* ([cited]).

[10] This assumes that emission allowance prices rise steadily to $100 a metric ton in 2030 from $15 in 2012.

[11] This calculation is based on allowances projected in H.R. 5424. See U. S. Library of Congress, *H.R. 2454: American Clean Energy and Security Act of 2009* ([cited).

[12] Louis Uchitelle, "Economists Warm to Government Spending but Debate Its Form," *New York Times*, January 7, 2008.

[13] This is the conclusion in Robert Pollin et al., "Green Recovery: A Program to Create Good Jobs and Start Building a Low-Carbon Economy," (Amherst, MA: Political Economy Research Institute and the Center for American Progress, 2008).

[14] Ibid.

[15] U.S. Department of Energy, *Annual Energy Review, 2008* ([cited]).

[16] You will recall that we each will need roughly 200 square meters of photovoltaic cells to supply 80 percent of our energy consumption (see Chapter 3). The Department of Energy projects that the lifetime cost of installed solar capacity should drop to about 3 dollars per peak watt. For a 15 percent efficiency square meter panel that produces 150 watts from 1,000 watts of sunlight, the installed cost would be $600 per square meter including inverter replacement and lifetime maintenance by 2020. For the full 200 the total cost would be $120,000. Since panels have a life expectancy of 35 years, this boils down to about $3,400 a year. The great virtue of solar is the absence of fuel costs. See U.S. Department of Energy, *Solar Energy Technologies Program: Multi-Year Program Plan* ([cited]). We also need to add the cost of wind energy for the other 20 percent of our energy supply, which will likely be no greater than solar (otherwise we will just do solar). This brings us up to a total of $4,250 a year for our energy desires. In fact, the cost per kilowatt hour for wind is projected to be around $.08 by 2030 while solar will be more like $.09. For the cost of wind, see U.S. Department of Energy, *20% Wind Energy by 2030: Increasing Wind Energy's Contribution to U.S. Electricity Supply* ([cited]).

[17] U.S. Department of Energy, *Annual Energy Review, 2008* ([cited]). The spending data is for 2006.

[18] U.S. Bureau of the Census, *The 2009 Statistical Abstract* ([cited]). Even if we stop buying oil from the Saudis, that doesn't necessarily mean they will cut their imports from us to zero. The reduction will depend on what ultimately happens to their incomes and spending power in the face of a global shift to clean energy and away from fossil fuels. They still might do comparatively well by focusing on solar energy production—they do have a lot of sunshine.

[19]Of course we will not be free of fossil fuel imports until 2050 or so if the measures described in these pages to move to green energy are implemented. By then we would be spending about $500 billion in today's dollars on petroleum imports if we don't unhook ourselves from fossil fuels. This number is based on an extrapolation of Energy Information Administration estimates through 2035. In sum, we are underestimating the actual number of jobs that will be created from freeing ourselves from imported energy. We will be diverting 500 billion, not 331 billion away from spending on energy imports by 2050, generating proportionately still more jobs in our domestic energy industry. For projections on future fossil fuel imports and prices, see Energy Information Administration U.S. Department of Energy, *Annual Energy Outlook, 2010* (U.S. Department of Energy, Energy Information Administration, 2010 [cited June 28, 2009]); available from http:// www.eia.doe.gov/oiaf/aeo/.

[20] I base this figure on the research in Pollin et al., "Green Recovery: A Program to Create Good Jobs and Start Building a Low-Carbon Economy." As already noted, they find that $100 billion in green spending leads to an added 2 million jobs. I reduce the employment estimate by .7 million simply for the sake of being conservative in the calculations.

[21] Joseph A. Schumpeter, *Capitalism, Socialism, and Democracy* (New York: Harper Torchbooks, 1950).

[22] Judging from recent experience, economic booms need to be managed with care.   Business and financial institutions are prone to irrational exuberance in the pursuit of the new and novel kinds of economic endeavors. Over investment seems to almost always be the inevitable result of bursts of economic activity, although at the time of this writing it appears we could use a little more economic "exuberance."

[23] Robert Pollin and Jeannette Wicks-Lim, "Job Opportunities for the Green Economy: A State-by-State Picture of Occupations That Gain from Green Investments," (Amherst, MA: Political Economy Research Institute, University of Massachusetts Amherst, 2008); U.S. Department of Energy, *Careers in Renewable Energy* (U.S. Department of Energy, 2001 [cited January 9, 2009]); available from http://www.nrel.gov/docs/fy01osti/28369.pdf.

[24] Peter S. Goodman, "A Splash of Green for the Rust Belt," *New York Times*, November 2, 2008.

[25] Ibid.

[26] Anderlik, *Rural Depopulation: What Does It Mean for the Future Economic Health of Rural Areas and the Community Banks That Support Them?* ([cited]).

[27] Ibid.([cited]); Jeffrey Walser and John Anderlik, "Rural Depopulation: What Does It Mean for the Future Economic Health of Rural Areas and the Community Banks That Support Them?," *FDIC Banking Review* 16, no. 3 (2004).

[28] Ellen M. Donoghue and Richard W. Haynes, "Assessing the Viability and Adaptability of Oregon Communities," in *PNW-GTR-540* (Portland, OR: USDA Forest Service, Pacific Northwest Research Station, 2002); Ernie Niemi and Ed Whitelaw, "Bird of Doom...Or Was It?," *Amicus Journal,* Fall (2000); Pacific Northwest Research Station USDA Forest Service, "Understanding the Social and Economic Transitions of Forest Communities," *PNW Science Update* Fall, no. 18 (2008).

[29] Pinchot Institute for Conservation, "Stewardship Contracting: A Summary of Lessons Learned from the Pilot Experience," (Washington D.C.: Pinchot Institute for Conservation, 2006); V. Alaric Sample et al., "National Forest Certification Study: An Evaluation of the Applicability of Forest Stewardship Council (FSC) and Sustainable Forest Initiative (SFI) Standards on Five National Forests," (Washington D.C.: Pinchot Institute for Conservation, 2007); USDA Forest Service, "Understanding the Social and Economic Transitions of Forest Communities."

[30] Intergovernmental Panel on Climate Change, *Climate Change 2007: Mitigation of Climate Change* ([cited).

[31] Pat Murphy, *Plan C: Community Survival Strategies for Peak Oil and Climate Change* (Gabriola Island, BC, Canada: New Society Publishers, 2008).

[32] U.S. Government Accountability Office (GAO), *Crude Oil: Uncertainty About Future Oil Supply Makes It Important to Develop a Strategy for Addressing a Peak and Decline in Oil Production* (U.S. Government Printing Office, 2007 [cited January 27, 2010]); available from http://www.gao.gov/new.items/d07283.pdf.

[33] R.W. Bentley, "Global Oil and Gass Depletion: An Overviews," *Energy Policy* 30 (2002); Energy Watch Group, *Coal: Resources and Future Production* (Energy Watch Group, 2007 [cited January 27, 2010]); available from http://www.energywatchgroup.org/fileadmin/global/pdf/EWG_Report_Coal_10-07-2007ms.pdf.

[34] U.S. Department of Energy, *Annual Energy Review, 2008* ([cited]); U.S. Department of Energy, *Annual Energy Outlook, 2010* ([cited]).

[35] See the above discussion on how we arrive at this number.

Chapter 14
Compact Green Living and the Future Land Use Pyramid

Compact living as described in these pages will cause us to rearrange our use of space, reduce our greenhouse gas emissions, and increase the amount of space we leave for undisturbed natural landscapes. We have described our arrangement of space with what I have called the "land use pyramid." At the peak of the pyramid is the amount of developed land we each use directly and intensively—buildings, streets and highways, parking lots, and parks. Farther down the pyramid is the amount of land we use indirectly and largely out of our daily view for food, wood fiber, mineral extraction, and energy production, the vast bulk of which falls in the first two categories. The land leftover outside the pyramid is for the most part naturally vegetated and serves as habitat for plant and animal species that do best in their own spaces free of human intrusion.

To get a better sense of the changes compact living brings to our spatial arrangements, we will now compare our possible—and I think likely—future as described in these pages with our current circumstances. This future is a mixture of hope and probable reality. To staunch global warming we will have to cap greenhouse gas emissions, a task which seems to be slowly gathering momentum in the global political arena. In the end, this will mean that the cost of getting around by car will increase along with the cost of living in big houses on big lots. Both will cause us to seek living at higher densities and to shift to public transit. This much is clear. Certainly our urban densities will rise, but whether they will double as I have suggested here is open to speculation. Increasing our average urban density to a level equal to the typical Canadian city seems plausible in the next 40 years, and if we do so our density will indeed double.[1] I hope this will happen and I hypothesize that our lives will improve if it does apart from any salutary environmental results. Dense populations make for interesting urban living. Similarly, I hope we adopt a compact green cuisine and green forestry practices, but I have no allusions that this will necessarily happen. Given the rising interest in organic food and environmentally friendly wood and paper products, compact cuisine and green forestry are not out of the question.

If we manage to double our urban densities, we will reduce our direct use of developed land from 1,500 to 1,250 square meters each taking into account our increased need to devote space to solar energy.[2] Shifting to a green compact cuisine will cut the amount of land we devote to corn on a per capita basis by about 500 square meters (a 50 percent reduction) and convert it to grasslands and prairie that will not only support cattle but also serve as natural habitat for grassland birds and other prairie species. We will be sharing this habitat with nonhuman species instead of completely appropriating it for ourselves. The same will be the case for old-growth forests under certification. If just a fourth of our commercial forests become certified, 1,000 square meters per capita of exploited forests will be eventually transformed through sustainable management practices into a natural state that will support a diverse collection of plant and animal species. Again, rather than totally dominating the landscape as we would in a plantation forest, we will now share forests with the rest of nature. To summarize, our personal land use pyramid under these assumptions would shrink from a total of 13,500 square meters (Developed, 1,500; agriculture, 7,000; timber, 4,300; rural, 700) down to 11,750 square meters (Developed, 1,250; agriculture, 6,500; timber, 3,300; rural, 700) given that we shift farm- and forestland shared with nonhuman species out of our personal land use pyramid into nature's space. As a consequence, the amount of land for nature would expand from 12,000 square meters per capita to 13,750 square meters.

In 40 years if all that I have suggested comes to past, we will have reduced our personal human spatial footprint as measured the area of our individual land use pyramids. Of course, such shrinkage for each of us could be offset for land use in total by a growing human population. Clearly, the one issue we still need to address is the effect of probable population growth over the next 40 years on human land use. So far we have focused on our personal (per capita) land use pyramid. Now it is time to shift the terms of discussion to our country's grand total land use pyramid.

Current projections suggest that by 2050 population in this country will rise to 439 million from 300 million today, which means a growth rate of just over 1 percent a year and a total population that is 46 percent above our current level.[3] If we succeed in doubling our current urban land use density, accommodate space needs for solar energy, and end up with 1,250 meters per capita for developed land, this would mean our total for this land use category would increase from 45 million hectares to about 55 million hectares to accommodate population growth.[4] This increase would not amount to much, roughly 1.3 percent of the total land area in the U.S.[5] The peak of our aggregate land use pyramid would need to expand, but not substantially.

The really huge potential affect of a larger population would be on our indirect uses of land farther down the pyramid, not on the direct uses at the pyramid's peak. Simply put, 46 percent more residents of the U.S. should lead to roughly a proportionate increase in food and wood fiber consumption, and a greater demand for land devoted to their production. On the face of it, the total amount of land we need for food and wood fiber should be driven to dramatically greater levels by a larger population. The only way we could get that land would be by taking over natural habitats currently free of significant human intrusion, and doing so would place numerous plant and animal species under the threat of extinction.

Probable future land use trends in agricultural and timber fortunately suggest a different scenario. We shouldn't have to take more land away from the world of nature even if population expands by 46 percent. We need to explain why.

Let's begin with agriculture. The amount of land devoted to agriculture in the U.S. between 1982 and 2003 dropped from about 223 million hectares to around 209 million. This is a continuation of a long-standing trend in this country toward less land under cultivation. Farmland decline has occurred despite expanding demand for food induced by population growth at a bit more than 1 percent a year. Simply put, over time we extract more food from a given amount of land devoted to agriculture. Agriculture features a long-term and enduring trend of growing productivity relative to both all inputs in general and land specifically.[6]   Despite population growth, less land is needed in the U.S. for agricultural production than in the past. We have no reason to doubt the continuation of such productivity growth in the future, and if the future of agricultural productivity growth is comparable to the past, then, despite a growing population, the total amount of land devoted to agriculture will continue its slow downward trend. Of course, if population grew at a slower pace than predicted, then the amount of land devoted to agriculture will trend down more quickly because of a lower rate of growth in demand for food, and more land could be given back to nature for the support of rare and threatened plant and animal species. Add to this the adoption of a compact "green cuisine" in the French tradition we could deeply cut our growth in demand for food to the benefit of our personal health and gustatory pleasures.

For somewhat different reasons, a similar tale can be told for wood fiber production. Between now and 2050 the U.S. Forest Service projects that timber harvests in this country for lumber and paper products will expand by 28 percent. Despite this increase, the volume harvested will come from a smaller forest area simply because forest growth will exceed the amount removed by as much as 50 percent each year between now and then.[7] The forests in this country are poised for a future of rapid growth. So even though we will be using more wood fiber because there will be more of us, the forest area required to feed our fiber demand will be less. Of course, the shrinkage of the forest area needed to meet our wood fiber demand would be even more if population growth were less.

Surprisingly, in this country we can handle a 46 percent larger population by 2050 and at the same time modestly shrink our total use of land for farms and timber. We will have to expand our developed land modestly (assuming a doubling of urban densities), but we still can return some of the land we currently use to nature and the threatened species that need it, especially if we adopt the measures suggested here for compact living, a compact green cuisine, and green forestry. This is not to say that I advocate a continued increase in our population. Obviously, if population growth were held below predicted trends, our human spatial footprint could be shrunk even further, leaving more for nature. A more compact, smaller population would also reduce the projected pace in demand growth for energy and ease the task of controlling greenhouse gases. I personally favor population stability, but I have no special insights about how to achieve that. I leave this question to others.

While the focus of our attention in this book is on the U.S. and by inference comparable affluent countries of the world, I would like to direct the reader to a recent fascinating study about the feasibility of feeding a global population of more than 9 billion in 2050 using environmentally friendly "organic" crops and moving away from confined animal feeding toward more humane free range approaches.[8] The study dispels the usual claim that organic agriculture is fine for the affluent, but we need high-technology fertilizer and pesticide based cropping systems along with confined animal feeding operations to provide the world's population including the poor with a healthy amount of calories and proteins.

The starting point for the study is the Food and Agricultural Organization's (FAO) projections for 2050 agricultural production and land use. A "business as usual" forecast yields a 9 percent cropland expansion relative to 2000 and an increase in crop yields per unit land of around 54 percent. Production rises in the future according to these projections primarily because of growth in agricultural yields as opposed to more expansive land cultivation. A review of the literature on organic agriculture suggests crop yields somewhat below conventional agriculture, except in developing countries where organic agriculture possesses a substantial potential to improve soil fertility and productivity. Organic crop yields worldwide are close enough to conventional agriculture to support healthy global diets for all in 2050 under expected trends. The study considers three methods of raising livestock for protein: intensive, humane, and organic. To allow animals to range freely (the humane option) requires 10 percent more feed input than confined feeding (the intensive option), and to adopt organic standards costs 20 percent more in feed than the intensive option. The study concludes that organic agriculture can likely feed a projected global population of 9.2 billion in 2050 without increasing land under cultivation by more than the 9 percent projected by the FAO. This added cropland can come out of the huge inventory now devoted to grazing globally while at the same time expanding free-range meat productivity through more intensive pasture management. The essential cost for us in U.S. and some of the other affluent countries of the world to accomplish all this will be a need to reduce our caloric and protein intake to lower, healthier levels, such as those in the French diet. Judging from the gastronomical pleasures the French enjoy (as discussed earlier), this shouldn't be too much of a problem. A huge environmental virtue of free-range animal husbandry and organic cropping would be a substantial reduction in greenhouse gases associated with our current fossil-fuel dependent agricultural system. On top of this, injections of excessive nitrogen from fertilizer runoff into our oceans that cause dead zones can be brought to a halt, and we can do this without the need to take away more of nature's space. The study also suggests that roughly 15 percent of our current global energy consumption can come from agriculture (mostly wastes and perennial grasses such as switch grass) while still meeting global food supply needs.

All this means that compact living at a global level is eminently feasible. We can get by with the current amount of land we use for cropping and grazing worldwide even with an increase in population to 9 billion.

Notes

¹ Newman and Kenworthy, *Sustainability and Cities: Overcoming Automobile Dependency.*

² Our current developed land use is 1,500 square meters each of which about 1,100 is urban. If we each live at double our current urban density, this would reduce our developed land to about 950 square meters. We will need another 300 square meters for solar energy, bringing the total back up to 1,250 for each of us.

³ U.S. Bureau of the Census, *The 2009 Statistical Abstract* ([cited]).

⁴ To get the projected 55 million hectares of developed land, multiply the per capita estimate—.125 hectares (1,250 square meters)—times population, 439 million.

⁵ The lower 48 states contains roughly 764 million hectares of which 10 million is about 1.3 percent. In this scenario our developed land will increase from 5.8 percent of the total (45 million hectares) to 7.1 percent (55 million hectares). The final 2050 amount of developed land includes the area need for solar energy production for the green energy scheme outlined in the pages above.

⁶ USDA Economic Research Service, *Agricultural Productivity in the United States* (USDA Economic Research Service, 2009 [cited June 8, 2009]); available from http://www.ers.usda.gov/Data/AgProductivity/.

⁷ Haynes et al., "The 2005 RPA Timber Assessment Update." We currently on net import timber products, but the volume of this is expected to stabilize over the next 50 years. In short, our current fairly modest dependency on forests overseas will remain about the same.

⁸ Karl-Heinz Erb et al., *Eating the Planet: Feeding and Fueling the World Sustainably, Fairly, and Humanely--a Scoping Study* (Institute of Social Ecology and PIK Potsdam, 2009 [cited November 13, 2009]); available from http://www.ciwf.org.uk/includes/documents/cm_docs/2009/e/ eating_the_planet_full_report_nov_2009.pdf.

Chapter 15
The Coming Good Green Economic Boom: Economic and Philosophical Foundations

Path Dependence

Even though most of us know the "qwerty" story, it is worth retelling to set the stage for our inquiry. Take a moment to look at the letters on your computer keyboard. The first six of the top row spells the nonsensical word, qwerty. Take a look at the arrangement of all the keys and ask yourself why are they configured the way they are? Is it to make typing easier and faster? The answer to that question is no. The keys on the so-called qwerty keyboard are arranged to minimize key jams on the original mechanical typewriters that now exist only in museums, antique stores, or your great grandparents' attic. Once technological advance produced the electric typewriter, and ultimately the personal computer, the rationale for the qwerty arrangement disappeared, yet to this day we stick with it. Why? Surely we would all be better off if all our computer keyboards had a more efficient arrangement.

Typing is one of those activities in life where doing it one way and one way only really pays. We need a standard. If there were two different key arrangements or five or ten, and we learned one of them, chances are we would go into a computer lab or get a job in an office where the keyboard arrangement differs from the one on which we learned. Anyone who has gone into an internet cafe in France or many other countries will have a heck of a time sending an e-mail because the keys on computers are arranged differently. The point is simple—life is much easier if there is one arrangement of keys. No matter where we find ourselves we can type with ease.

Shifting to a more efficient keyboard configuration would in the end benefit us all, but to get everyone to retake typing would be a huge undertaking that no doubt would meet with stiff resistance. Better the devil we know than the one we don't. Most of us won't really want to bother making the change to something with which we are unfamiliar. So as a society we stay stuck with an inefficient, suboptimal keyboard. We don't like change to an uncertain future. There is a second problem as well. Even if we all favored changing to a more efficient arrangement, doing so is a collective act. The benefits of change will be so highly dispersed and so small for each of us, it won't pay any of us individually to take charge and start the "new keyboard movement."

You might think this is a trivial affair—and you would be right—but it illustrates rather nicely the idea of "path dependence." Two different paths of some kind exist; we are on one but we would in the end find ourselves better off on the other; but to shift from one to the other, everyone must do it. Two huge barriers prevent the shift. First, we have intimate familiarity with the path we are on and may know little about, and fear the uncertainty of, the alternative.   Second, it won't pay anyone to bear the costs of getting the political ball rolling to spark the collective shift between paths.   In essence, we become hooked to the bad path and can't move to the good.   This is path dependence.[1]

Which Path to Choose for our Personal Well Being: Compact or Spatially Expansive Living?

Most of us today possess a comfortable familiarity with the spatially expansive, suburban mode of life that constitutes our daily experience.   The path we are on continually finds reinforcement as the best of all possible worlds in the power of advertising and the attractions of popular culture.   The consumer life on which our economic prosperity depends possesses heavy suburban roots.   The material virtues of a low density suburban life are well known and need little further comment except to say that most of us are probably quite happy with our current surroundings.   After all, most of us have freely chosen where we live.

While we may have some inkling of what the alternative path of compact living would be like from trips to Europe or spending time in revitalized American central cities, we probably still feel uncertain about whether we could live well in a spatially compact environment.   Why take a chance on upending our lives if we lack good reasons for doing so?   Why move from the path we are on to one that we don't know much about?   In short, to be willing to adopt spatial compactness, we have to be really clear on the advantages of doing so for our own personal lives.   This of course is the key purpose of this book, to explain the pluses of compact living.

Let's bring all that we have said so far together into a philosophical framework.   After all, choosing how to live is a philosophical question, especially when faced with a need for change.   Digging ourselves out of the environmental hole that we currently occupy will necessarily push us from our current path to an uncertain alternative.   Whether we will accept change, or push against it, depends heavily on our judgment about the feasibility of us and our descendants living well in a substantially altered future.   If you are a person of a certain age, you need to recognize that we are talking mainly about how your children will live.   After all, 2050 is forty years off, and the changes we are talking about will occur at a fairly slow pace over time.   The process of density increases caused by a greenhouse gas reduction induced move to compact living in city and suburb will occur slowly and, for many of us, go unnoticed in our daily lives.

Take a moment and imagine what you own life might be like in an urban world at least twice as dense as the one you occupy today (assuming you live in a suburb like I do).   Chances are you will be living in a condominium, or perhaps a townhouse.   On your way to work, you may well walk your kids to the neighborhood school if they are young.   You will probably hop a subway, light rail, or bus to get to your job (If you live close enough, you could walk or jump on your bike for the commute). Along the way, if you're like me, you will duck into a coffee shop or sidewalk cafe for a quick morning espresso and a look at the paper. After this you may stroll across a nicely landscaped square or park to get to your office. Lunch will be much as it is today, except you will likely go out for a walk to a local cafe as opposed to driving. If you adopt European tastes, your midday meal will be a leisurely and social affair, and you will stay later at work to compensate. You might stop on the way back from lunch in a local book store to peruse the latest best sellers, or maybe instead of a big midday meal, you will use the time to go for a run through a local natural area or green space. If you are of a religious bent, you might frequent a local church for a few minutes reflection, or if you are a pantheist you may take some time in a local park near water for a quiet connection with nature's wonders. On the way home from work, you might pick up some fresh bread at a bakery you love or stop for a bottle of good wine to have with dinner. Instead you might take the time to shop for a new coat in the many retail shops found in a dense city environment. You will probably spend less time than you do now shopping in auto oriented big box outlets and may end up paying a bit more for your purchases as a consequence. In spring or fall, you might head to a soccer field to watch your daughter's team, or you might even go there to play yourself. One could think of many other options to plug in here for after work activities— pick up you kids and walk them home from school, stop for a book at the library, attend a meeting of the Sierra Club or Kiwanis, take some time to in a coffee shop or elsewhere to collect you thoughts about the day and watch the world go by, meet with friends for a drink and discussion about life's meaning or public affairs, and so on. When you get home, your dwelling will have all the usual comforts, but will be relatively compact in its arrangement. If you have young children, you might head to the local playground for a time before dinner.

The point of this reflection is simple. Your life would not change that much in a denser world except for your use of the spatial environment around you. You will still enjoy life's pleasures, but you will get around more often using mass transit and you will spend more time in public spaces. You may even have more opportunities as a consequence for social intimacy and connection than you do now—chance meetings occur more typically where people publicly congregate in significant numbers. Rather than driving from place to place in the private confines of your motor vehicle, you will be more inclined to either walk or take public transit and in the process spend time in a shared environment. Rather than the comforts and amenities of a car, you will instead enjoy the pleasures of movement through public spaces—the stimulation of life on the sidewalks, the beauties of urban architecture, the visual appeal of urban green space, the sounds of street musicians, the ease of stopping for refreshment at a pleasant sidewalk cafe.[2] Shopping malls will remain a significant part of your life, but you will probably spend less time in them simply because you will be less auto oriented. Cars will still be important to you, but you will probably be less inclined to own more than one and will rely on rentals more.   Intimate dinners in the confines of our private dwellings will continue, but one could imagine gathering at roomier restaurants more often for life's larger celebrations with their longer guest lists. Outdoor gatherings will more likely be moved from backyards to more spacious local parks or other public places in a more compact world. With greater density, public attractions, such as museums, theaters, and concert halls, will be more readily accessible and more frequently used for social enjoyment as opposed to watching television or listening to music at home. Voluntary group opportunities should continue undiminished in a more compact environment.   Getting together with others for soccer or baseball games, philosophical discussions, knitting, political agitation, community improvement projects, bike rides, or any other voluntary purpose should be no less of a problem in a compact community than currently, and might even be eased a bit if we all live closer to one another.

Seeking out your own personal passions in life will still be at least as feasible in a denser world as it is today, whether at work or elsewhere. Employment today flows predominantly to where people desire to live, whereas in the past people moved to where work could be found. Manufacturing in its heyday needed to locate in cities for access to transportation hubs and local markets, so population flowed to large urban centers.   To communicate and cut deals, people who worked in offices in support of industry required immediate proximity to one another, so they located in urban centers as well.   This pattern of people following jobs reversed itself with the suburban revolution after World War II.   Freeways and a government backed mortgage financing system opened up the suburbs to homeownership and people quickly pursued this new opportunity. For a time many commuted back to central cities for their jobs, but soon businesses moved out as well, transforming the landscape with spatially expansive, auto oriented facilities.   Jobs followed people.[3]   Today with our economic interactions taking on an increasingly virtual character, people can live almost anywhere they desire, and business and employment will follow. The attractions of the Paris's, Toronto's, and San Francisco's of the world today are less economic than cultural and social.   People increasingly desire compact cities simply because they are interesting places to be. If we choose to live more densely, regardless of whether it is good for us or good for the global environment, then business and employment will adapt.

Such adaptivity is augmented by the modern knowledge worker's capacity to flourish in either a suburban office park or in high rise offices at the center of large cities.   Silicon Valley with its dominance in computer technology development illustrates the first case while San Francisco's late 1990s boom in online businesses and web development portrays the second. The spatial configuration of economic activity will become denser in compact world but will unlikely shift around dramatically.   Single story manufacturing and distribution operations will still be found largely on the outer rim of metropolitan areas near freeways and rail lines, much as it is today in the more compact modern cities of the world such as Toronto and

Paris. Because of their hub-and-spoke configurations, the expansion of mass transit systems, such as light rail, in the quest for energy efficiency and urban compactness will serve to reinvigorate economic activity at urban centers. The central city will recapture its locational advantage of old by being easily accessible from all parts of its metropolitan area by public transit. This in turn will help expand service sector employment opportunities in such places as hospitals, retail shops, restaurants, hotels, and office buildings for lower income residents who live in the ring of older dwellings surrounding downtown areas. If configured right, mass transit could even facilitate reverse commuting from these neighborhoods to manufacturing and distribution businesses located on the urban periphery, opening up employment opportunities for low-income inner city residents from which they are currently excluded by the barriers of reverse commuting and the expense of motor vehicle ownership.

If anything, compact living should expand the opportunity for employment and the possibility of personal fulfillment on the job. Because clean energy functions as a necessary component of compact living, an array of clean energy jobs will be created in a compact world that can accommodate a range of interests and personal skills. The fossil fuel industry, underlying suburban spatial expansiveness, possesses much less labor intensity than clean energy, as already noted earlier. Shifting from the former to the latter will give a boost to employment opportunities throughout much of the country.

This discussion of satisfying one's passions in the economic arena is all well and good insofar as it goes, but the universe of commerce and government work is ultimately under the thumb of large bureaucratic institutions. In such settings, to satisfy the human need for creative acts is at best a challenge. In the end, many of us will have to look outside the world of work for those endeavors that give value to our lives. To do this, we will need access to supportive institutions and like-minded others. Compact living shrinks physical distances between people and places, greasing the skids of interactions essential for the fulfillment of human passions. Aspiring actors need theaters and other actors; starving artists need cheap studios and art galleries; writers need libraries; musicians need each other and places to perform; amateur soccer enthusiasts need teams and fields; political activists need similar-minded others and the halls of government; baseball fans need proximity to stadiums in which to watch and play; hobbyists need access to suppliers and clubs of the like-minded; philosophers need cafes to meet in and mull over life's meaning; and photographers and other chroniclers of urban life need to be in the center of things. All this will be much easier in densely packed cities.

In the East Williamsburg section of Brooklyn, starving artists and musicians have found a place to live in expensive New York City. The so-called "McGibbin dorms" offer a home to newly arriving collegiate artistic types in two large, nearly identical, old factory buildings that have been converted into lofts where living space can by had for anywhere from $375 to $800 a month. The accommodations are "warren-like" but legal and work for any young, new-arrival to the city who wants to try cracking into its diverse cultural job market. While no one envisions spending a lifetime in such a surrounding—it has both the virtues and drawbacks of dorm life including noise, loud music, and obnoxious neighbors—vacancies don't last for long.[4] You won't find anything comparable in the suburbs. At the McGibben, one can survive on the part time wages of a waiter or hotel desk clerk while looking for that dream job in theater, music, or an art studio.

Economical rents allow one to get along on less paid work and income, freeing up time for truly desired activities. The same is the case for high density urban environments where public facilities and spaces substitute for private. Given efficiently functioning public transit and plenty of ways to enjoy life outside the home, one can avoid the expense of a car and a spacious house and yard. One doesn't need to worry about sustaining a costly suburban style of living to enjoy life's pleasures and passions where those are ready at hand in a culturally and social diverse city environment.

On top of opportunities for private activities, the capacity for finding solace and meaning beyond our personal selves should remain undiminished in a denser world. A religious ascetic can probably find meaning serving the poor in the streets of a crowded Asian city or seeking a personal vision through meditation in a remote mountain temple or a suburban ashram. The capacity to reconcile oneself with the pains and tragedies of life, to decide whether existence in any sense extends beyond death, and to feel a connection to the larger world around us, I suspect, has little to do with whether we live in a spatially expansive suburb or a spatially compact city. One could argue that a less intensely materialistic life than that found in the suburbs today might facilitate greater spirituality, but I don't know of any way to prove the point.

To summarize, compact living will give us at least the same freedom to pursue life's pleasures, engage socially with others, and follow personal propensities for creative or spiritual activity as suburban spatial expansiveness. For those iconoclasts who look beyond the economic realm for personal satisfaction, a movement to compact living will likely increase opportunities for fulfillment of their particular quests. Yet our present experience with an expansive suburban spatial environment undoubtedly dominates our judgment about how we should live in the future. If we have had limited contact with a compact form life and know little about it, we will tend to stick with what we have. This creates a dilemma for us in deciding how to arrange our lives. A compact form of life could well turn out to be superior to how most of us live currently, but we have no way of knowing ahead of time. This is where "path dependence" rears its ugly head. We come to depend on the path we are on and fear moving to a potentially more beneficial alternative.

Economic Thinking and Path Dependence: Achieving Spatial Compactness

If we underestimate the importance of the "path dependence" and the challenges it creates, we do so at our peril. To fully understand the nature of the problem, we need to take a detour into the way economists think about the human social decision process. I am by training an economist, but the readers of this book so far who have some familiarity with the discipline might not be able to tell. My own conception of social decision making parts company from orthodox economic thinking. Explaining why will help us pick apart the dilemma of deciding whether we should choose the unfamiliar over the certain.

Lately I have been worried about toothpaste. Until recently I used a store brand with a tasty mint flavor that desensitizes my teeth near the gum line and reduces the pain of a teeth cleaning in my semiannual visit to the dentist. Sometimes I have a bit of soreness on the gums themselves and I find that a bit of baking soda heals things up. Recently I tried Tom's natural baking soda toothpaste. I don't get the mint hit anymore, and my tooth sensitivity will probably go up, but my gums feel really healthy, and Tom's is made here in the U.S. in contrast to my store brand which suddenly comes from India. So I have decided to switch to Tom's.

The suburb in which I live recently passed a controversial bond issue to build a new library with more space and up-to-date facilities. Some argued against the proposal on the grounds of its costs. Others pointed to certain advantages of a new library, such as more pleasing spaces for reading and contemplation, a more attractive setting for social interactions, better facilities for children that would give a boost the library's educational role, and a source of community pride. The advocates for the library won the day, although the vote was close.

In life we continuously modify how we live in small ways that have modest consequences. In doing so we take our preferences as given and make a judgment about how a particular action affects us. This occurs at the individual level in our consumer choices, such as in deciding whether to change the brand of toothpaste or anything else we use on a daily basis. It also occurs at a collective level in our local units of government where, for example, we might be trying to figure out whether to build some new public facility, such as a library. The task in either case is to measure the costs and benefits of change. If benefits exceed costs the change is warranted; if the reverse is the case, we stick with the status quo. This is the way economists think about the world.

Tempting as it may be, to extend this line of reasoning to big, discontinuous changes in the way we live poses deep conceptual problems. Life in spread-out suburbs we understand because of our personal experience. What life would be like in an urban setting where density is twice current levels and light rail, buses, walking, and biking become important ways of getting around, most of us can't really say. The small proportion of us who have visited Toronto, Paris, San Francisco, or Portland, Oregon may have a glimmer of spatial compactness reality, but many of us will instead recall with fear a drive or walk through a degraded and dangerous, densely packed neighborhood in one of our own central cities. In a stable environment, current values and preferences serve as a reasonable guide to judging small changes. Big changes in all likelihood will transform our take on the world and what's important in it to us (and especially to our children). If our world shifts in dramatic ways, causing us to have substantially new experiences, we will change. In the end, we can't fully know how we will value a new world until we have experienced it. We may love it, or we may hate it, but we can't say for sure ahead of time.

Adaptability seems to be the hallmark of the human psyche. People bounce back from many, although not all, personal tragedies that markedly change their lives.[5] The one economic change that seems to have lasting damage is suffering a substantial period of unemployment. Conversely, people who receive unexpected boons in their lives, such as multimillion dollar lottery winners, experience an initial surge in their happiness, but soon return again to their pre-lottery feeling state.[6] If we gain or lose financially, the respective positive or negative affect on our happiness ultimately disappears, at least if we are not driven into destitution.[7]

Put a suburbanite in a dense central city or take a cosmopolitan urbanite and plunk her down in a suburb and both will probably feel unhappy for a time, but they will likely recover.[8] In short, felt well being may be an unreliable means for judging whether a move from an existing path through life to an entirely new one is the right thing to do. Chances are changes of any kind will cause an initial surge of either happiness or unhappiness, but should we judge how we live by temporary and fleeting positive or negative increments to how we feel? Happiness can probably be found by most of us in either an attractive, green spread-out suburb or a well-designed, pedestrian friendly, safe compact city. If this is so, how do we judge which is best? The usual cost-benefits analysis, which is simply a way of evaluating in a careful and rational way how a course of action will affect our happiness, fails us because of the vagaries of our personal preferences and the internal momentum of our prevailing feeling state. Big changes in our course of life will likely alter our outlook and personal values, but resulting bumps in our happiness or unhappiness will tend to disappear over time. Barring anything that will make our lives persistently miserable, a big change in the way we live that leaves us with reasonable opportunities to seek our pleasures, social connections, personal passions, and meanings in life will not likely have a long-run affect our felt happiness or personal satisfaction. We may experience either a dip or a surge as we adjust to a new and different environment, but we will likely adjust back to our personal norm.

In the pages of this book I have chosen a different approach to evaluating compact living, one rooted more in philosophy than economics. This amounts to making a judgment about whether spatial compactness delivers the essential conditions for a good life broadly conceived. While my biases obviously favor compact living, in the end I don't want to make so strong a claim as saying that spatial expansiveness is a miserable mode of life and that spatial compactness will take us to paradise. What I do claim so far is that either form will do for satisfying our basic human desires for material pleasures, interactions with others, personal accomplishments, and connections beyond the self. Compact living I judge is at least as good for living decently as the current spatially expansive alternative. The patterns of life will differ under compact living but they will not be so radically altered as to make very many people, if any, truly miserable. Some, and maybe even most, will find that they flourish in a compact world. Of course, all this in itself doesn't argue very strongly for compact living's adoption. If the spatially expansive mode of life allows the vast majority to live decently and comfortably, why change it? To set out a compelling argument, we need both philosophy and ecology. Remember two things as we go through this. A shift to compact living is unlikely to dampen our opportunities for living well and maybe even will enhance them. Remember also that ecological imperatives are pushing us in the direction of compact living anyway, but we have the choice to embrace it or resist it. The question is, what should we do? The distinction between the notions of "doing well" and "doing good" will help us sort out this issue.

Saving the Environment through Spatial Compactness: An Ethical Free Lunch

Mother Teresa, a Roman Catholic nun born in Albania, spent most of her life in India ministering to the destitute in Calcutta. Her passion in life was to care for the poorest of the poor, orphans, the blind and disabled, the sick, and especially those near death. In her eyes the poor of the world who "lived like animals" should be able to "die like angels—loved and wanted."[9] She ultimately established the Missionaries of Charity, whose efforts grew to become global in extent. If anyone exemplifies the pursuit of good in the world, it has to be Mother Teresa. Yet her work has not gone without criticism, including claims that she focused on conversions to Catholicism rather than good medical practices, romanticized poverty, and lacked scruples when it came to fundraising.[10] Nonetheless she received the Nobel Peace Prize for her efforts, was beatified by the Vatican following her death in 1997, and is amongst the most admired public figures in recent history.

Not everyone rises to the standard of moral action in the world set by mother Teresa. A more obscure historical figure who also possesses a passion in life is described by another Nobel Prize winner (for literature, not peace), V. S. Naipaul, in his "autobiographical" *The Enigma of Arrival*.[11] For a time, Naipaul lived in the English countryside, sticking largely to himself, but carefully observing local interconnections between people, domiciles, and the local landscape. A key figure in his novel about this experience is Jack who lived in a cottage with his wife on an estate devoted to farming near Stonehenge and Salisbury. Because of his garden, Jack gains Naipaul's interest. Jack, a farm worker on the estate, keeps a garden in front of his cottage with a well clipped hedge that marked a boundary between carefully pruned fruit trees next to the house, and a flower garden planted in annuals with some vegetables each year. The purpose of the garden was not extra money or killing time—it was instead "fulfillment". Jack relished his garden where, bare backed on summer days, he worked with an intensity that no other task received on the estate. When Naipaul first arrived, he saw the local landscape as timeless and permanent, but he soon noticed inexorable change at work. The old ways of farming were disappearing as aged buildings came down and machinery replaced farm workers. Change of a more personal kind came to Jack's world as illness and slow decline. Jack's final public act was to get in his car as he did every Sunday for a drive to the pub for a beer, but his life comes to its end with the garden soon to follow.

Philosophical notions of the good life cover both doing well (experiencing pleasure, enjoying the company of others, exercising one's talents, and developing a life of meaning) and doing good (giving one's children a decent start in life, defending the country against terrorism, reducing homelessness, or saving the environment). The two sometimes blend, such as in the case of Mother Teresa relishing her work aiding the destitute of Calcutta. Just as often life's passion is a personal affair contributing to an individual's private well being, but not extending much further. Naipal's Jack devoted himself to his garden beside his remote cottage, but he does it only for himself. We don't have to be Mother Teresa to have a good life, and more often than not our smaller daily acts inadvertently make a positive difference in the lives of those around us. Jack certainly was unaware of how much his garden was enjoyed by his neighbor. If we have a passion for some activity in our life, chances are it will rub off on others. Doing well and doing good will often blend, as happiness researchers find.[12]

I suspect that Mother Teresa, Jack, and the rest of us want in our hearts to do the right thing for both humanity and the world of nature given the opportunity, even if doing so were not the central focus of our daily life. This is the case in deciding whether we should continue our current mode of spatial existence, or support the pulling in of our spatial horns and leading a more compact form of life. For most of us, moving to spatial compactness will never be the driving passion of our lives, but we have the choice of accepting larger forces pushing us in this direction, or of resisting them. I am suggesting here that accepting these trends and supporting them personally and politically will be a small but worthy act for each of us.

Ghoramara Island sits in the Bay of Bengal, but it won't be there much longer. The Island is sinking in the face of higher and higher, cyclone driven tidal surges caused by climate-induced rising sea levels and flooding from the rivers that flow down to the Bay from the Himalaya Mountains. Forests in the Himalayas used to behave like a sponge, absorbing monsoon rains and releasing them slowly and steadily, but now rains charge rapidly down denuded mountain slopes feeding floods that eat away at Ghoramara and other members of the Sundarbans, a chain of low-lying Islands in the Bay of Bengal river deltas. At low tide the remaining residents of Ghoramara can see the wreckage of their old village, but the vegetable gardens and paddies they used to cultivate by hand have long disappeared. More than 31 square miles of the Sundarbans has been lost over the past 30 years.[13] Climatic warming appears to be dooming low-lying islands, such as Ghoramara to a permanent inundation.

Unlike the Sundarbans, New Orleans, over half of which lies below sea level, enjoys substantial barriers against flooding such as levees and floodwalls, but those defenses succumbed to the power of Hurricane Katrina. The hurricane hit the Louisiana coast in the early morning on Monday, August 29, 2005. Levees were breached and much of the city was flooded, causing more than 1,500 residents to lose there lives and more than 100,000 to become homeless.[14] As we all know from news reports, one of the hardest hit sections of the city was the lower Ninth Ward which suffered inundation from a serious breach in the so-called Industrial Canal fed by surging waters from the Mississippi River. Undeterred by their poverty, many of the nearly all-black Ninth Ward residents had managed to become homeowners, and some families had lived in their shotgun-style houses for generations and were mortgage free.[15] To this day, much of the low-income Ninth Ward remains devastated. Despite being discouraged by city leaders who want residents to relocate to higher ground, more than 1,000 of the areas original 14,000 citizens have returned and have taken the work of reconstruction into their own hands.[16] By any standards, the process of rebuilding the city has been as slow and fitful as was the immediate disaster response.[17] While no one can prove that the intensity of Hurricane Katrina resulted from climate warming, storms of this size will likely increase in frequency because of more heat in ocean waters. Ocean heat is the central driver of the cyclonic force of hurricanes and typhoons. Nor can one prove that increases in sea levels played a significant role in the flooding of New Orleans, but with elevated future sea levels, storm surges will begin from a higher baseline and will be more damaging to coastal cities and landscapes. Hurricane Katrina could well be a preview of unwanted coming attractions.

The devastation of New Orleans by hurricane Katrina severely taxed the capacity of the wealthiest country in the world to respond to a severe weather event of the kind that could well become more dangerous and frequent under a warming climate. If the richest countries are stretched to contend with storms and floods, poor countries will have little option but to passively accept whatever our climate future brings them.

In a warmer world both too much and too little water can bring quick and dramatic death and destruction. The 2009-wildfires in the Melbourne, Australia area suggest that contending with drought and fire can be as challenging as dealing with storms and flooding. In Australia, just as in the U.S., people want their little bit of paradise in the wild just beyond metropolitan borders. This creates a special danger in fire-prone landscapes of death and property destruction from intense and rapidly moving

wildfires.[18]   The death toll in the Australia fire exceeded 200, over 450,000
hectares burned (1.1 million acres), and more than 1,000 homes were
destroyed.   Again, climate change cannot be directly implicated in the
Australia fire, although the country has suffered from a decade-long drought
that undoubtedly contributed to the fire's extent and intensity.   Drought in
Australia and other arid areas of the world will become more prevalent as
global warming intensifies, and tough to control large wildfires will become
a fact of life. Just as the U.S. had a tough time responding to the devastation
of Katrina, so did Australia to its worst bushfire disaster ever. Adaptation to
a warmer world will clearly have its challenges, and probably its failures, if
this bit of history is any lesson.

As these events suggest, meddling with the climate could turn out to be a
dangerous business.   At one extreme of possibilities we could in the end
threaten our current way of life and create substantial pain and suffering for
the poor of the world. To avoid this alternative, adopting a compact form of
life and bringing about a halt to warming will be in our own best interests.
To halt climate change in these circumstances is less a philosophical question
than a matter of self-preservation.

The Intergovernmental Panel on Climate Change (IPCC) euphemistically
calls those threats that pose a serious challenge to human well being "key
vulnerabilities."[19]   The IPCC's lengthy list of such vulnerabilities includes
the melting of the Greenland ice sheet, increasingly powerful typhoons and
hurricanes, and drought in the lower latitudes.   If such vulnerabilities occur,
we can expect massive population displacements in the river deltas of India
and Bangladesh, more Hurricane Katrinas hitting our coastal cities, increases
in the frequency of African famines, and increasingly intense fires in
Australia and the western U.S. that will be difficult to control. The ocean's
of the world are already expanding and rising because of the additional heat
they absorb from climate warming, and they will continue to do so for
decades to come as heat eventually makes its way into the deepest waters.
On top of this, with global warming of 3-5 degrees centigrade, total melting
of the Greenland ice sheet becomes a distinct possibility. This will mean an
added increase in ocean levels on top of thermal expansion amounting to
anywhere from 2 to 7 meters (around 6 to 21 feet).[20]   Visions of lower
Manhattan under water will no longer seem as fantastic as it might today.
Worse than this will be the total inundation of low-lying, heavily populated
river delta lands in such countries as India and Bangladesh. The fate of the
Ghoramara Islands of the world will become the wave of the future. Heat in
water not only drives thermal expansion and increased sea levels, but it also
provides added power to hurricanes in the Atlantic and typhoons in the
Pacific and elsewhere. Stronger storms combines with higher sea levels is a
potent weapon for flooding and destroying the world's coastal landscapes.

Under a less dire climate scenario, adjustment to global warming may
turn out to be feasible without substantially disturbing our own economic
way of life. We may need to fortify our coastal areas from storm surges and
flooding, develop drought resistant crop varieties, improved water

conservation and rainfall capture, expand our disaster relief and wildfire fighting capacities, and offer more special heat emergency healthcare assistance. Such efforts will be costly, but they will also create employment opportunities. For the poor of the world, adjustments to climatic warming will no doubt be more difficult. Many of those living on low-elevation islands or in flood-prone river deltas will have to be relocated, and the global capacity to respond to drought-induced famines will need to be enlarged. Drought-prone poor countries commonly found in the subtropical and tropical latitudes will face special difficulties in adapting their already fragile agriculture to a drier and hotter climate.[21]

An attractive option for wealthy countries is to avoid all this by seriously reducing their carbon emissions—the affluent countries of the world plus China account for the vast majority of greenhouse gases. Driving greenhouse gas emissions to near zero can be accomplished fairly painlessly by adopting a compact mode of living as described in this book and would be the right thing to do for the world's poor who lack the resources to adapt to climate change on their own. The other option for wealthy countries of course would be to continue their existing mode of life, let climate change take place, and simply pay for needed adaptations in poor countries, but why would we want to pay the cost of adaptation if we don't have to? If we choose compact living and a stable climate instead, we get out from under adaptation costs. Simply allowing the poor to fend for themselves in a world made warmer by the greenhouse gas emitting actions of the affluent is a possible option of course, but one that I believe most of us would find morally repugnant. Compact living allows us to have our "doing good" cake and to eat it too by simultaneously "doing well."

This brings up a sore point I have with my profession. Economist love to claim, "There is not such thing as a free lunch." If we are to bring climate change to a halt, we will have to pay the piper. I would beg to differ. We currently have an economy with ample unemployed resources; creating a good green boom through the measures described herein will spread economic prosperity to all reaches of the income distribution; and chances are high that many if not most of us will end up liking compact living just as much as, if not more than, our current spatially expansive suburban mode. Granted we will have to vastly shift our economic resources around, but I conjecture that in the end we will end up with world in which most of us see ourselves as better off. In the bargain we will have prevented the poor of the world from having to suffer the pains and indignities that climate change will bring. To repeat my standard refrain, what could be better? Is this not a kind of free lunch? Simply put, we can simultaneously do well in our own lives and do good for others if we embrace the move to compact living.

For the sake of argument, let's suppose that adapting to climate change turns out to be no better or no worse for global economic opportunities and human material well being than shifting to compact living and climate stability. We would be just as happy doing either and the poor of the world would be equally well off materially under either adaptation to global warming or climate stability. Why would we still want to fight climate change and adopt a compact way of life? Here is another sixty-four dollar question, one that involves nonhuman nature.

For some species global warming will mean actual habitat loss—a fate that is already being experienced by *Ursus maritimus,* the polar bear we all know and love from our trips to the zoo. Polar bears get the bulk of their nutrition by preying on seals that breed on circumpolar sea ice. In their quest for food the bears wander thousands of kilometers each year on the ice, but breeding females need land access as well to den for 5-7 months in the winter and birth their offspring. Because global warming, sea ice is virtually melting out from under the feet of polar bears in the summer season, causing them to seek refuge for increasing periods on land where they lack food supplies.[22] For this very reason, in 2008 the U.S. Department of Interior designated the polar bear as threatened under the Endangered Species Act.[23] If global warming continues at its current pace, by the end of the century summer polar sea ice could be a thing of the past.

Closer to home (for most of us), the polar bear's cousin, *Ursus arctos horribilis*, the federally threatened grizzly bear, who some of us may have been lucky enough to see (unluckily if too close) in Yellowstone National Park, is facing its own challenges which will intensify because of global warming. To fully understand how climate change can affect the grizzly in the Yellowstone area, we need to backup and talk about the whitebark pine tree. Whitebark pine favors high elevations in the Wyoming Rocky Mountains just below treeline in the 5,000 to 10,000 foot range (1,500-3,000 meters). The energy-laden whitebark pine seed serves as a key food source for a variety of wildlife, especially the Clark's Nutcracker, red squirrels, and the grizzly bear. The nutcracker pecks the seeds out of the pine cones and helps propagate the tree by burying seeds all over the place at ideal depths for seedling growth. Red squirrels bury pinecones and their seeds in huge middens that the grizzlies love to raid. In the Yellowstone area, grizzlies prefer to forage in the uplands for the energy-rich whitebark seeds to searching for food at lower elevations in high seed production years. This improves the grizzly's prospects for weight gain and winter survival because of the concentrated food source the seeds provide. Grizzlies face their most serious mortality threat at lower elevations where they are more likely to get into trouble from human confrontations. Whitebark pine nuts in effect keep grizzlies at higher elevations and away from the dangers of human contact. The fate of the whitebark pine and the grizzly are consequently intertwined.

Unfortunately, the whitebark pine faces two special threats to its survival from global warming. First, the tree suffers from infection by a pathogen called white pine blister rust. Wisconsinites such as myself know about the disease because it has accelerated the loss of the stately white pines that used to dominate our northern forests. Since blister rust prospers at warmer temperatures, it isn't much of a threat currently at cool high elevations, but with climatic warming the pathogen will spread upward more readily and cause more whitebark pine mortality. Second, the whitebark does well where it lives precisely because it is better adapted to a cold climate and harsh weather. As the climate warms, lower elevation species will more easily gain a foothold farther up and eventually out-compete the whitebark. The tree could in effect move up to cooler, higher elevations with the help of the seed-spreading Clark's Nutcracker, but as one goes up a cone-shaped, steep-sided mountain, habitat for any kind of tree shrinks in availability and beyond the summit totally disappears. The whitebark pine's days appear to be numbered if global warming continues, and the Yellowstone grizzly bear will face an increasing probability of extinction with the loss of a critical, energy-rich food source.[24]

Yellowstone's special habitats and geological features make it a national natural treasure. A very special kind of ecosystem—coral reefs found in shallow tropical waters—constitute what many would agree is a global natural treasure. Coral begins as free-floating planula larvae formed by the combining of male and female gametes released from mature coral polyps. The planula eventually settles out of the surface waters onto a reef substrate where they transform themselves into immobile polyps. The polyps build reefs by encasing themselves at their base in calcite, a substance composed of calcium carbonate (which is essentially the same material as marble). From the head of the polyp extends tentacle-like appendages that wave back and forth in the ocean currents and contain stinging cells (nematocysts) that fire poisonous stingers when touched and capture small prey. The bulk of a coral's nutrition comes not from capturing prey, but less visibly from symbiotic algae that live within the polyp and supply it with part of the energy they produce. This energy supplying mechanism confines coral to clear, shallow water where the sun's light is strong enough to support photosynthesis. In our visits to aquariums with coral reef tanks, we get a sense of the biodiversity corals support by the number of fish (I love the clown fish) and other organisms we see on and near the reef polyps. Coral reefs provide habitat to upwards of one-fourth of all marine species.

Corals possess a special sensitivity to their environmental conditions. Two are the focus of particular concern among scientists—water temperature and acidity. A warming of ocean waters around coral reefs causes "coral bleaching." Simply put, coral polyps whiten in color by expelling their symbiotic algal tenants when waters get too warm. They do this as an stress-reaction to reduce the burden that algae impose on them, and if the polyps ultimately survive, they can take new symbiotic partners later on. If the warm waters persist, the coral will die.[25] A critical role of oceans in the process of global climate change is the absorption of added heat. As oceans warm, coral bleaching will increase in extent and intensity, and coral will face extinction.

If you have spent time around old, marble buildings, you may have noticed that the stone surface is often pockmarked and eroded. Acid deposition causes this deterioration. As we learned in chemistry, acids react with chemicals in many different kinds of materials and cause them to break down. Acid attacks calcium carbonate with special vigor and threatens any shell-building ocean species, including coral polyps. Along with warming the air and ocean waters, the buildup of CO_2 in the atmosphere accelerates its absorption into the oceans (a major sink for the gas) creating carbonic acid in the water. The acidification of ocean waters reduces the ability of coral polyps to build up coral reefs and adds to the threat of coral bleaching.[26] The only place we may be able to see coral reef species in the future could turn out to be aquariums.

Just as we love to visit aquariums and gain a window into natural wonders such as coral reefs that we may never see in person, we also love to visit beaches, not just to lie in the sand, but to enjoy finding sea shells, digging for clams, watching sea birds, or even fishing. Our visits to ocean beaches, especially in the winter, benefit visually from being able to watch groups of long-legged peeps dodging the surf looking for goodies to eat. The American subspecies of the Red Knot, one of the largest of the sandpiper-like peeps, migrates over 9,000 miles every year from its wintering grounds on the coast of South America to its breeding ground in the arctic tundra. While it currently numbers in the millions, this species still faces significant threats from human actions. The knot's migration is timed to take advantage of spawning horseshoe crabs in Delaware Bay where thousands of the bird take a break to feed on the crab's eggs. Recently, horseshoe crab harvests for commercial fishery bait have diminished the supply of spawn to the knot. On top of this, global warming in future years will shrink the tundra habitat the knot depends on for reproducing, and rising oceans will inundate some of its key migratory stopovers. The Red Knot is but one of the many migratory bird species that will face significant challenges from climate change down the road.[27]

Neither the polar nor grizzly bear does much for us, other than to provide a little entertainment when we go to the zoo or on our trips to Yellowstone. Unless we are wealthy enough for a scuba diving vacation, most of us will not likely experience the beauties of an actual coral reef, although many of us have no doubt seen replicas in aquariums. Because of the many birdwatchers among us, we might feel the loss of migratory birds such as the Red Knot more deeply than, say, coral reefs or whitebark pines. Since we don't depend on them very heavily for material resources, the economic loss from the climate-induced extermination of such species will be modest at best. The loss of these natural beings wouldn't amount to much in for the quality of our daily lives.

The question that always arises in talking about species extinctions is this: Why should we care, apart from our own self-interest? In such discussions, someone usually concludes that if we don't stop extinctions, at some point we will be next. Other species matter for our own survival. While we do depend on certain key species for our own material welfare, given our innate adaptability we may well survive mass extinctions with little real harm. The species we use prosper exactly because we desire them. Corn is such a successful species because in evolutionary terms it has figured out how to get human beings to propagate it on a massive scale. It will be in our interest to make sure species of this kind remain healthy. This will not be the case for all those species that don't contribute to our physical presence and success in the world.

Scientists say we are going through a major extinction event on par with those of the past including the disappearance of the dinosaurs. The essential driver of species endangerment to this point in human history is the loss of usable habitat. Like humans, plants and animals need space. Owls, woodpeckers, grouse, and grassland birds all need the space that is being taken away from them by human expansion. In the future, global warming will compound the threats to both plants and animals from habitat loss and accelerate the pace of species extinctions. According to the Intergovernmental Panel on Climate Change, 20 to 30 percent of plant and animal species could be threatened with extinction due to climate warming.[28]

So why would we want to take a chance on compact living and a green energy system simply to help out species for which we lack a concrete use? This is a philosophical question having to do with meanings we attach to life. What do we identify with and find inspiring, or meaningful, or even astonishing? Art, music, architecture, literature, beautiful cities, love, the sensuous human form, friendship, spiritual values or icons, meditative visions, organized human ventures, the mall of America, the shops on Avenue des Champs-Élysées, or natural landscapes and the species who live in them? Maybe everything in the list, or just some things in it, or something not in it, or, in particular, the last item in the list imprints you with a sense of amazement about existence in the world. That which astonishes us positively will be something whose continued presence we will desire to see for our own sake, the sake of others, and the sake of the being itself. If the presence of wild orchids deeply moves us, then we will want to defend their continued presence in the world apart from any material benefit we get from them. We may even want orchids in the wild that we never observe or experience to continue on their evolutionary path through life.

Survey researchers find that most of us care at least to some degree about nonhuman species and we do so independently of what they do for us in any material sense.[29] In other words, we care for them because we believe it to be the right thing to do. We see nonhuman species and the habitats in which they live as that part of being we should care for, defend, and protect from our own carelessness. To borrow from Aldo Leopold's "Land Ethic," we include the "land"—Leopold's term for the whole of nature—in our community of beings from which we gain meaning, astonishment, or inspiration. [30] The discipline of environmental ethics spends the bulk of its energy parsing and attempting to justify this position, but what it concludes in the end boils down to the idea that nature ought to exist for its own sake, not just for ours.

To survive in the world, plant and animal species need space and many need climate stability as well. Insuring such survival in my mind is the final justification for adopting a compact form of life. If I believed that compact living would be exceedingly painful for human existence, I would have to rethink this position. As the pages of this book argue, compact living will allow us to both live well in the world and give us the opportunity to do the right thing. What more could we ask for?

Let's sum up. Climatic warming is increasingly looking like an unprecedented global threat to human well being and nature's biological riches. We humans as a species may be able to adapt and even flourish in a warmer world, although the probability of that being the case shrinks with increasingly dire findings on how greenhouse gas accumulations are affecting the earth and its natural systems. Prospects for us doing well in a warmer world are becoming less and less probable as time passes and scientific knowledge increases. Even if we feel confident about our adaptability, we know that many nonhuman species can't handle the kind of climate warming we can reasonable expect in the next century. As a species, I don't believe we want to be responsible for a major extinction crisis.

Given the magnitude of the climate change problem and the opportunities solving it presents for economic prosperity, I suspect that we will stumble toward a solution. Current efforts to address the problem at least seem to be moving us down the right path, although the course of politics never runs smooth.

Resistance to change inheres in the path dependence phenomenon. A host of economic interests benefit from the existing fossil fuel energy path. Big oil companies, motor vehicle producers, highway construction businesses, and suburban developers have all prospered from decades of an auto oriented transportation system. They see a shift to compact living and green energy as a threat to their prosperity and have the economic resources to invest in political action against change. The potential for economic interests to unduly influence action by governments to address key society-wide problems like global warming is a troublesome feature of democratic political institutions. The political game is rigged for large, powerful economic institutions that have much to gain by opposing changes harmful to their own interests but beneficial to a substantial majority. Each of us may judge the fight against global warming to be in our interest and may be willing to see our energy costs go up by significant amounts to achieve climate stabilization. In the political arena large groups whose members support stabilizing climate will have problems organizing politically to realize what they desire in contrast to large, wealthy economic institutions.

Economists refer to this issue as the free rider problem. In a large group, my own contribution to political action won't amount to much compared to the total needed, so I will be inclined to let others step up to the plate. In short, I will free ride on those who are truly committed to the cause, and so will many others. The free rider problem often dooms to failure political action by large groups.

For large cash-rich businesses, coal-dependent utilities to take an example, the problem of organizing politically is much less daunting than for the public at large. Each utility, for instance, has much to gain by forestalling a climate stabilizing cap and trade approach and requirements to buy emission allowances. Consequently, the individual contribution of each utility to political action (lobbying, campaign contributions, and public relations campaigns) will matter and utilities as a whole will have a huge incentive to voluntarily come together for joint political efforts against cap and trade.

Fortunately for democracy's sake moments in history occur where the free rider problem is overwhelmed by the intensity of public desire for change.[31] In such situations politicians must pay attention to the demands of the moment or face defeat at the polls despite the political efforts of powerful interest groups. With the election of Barack Obama to the presidency, we seemed to be at such a moment. The capacity of the Obama campaign to raise huge amounts of money from a host of small contributors on the internet is an unprecedented political feat that substantially trumps the power of organized political interests.[32] This appeared to give President Obama a rather unusual degree of political freedom in fulfilling the desires of the political majority.

The initial foray of the Obama administration into moving us onto a new clean energy path is impressive in its size and scope. The stimulus plan alone includes a huge volume of spending on clean energy projects, adding up to some $83 billion.[33] On top of this the Administration has adopted stringent new fuel efficiency standards for motor vehicles, better known as CAFE (Corporate Average Fuel Economy) standards. The current fleet-wide average requirement for all cars and light trucks stand at a little over 25 miles per gallon of gasoline. The new requirement, to be achieved by 2016, will be 35.5 miles per gallon, a 40 percent increase. For the first time cars and light trucks will be brought under the same umbrella instead of separate standards for each category.[34] Auto industry leaders stood beside environmentalists at the announcement of the new rules by the President, indicating the industry's acceptance of the need for more fuel efficiency, which is perhaps unsurprising given that the government has taken a huge financial stake in both General Motors and Chrysler because of the auto industry bailout. At this historic moment, auto industry opposition to addressing climate warming has virtually evaporated in the face of the industry's financial crisis and the government's intervention to keep GM and Chrysler from disappearing. Just a month before this announcement, the Environmental Protection Agency (EPA) for the first time declared greenhouse gases to be pollutants covered under the Clean Air Act. This allows the EPA to establish regulations limiting the emissions of such gases.[35] In short, one way or another the federal government will place limits on greenhouse gases. If Congress fails to ultimately approve cap and trade or an equivalent carbon tax, the EPA already has the authority to regulation emissions directly and is showing clear signs that it will do so. Such regulation, as messy as it might be, will inevitably drive up the cost of fossil fuel energy in the same fashion as either cap and trade or a carbon tax.

Since moving toward climate stability is on its way to becoming a reality, we will soon start unhooking ourselves from fossil fuels. Not to do so would be the height of stupidity given the coming peak in oil production and the huge economic benefits from creating a domestic clean energy industry. Because the nuclear energy option is publicly viewed as too dangerous, and since greenhouse gas capture technology seems unlikely to pan out at a reasonable cost, I suspect we will replace fossil fuels with predominantly solar and wind energy. We will also become more devoted to energy conservation, the cleanest and greenest energy source of all. The kinds of economic incentives and public spending that will push us toward clean energy will simultaneously move us in the direction of compact living. Greater spatial compactness will not only reduce the pace of climatic warming, but it will help contain our human footprint on the earth's surface, leaving more space for nonhuman nature. This, along with less global warming, will help forestall a mass species extinction event that currently appears on the horizon. An inevitable trend towards compact living can either be embraced because it is both good for the global environment and a decent way to live, or it can be resisted in a quest to preserve our traditional low density suburban way of life. The choice is ours individually and politically. If we embrace compact living, I believe we will be rewarded with an economic boom that creates widespread prosperity. Indeed, what could be better?

Notes

¹ Paul A. David, "Clio and the Economics of Qwerty," *American Economic Review* 75, no. 2 (1985).

² Of course, travel by motor vehicle in the suburbs and moving about in densely packed cities both carry with them their own unique frustrations and displeasures.

³ For a summary of this process, see my own work, Booth, *Searching for Paradise: Economic Development and Environmental Change in the Mountain West.*

⁴ Cara Buckley, "Young Artists Find a Private Space, One without the Privacy," *New York Times*, May 7, 2008.

⁵ The degree of the recovery depends on the event. People bounce back from divorce and widowhood, but less so from unemployment and disability. Richard E. Lucas, "Adaptation and the Set-Point Model of Subjective Well-Being: Does Happiness Change after Major Life Events?," *Current Directions in Psychological Science* 16, no. 2 (2007).

[6] Martin E. P. Seligman, *Authentic Happiness: Using the New Positive Psychology to Realize Your Potential for Lasting Fulfillment* (New York: Free Press, 2002).

[7] Apart from unemployment, it is mainly the non-economic arena of our life that influences our permanent, set-point level of happiness. See Ed Diener, Richard E. Lucas, and Christie Napa Scollon, "Beyond the Hedonic Treadmill: Revising the Adaptation Theory of Well-Being," *American Psychologist* 61, no. 4 (2006); Richard A. Easterlin, "Explaining Happiness," *Proceedings of the National Academy of Sciences* 100, no. 19 (2003).

[8] Recall our earlier report that population density has no statistical impact on happiness. Rehdanz and Maddison, "Climate and Happiness."

[9]Kathryn Spink, *Mother Teresa: A Complete Authorized Biography* (New York: HarperCollins, 1997).

[10] For perhaps the more entertaining of the critiques, see Christopher Hitchens, *The Missionary Position: Mother Teresa in Theory and Practice* (London: Verso, 1995).

[11] V.S. Naipaul, *The Enigma of Arrival* (New York: Random House, 1987). My examples here are a product of my own idiosyncratic interests and a chosen simply to make a point.

[12] On this issue, see Seligman, *Authentic Happiness: Using the New Positive Psychology to Realize Your Potential for Lasting Fulfillment.*

[13] Somini Sengupta, "Sea's Rise in India Buries Islands and a Way of Life," *New York Times*, April 11, 2007.

[14] Ivor van Heerden, "The Failure of the New Orleans Levee System Following Huricane Katrina and the Pathway Forward," *Public Administration Review* 67, no. s1 (2007).

[15] Susan J. Popkin, Margery A. Turner, and Martha Burt, "Rebuilding Affordable Housing in New Orleans: The Challenge of Creating Inclusive Communities," (Washington D.C.: The Urban Institute, 2006).

[16] Bill Sasser, "New Orleans Lower Ninth Ward Stirs and Rebuilds," *Christian Science Monitor*, November 5, 2008.

[17] Adam Nossiter, "Largely Alone, Pioneers Reclaim New Orleans," *New York Times*, July 2, 2007.

[18] Patrick Barta and Rachel Pannet, "Australia Fires Point to Risks of Shifting Population," *Wall Street Journal*, February 10, 2009.

[19] Intergovernmental Panel on Climate Change, *Climate Change 2007: Impacts, Adaptation and Vulnerability* (Cambridge University Press, 2007 [cited January 10, 2009]); available from http://www.ipcc.ch/ipccreports/ar4-wg2.htm. See Chapter 19.

[20] Ibid.([cited]).

[21] Ibid.([cited]).

[22] Ibid.([cited]).

[23] Office of the Secretary U.S. Department of the Interior, *Secretary Kempthorne Announes Decision to Protect Polar Bears under Endangered Species Act* (U.S. Department of the Interior, 2008 [cited January 19, 2009]); available from http://www.doi.gov/news/08_News_Releases/080514a.html.

[24] Laura Koteen, "Climate Change, Whitebark Pine, and Grizzly Bears in the Greater Yellowstone Ecosystem," in *Wildlife Responses to Climate Change: North American Case Studies*, ed. Stephen H. Schneider and Terry L. Root (Washington D.C.: Island Press, 2001).

[25] Intergovernmental Panel on Climate Change, *Climate Change 2007: Impacts, Adaptation and Vulnerability* ([cited]).

[26] Ibid.([cited]); Second International Symposium on the Ocean in a High-CO_2 World, *Monaco Declaration* (Second International Symposium on the Ocean in a High-CO_2 World, 2008 [cited March 30, 2009]); available from http://www.igbp.net/documents/MonacoDeclaration2009.pdf.

[27] Intergovernmental Panel on Climate Change, *Climate Change 2007: Impacts, Adaptation and Vulnerability* ([cited); Northeast Region U.S. Fish and Wildlife Service, *The Red Knot (Calidris Canutus Rufa)* (U.S. Fish and Wildlife Service, Northeast Region, 2008 [cited April 1, 2009]); available from http://www.fws.gov/northeast/redknot/index.html.

[28] Intergovernmental Panel on Climate Change, *Climate Change 2007: Impacts, Adaptation and Vulnerability* ([cited]).

[29] Willett Kempton, James S. Boster, and Jennifer A. Hartley, *Environmental Values in American Culture* (Boston: M.I.T. Press, 1996).

[30] Aldo Leopold, *A Sand County Almanac: With Essays on Conservation from Round River* (New York: Ballantine Books, 1970).

[31] This was the case for the environmental movement in the 1960s and early 1970s when Congress passed a variety of landmark environmental legislation such as the Clean Air and Clean Water Acts. See Anthony Downs, "Up and Down with Ecology--the 'Issue-Attention Cycle'," *Public Interest* 28 (1972).

[32] Geoff Norquay, "Organization without an Organization: The Obama Networking Revolution," *Policy Options*, October 2008.

[33] Hossain et al., *New York Times* ([cited]).

[34] Broder, "Obama to Toughen Rules on Emissions and Mileage."

[35] John M. Broder, "E.P.A. Clears Path to Regulate Heat-Trapping Gases for First Time in the U.S.," *New York Times*, April 18, 2009.

Afterword

A Clean Energy Employment and Debt Reduction Act of 2013

With the tea-party and big-money fed Republican takeover of the House in the 2010 midterm elections, the far right in American politics will be able to frustrate any legislation increasing government involvement in the economy no matter how rational and market oriented. This means cap and trade proposals will be shelved and the fossil fuel industry will recapture its political dominion, at least for the time being. As the global economy recovers down the road, peak oil will kick in with a vengeance and bring forth upward spikes in energy prices, enriching petroleum oligarchs, sheiks, and dictators. This will be the harsh alternative reality to a more measured process of adjustment offered by cap and trade. About this the American electorate will not be pleased, and the present public grumpiness with government will look pale by comparison. Putting cap and trade in effect sooner rather than later would decapitate peak oil and its upward price surges. In two years time when the current political craziness abates, cooler heads will hopefully prevail and cap and trade can be brought back off the shelf in time to do some good. I do believe that such legislation carries with it so much potential for solving this country's economic and fiscal problems, that it is bound to ultimately reappear on the legislative docket, especially if it is repackaged and simplified to place its real benefits in sharper focus and renamed something like the "Clean Energy Employment and Debt Reduction Act of 2013." Let me explain the virtues of this approach with some simple 'back of the envelope' calculations.

We in the U.S. spent nearly $500 billion on imported petroleum in 2008. The U.S. Department of Energy projects that the average price of such imports will rise in inflation adjusted terms by about 1 percent a year through 2035 while our imported petroleum consumption will decline by .3 percent a year. If we extend this projection another 15 years, by 2050 our spending on imported petroleum will rise to $650 billion annually, given continued reliance on fossil fuels as our primary energy source.

The essential macroeconomic effect of our import spending is to generate demand for goods, employment, and income in foreign countries, not in the U.S. The more we spend on imported oil, the greater the income earned by foreign oil producers, and the richer the Saudi Arabia's of the world become. Such increases of foreign wealth will create demand for a few U.S. products such as Cadillac Escalades and Boeing aircraft, but only a small share of our spending on imported oil will return to the U.S. shores through the sale of U.S. exports. Saudi Arabian acquisition of U.S. goods amounts to only about 25 percent of our spending on their oil.

If the emission caps of H.R. 2454 (the 2009 House-passed cap and trade bill) were implemented, carbon emissions would drop to 17 percent of 2005 levels by 2050. This will mean the virtual disappearance of the petroleum industry and its replacement by domestic clean energy. In short, cap and trade will create a new U.S.-based energy industry to replace petroleum, and this will cause a redirection of spending from energy imports to the domestic economy. The beneficiaries of this shift will be the owners and employees of businesses in wind and solar energy as well as energy conservation. Such gains from an expansion of clean energy will ripple throughout the total economy with incomes earned by wind generator mechanics and solar panel installers triggering new spending on restaurant meals, clothing, electronic gadgets, and other items, lending a further stimulus to economic activity and employment. Cap and trade, in sum, will take American spending out of the hands of Arab oil sheiks and petroleum dictators and return it to our own citizens.

Predicting future employment is a perilous task in any circumstance, but we can nonetheless get some ideas about the order of its magnitude for the creation of a domestic clean energy industry. The first step is to establish roughly how much spending will be redirected from petroleum imports to our domestic economy by cap and trade. The total amount of projected spending on imported petroleum for the period 2012 to 2050 equals roughly $21 trillion. With carbon caps, such spending will shrink annually over time as the number of available carbon emission allowances diminish. Given fully implemented H.R. 2454 caps from 2016 on, allowances will begin at 5.4 billion tons of CO_2 and will decline steadily to 1.3 tons by 2050. Caps will force a reduction in the consumption of domestically produced and imported petroleum over time, and we Americans will spend roughly $8.9 trillion less on imported petroleum through 2050 than we would without cap and trade.[1]

Energy expenditures per household will increase very little if at all from cap and trade because of increases in energy efficiency and scale economies in clean energy production, and the share of this we now spend on imported petroleum will be redirected to our domestic energy industry. To compensate for likely spending drains to imports of clean energy equipment and losses in exports to oil producing countries, we will assume that 75 percent of reduced U.S. petroleum imports will equal the upward shift in expenditures for the economy as a whole, rising to a permanent increase of $400 billion by 2050. As explained in Chapter 13, each $100 billion in additional annual clean energy spending creates approximately 2 million jobs in an unemployment economy. Beginning in 2016, the addition to clean energy induced-jobs will equal 154,000 and will rise to 8 million by 2050 and continue at that level thereafter. Once implemented, cap and trade will be a job creating machine.

Besides generating employment, cap and trade will also produce substantial revenues from government auctions of emission allowances. If allowance prices rise to $100 a metric ton of carbon dioxide emissions by 2030 and remain there (as explained in Chapter 13), the total potential revenues for 2012-2050 will add up to something like $8.3 trillion. If the government used all these revenues to reduce the federal debt, a drag on consumer and business incomes would occur, dampening employment increases from the creation of a new clean energy industry. The cap and trade bill (H.R. 2454) avoids this problem by returning most of the emission allowance revenues to the public through 2030.

The beauty of the cap and trade bill is this: it will create enduring additions to employment and a source of future government revenues that can permanently reduce the federal debt to the tune of up to 4 trillion dollars if all emission allowance auction collections after 2030 are devoted to this purpose. In short, we can let the employment creation machine run for the next twenty years by returning cap and trade revenues to the public, and after that we can direct such revenues to debt retirement. We could even accelerate employment recovery by increasing government spending on clean energy in the next two decades (as suggested in Chapter 13) and finance it with bonds to be retired after 2030 from emission allowance revenues. With a near-full employment economy by 2030, the economic drag created by debt retirement will not be much of a problem and may even be welcome to push against the winds of economic overheating and inflation.

Predicting the distant future is a dangerous business—most who do so turn out to be wrong. Even if one assigned a 50 percent range of error to my 'back of the envelope calculations', doing what I suggest would still be worthwhile. The underlying logic of my argument here is incredibly simple. Creating a domestic clean energy sector to replace imported petroleum can't help but create jobs, and cap and trade can't help but generate substantial government revenues, some of which can be applied to government debt reduction.

Notes

1 See Chapter 13 for an explanation of all the calculation methods and sources used in this afterword.

Bibliography

Adams, William Howard. *The Paris Years of Thomas Jefferson*. New Haven: Yale University Press, 1997.

Aguilar, Francisco X., and Richard P. Vlosky. "Consumer Willingness to Pay Price Premiums for Environmentally Certified Wood Products in the U.S." *Forest Policy and Economics* 9, no. 8 (2007): 1100-12.

American Forest & Paper Association. *Country Report: United States of America*. FAO Advisory Committee on Paper and Wood Products, 2008 [cited April 29, 2009]. Available from http://www.fao.org/forestry/media/15367/1/0/.

Anderlik, John. *Rural Depopulation: What Does It Mean for the Future Economic Health of Rural Areas and the Community Banks That Support Them?* FDIC, 2006 [cited January 13, 2009]. Available from http://www.chicagofed.org/community_development/files/07_2006_rural_depopulation.pdf.

Barham, Bradford L., Jeremy Foltz, and Ursula Aldana. "Expansion, Modernization, and Specialization in the Wisconsin Dairy Industry." In *Research Summary*. Madison, WI: Program of Agricultural Technology Studies, University of Wisconsin, Madison, 2005.

Barta, Patrick, and Rachel Pannet. "Australia Fires Point to Risks of Shifting Population." *Wall Street Journal*, February 10, 2009, A6.

Bentley, R.W. "Global Oil and Gas Depletion: An Overview." *Energy Policy* 30 (2002): 189-205.

Berry, Linda G., Marylyn A. Brown, and Laurence F. Kinney. *Progress Report of the National Weatherization Assistance Program*. Oak Ridge National Laboratory, 1997 [cited December 6, 2008]. Available from http://apps1.eere.energy.gov/weatherization/pdfs/con450.pdf.

BikePortland. *About Bikeportland*. PedalTown Media Inc., 2009 [cited May 8, 2009]. Available from http://bikeportland.org/about/.

Booth, Douglas E. *Land Trusts and Biodiversity*. Milwaukee, WI: Driftless Conservation Books, 2007.

———. "Municipal Socialism and City Government Reform: The Milwaukee Experience, 1910-1940." *Journal of Urban History* 12, no. 2 (1985): 51-74.

———. *Searching for Paradise: Economic Development and Environmental Change in the Mountain West*. Lanham, MD: Rowman and Littlefield, 2002.

———. *Valuing Nature: The Decline and Preservation of Old-Growth Forests*. Lanham: Rowman and Littlefield, 1994.

Bounds, Gwendolyn. "About the House: Saving Energy on the Cheap." *Wall Street Journal*, October 2, 2008, B2.

Broder, John M. "E.P.A. Clears Path to Regulate Heat-Trapping Gases for First Time in the U.S." *New York Times*, April 18, 2009, A15.

———. "Obama to Toughen Rules on Emissions and Mileage." *New York Times*, May 19, 2009, A1.

Buckley, Cara. "Young Artists Find a Private Space, One without the Privacy." *New York Times*, May 7, 2008, A1.

California Public Utility Commission. *California's Decoupling Policy.* California Public Utility Commission, 2009 [cited May 21, 2009]. Available from http://www.cpuc.ca.gov/cleanenergy/design/docs/Deccouplinglowres.pdf.

Cammen, Hans van der, ed. *Four Metropolises in Western Europe: Development and Urban Planning of London, Paris, Randstand Holland and the Ruhr Region.* Amsterdam: Van Gorcum, Assen/Masstricht, 1988.

Carmona, Michel. *Haussmann: His Life and Times, and the Making of Modern Paris.* Chicago: Ivan. R. Dee, Inc., 2002.

Carolina Sandhills National Wildlife Refuge. *The Longleaf Pine/Wiregrass Ecosystem.* U.S. Fish and Wildlife Service, Carolina Sandhills National Wildlife Refuge, 2005 [cited October 12, 2005]. Available from http://www.fws.gov/carolinasandhills/longleaf.html.

Center for Biological Diversity, and Defenders of Wildlife. *Petition to List the Cactus Ferruginous Pygmy Owl as a Threatened or Endangered Species under the Endangered Species Act.* Center for Biological Diversity, 2007 [cited May 28, 2009]. Available from http://www.biologicaldiversity.org/species/birds/cactus_ferruginous_pygmy_owl/pdfs/petition-to-list-cactus-ferruginous-pygmy-owl-03-2007.pdf.

Cervero, Robert, and Michael Duncan. "Transit's Value-Added Effects: Light and Commuter Rail Services and Commercial Land Values." *Transportation Research Record* 1805 (2002): 8-15.

Chen, David W. "In the Future, the City's Streets Are to Behave." *New York Times*, May 20, 2009, A23.

Chernova, Yuliva. "Consumers as Producers: When Homeowners Supply More Energy Than They Need, They Want to Be Paid for It: Not So Fast, Critics Say." *Wall Street Journal*, November 17, 2008, R11.

City of Brookfield. *2020 Master Plan.* City of Brookfield, 1999 [cited April 21, 2009]. Available from http://www.ci.brookfield.wi.us/index.asp?NID=237.

———. *Fact Book 2007.* City of Brookfield, 2007 [cited April 21, 2009]. Available from http://www.ci.brookfield.wi.us/DocumentView.asp?DID=6.

Clark, Andrew E., Paul Frijters, and Michael A. Shields. "Relative Income, Happiness, and Utility: An Explanation for the Easterlin Paradox and Other Puzzles." *Journal of Economic Literature* 46, no. 1 (2008): 95-144.

Coalition for Sonoran Desert Protection. *Open Space Bond Acquisitions.* Coalition for Sonoran Desert Protection, 2006 [cited May 28, 2009].

Available from http://www.sonorandesert.org/learning-more/open-space-bond-acquisitions.

Cohen-Solal, Annie. *Jean-Paul Sartre: A Life*. New York: New Press, 2005.

Conant, Richard T., Keith Pustian, and Edward Elliott. "Grassland Management and Conversion into Grassland: Effects on Soil Carbon." *Ecological Applications* 11, no. 2 (2001): 343-55.

Daniels, Tom, and Deborah Bowers. *Holding Our Ground: Protecting America's Farmland*. Washington D.C.: Island Press, 1999.

David, Paul A. "Clio and the Economics of Qwerty." *American Economic Review* 75, no. 2 (1985): 332-37.

Demographia. *Large USA Urban Areas: 1950 to 2000*. Demographia and the Public Purpose, 2005 [cited April 21, 2009]. Available from http://www.demographia.com/db-uza2000.htm.

———. *Paris Arrondissements: Post 1860 Population & Population Density*. Demographia and the Public Purpose, 2005. Available from http://www.demographia.com/db-paris-arr1999.htm.

———. *Paris Urban Area: Population, Area & Density from 1807*. Demographia and the Public Purpose, 2005. Available from http://www.demographia.com/db-parisua.htm.

DeRamus, H. Alan, Terry C. Clement, Dean D. Giampola, and Peter C. Dickison. "Methane Emissions of Beef Cattle on Forages: Efficiency of Grazing Management Systems." *Journal of Environmental Quality* 32 (2003): 269-77.

Diener, Ed, Richard E. Lucas, and Christie Napa Scollon. "Beyond the Hedonic Treadmill: Revising the Adaptation Theory of Well-Being." *American Psychologist* 61, no. 4 (2006): 305-14.

Dill, Jennifer, and Theresa Carr. "Bicycle Commuting and Facilities in Major U.S. Cities: If You Build Them, Commuters Will Use Them." *Transportation Research Record* 1828 (2003): 116-23.

Dittgen, Alfred. "Housing and Household Size in Local Population Dynamics: The Example of Paris." *Population* 60, no. 3 (2005): 259-98.

Donoghue, Ellen M., and Richard W. Haynes. "Assessing the Viability and Adaptability of Oregon Communities." In *PNW-GTR-540*. Portland, OR: USDA Forest Service, Pacific Northwest Research Station, 2002.

Downie, David. *Paris, Paris: Journey into the City of Light*. Fort Bragg, CA: Transatlantic Press, 2005.

Downs, Anthony. "Up and Down with Ecology--the 'Issue-Attention Cycle'." *Public Interest* 28 (1972): 38-50.

Easterlin, Richard A. "Explaining Happiness." *Proceedings of the National Academy of Sciences* 100, no. 19 (2003): 11176-83.

Energy Watch Group. *Coal: Resources and Future Production*. Energy Watch Group, 2007 [cited January 27, 2010]. Available from http://www.energywatchgroup.org/fileadmin/global/pdf/EWG_Report_Coal_10-07-2007ms.pdf.

Engstrom, R. Todd, and Felicia J. Sanders. "Red-Cockaded Woodpecker Foraging Ecology in an Old-Growth Longleaf Pine Forest." *Wilson Bulletin* 109 (1997): 203-17.

Erb, Karl-Heinz, Helmut Haberl, Fridolin Krausmann, Christian Lauk, Christoph Plutzar, Julia K. Steinberger, Christoph Muller, Alberte Bondeau, Katharina Waha, and Gudrun Pollack. *Eating the Planet: Feeding and Fueling the World Sustainably, Fairly, and Humanely-- a Scoping Study.* Institute of Social Ecology and PIK Potsdam, 2009 [cited November 13, 2009]. Available from http://www.ciwf.org.uk/ includes/documents/cm_docs/2009/e/ eating_the_planet_full_report_nov_2009.pdf.

Erlanger, Steven. "French Plans for Energy Reaffirm Nuclear Path." *New York Times*, August 17 2008, A.6.

Eto, Joseph. *The Past, Present, and Future of U.S. Utility Demand-Side Management Programs.* Ernest Orlando Lawrence Berkeley National Laboratory, 1996 [cited May 21, 2009]. Available from http:// www.osti.gov/bridge/servlets/purl/491537-Ttec7Y/webviewable/ 491537.pdf.

European New Towns Platform. *Home Page for St. Quentin En Yvelines.* Europeans New Town Platform, 2009 [cited November 4, 2009]. Available from http://www.newtowns.net/Members/st-quentin-en- yvelines/home-page-for-st-quentin-en-yvelines.

Farrell, Alexander, Richard J. Plevin, Brian T. Turner, Andrew D. Jones, Michael O'Hare, and Daniel M. Kammen. "Ethanol Can Contribute to Energy and Environmental Goals." *Science* 311 (2006): 506-08.

Ferguson, Andrew R.B. "The Logical Foundations of Ecological Footprints." *Environment, Development and Sustainability* 1, no. 2 (1999): 149-56.

Forest Stewardship Council. *Revised Final Pacific Coast (USA) Regional Forest Stewardship Standard.* Forest Stewardship Council, 2005 [cited November 29, 2008]. Available from http://www.fscus.org/ images/documents/2006_standards/pcwg_9.0_NTC.pdf.

————. *Some History.* Forest Stewardship Council, 2008 [cited November 28, 2008]. Available from http://www.fsc.org/history.html.

Frank, Douglas A., Michelle M. Kuns, and Daniel R. Guido. "Consumer Control of Grassland Plant Production." *Ecology* 83, no. 3 (2002): 602-06.

Franklin, J. F., K. Cromach Jr., W. Denison, A. McKee, C. Maser, F. Sedell, F. Swanson, and G. Juday. " Ecological Characteristics of Old-Growth Douglas-Fir Forests." In *GTR, PNW-8.* Portland, OR, 1981.

Freyfogle, Eric T. *The Land We Share: Private Property and the Common Good.* Washington D.C.: Island Press / Shearwater Books, 2003.

Freytak, T. "Making a Difference: Tourist Practices of Repeat Visitors to the City of Paris." *Social Geography Discussions* 4, no. 1 (2008): 1-25.

(GAO), U.S. Government Accountability Office. *Crude Oil: Uncertainty About Future Oil Supply Makes It Important to Develop a Strategy for Addressing a Peak and Decline in Oil Production.* U.S. Government Printing Office, 2007 [cited January 27, 2010]. Available from http://www.gao.gov/new.items/d07283.pdf.

Garreau, Joel. *Edge City: Life on the New Frontier.* New York: Doubleday, 1991.

Gates, Paul W. *The Jeffersonian Dream: Studies in the History of American Land Policy and Development.* Albuquerque: University of New Mexico Press, 1996.

Goodman, Peter S. "A Splash of Green for the Rust Belt." *New York Times,* November 2, 2008, B1.

Guiliano, Mireille. *French Women Don't Get Fat.* New York: Vintage Books, 2007.

Gunnison Sage-Grouse Local Working Group, Gunnison Basin. *Gunnison Sage Grouse Conservation Plan: Gunnison Basin, Colorado.* Colorado Division of Wildlife, 1997 [cited May 29, 2009]. Available from http://wildlife.state.co.us/NR/rdonlyres/30FDBAF5-1C11-48F9-A797-9827CA6181CF/0/GunnisonSageGrouseLocalPlan_GunnisonBasin.pdf.

Gunnison Sage-Grouse Rangewide Steering Committee. *Gunnison Sage-Grouse Rangewide Conservation Plan.* Colorado Division of Wildlife, 2005 [cited May 29, 2009]. Available from http://wildlife.state.co.us/WildlifeSpecies/SpeciesOfConcern/Birds/GunnisonConsPlan.htm.

Gutfreund, Owen D. *Twentieth-Century Sprawl: Highways and the Reshaping of the American Landscape.* New York: Oxford University Press, 2004.

Hansen, James. *The People Vs. Cap-and-Tax.* SolveClimate, 2010 [cited January 14, 2010]. Available from http://solveclimate.com/blog/20100113/people-vs-cap-and-tax?utm_source=feedburner&utm_medium=feed&utm_campaign=Feed%3A+solveclimate%2Fblog+(Solve+Climate%3A+Daily+Climate+News+and+Analysis).

Hargrove, Eugene. "Anglo-American Land Use Attitudes." *Environmental Ethics* 2 (1980): 121-48.

Harmon, Mark E., William K. Ferrell, and Jerry F. Franklin. "Effects on Carbon Storage of Conversion of Old-Growth to Young Forests." *Science* 247 (1990): 699-702.

Harper, L.A., O.T. Denmead, J.R. Freney, and F.M. Byers. "Direct Measurements of Methane from Grazing and Feedlot Cattle." *Journal of Animal Science* 77, no. 6 (1999): 1392-401.

Haynes, Richard W., Darius M. Adams, Ralph J. Alig, Peter J. Ince, John R. Mills, and Xiaoping Zhou. "The 2005 RPA Timber Assessment Update." In *PNW-GTR 699a.* Portland, OR: USDA Forest Service, Pacific Northwest Research Station, 2005.

Heerden, Ivor van. "The Failure of the New Orleans Levee System Following Huricane Katrina and the Pathway Forward." *Public Administration Review* 67, no. s1 (2007): 24-35.

Helliwell, John F. "How's Life: Combining Individual and National Variables to Explain Subjective Well-Being." *Economic Modeling* 20, no. 2 (2003): 331-60.

Herkert, James R. "Status and Habitat Selection of the Henslow's Sparrow in Illinois." *Willson Bulletin* 106, no. 1 (1994): 35-45.

Hitchens, Christopher. *The Missionary Position: Mother Teresa in Theory and Practice*. London: Verso, 1995.

Honda Motor Co. *Hydrogen Station: The Honda FCX*. Honda Motor Company, 2009 [cited May 14, 2009]. Available from http:// world.honda.com/FuelCell/FCX/station/.

Hossain, Farhana, Amanda Cox, John McGrath, and Weitberg. *New York Times*. New York Times, June 7, 2009 [cited June 8, 2009]. Available from http://projects.nytimes.com/44th_president/stimulus.

Huckelberry, Chuck. "The Sonoran Desert Conservation Plan." *Endangered Species Bulletin* 27, no. 2 (2002): 12-15.

Inglehart, Ronald, Roberto Foa, Christopher Peterson, and Christian Welzel. "Development, Freedom, and Rising Happiness." *Perspectives on Psychological Science* 3, no. 4 (2008): 264-85.

———. *Happiness Trends in 24 Countries, 1946-2000*. World Values Survey, 2008 [cited May 5, 2009]. Available from http:// www.worldvaluessurvey.org/happinesstrends/.

Institut National de la Statisque et des Etudes Economiques. *Les Villes Nouvelles: Atlas Statistique, 1968-1999*. Insee, 2004 [cited November 5, 2009]. Available from http://www.insee.fr/fr/themes/ document.asp?ref_id=9056.

Institute of Portland Metropolitan Studies. *Measure 37 Database*. Portland State University, Institute of Portland Metropolitan Studies, 2007 [cited May 27, 2009]. Available from http://www.pdx.edu/ims/ measure-37-database#regioncounty.

Intergovernmental Panel on Climate Change. *Climate Change 2007: Impacts, Adaptation and Vulnerability*. Cambridge University Press, 2007 [cited January 10, 2009]. Available from http://www.ipcc.ch/ ipccreports/ar4-wg2.htm.

———. *Climate Change 2007: Mitigation of Climate Change*. University of Cambridge Press, 2007 [cited December 3, 2008]. Available from http://www.ipcc.ch/ipccreports/ar4-wg3.htm.

International Energy Agency. *Key World Energy Statistics: 2008*. International Energy Agency, 2008. Available from http:// www.iea.org/textbase/nppdf/free/2008/key_stats_2008.pdf.

Jackson, Kenneth T. *Crabgrass Frontier: The Suburbanization of the United States*. New York: Oxford University Press, 1985.

Jacobs, Jane. *The Death and Life of Great American Cities*. New York: Vintage, 1961.

Jacobson, M. Z., and W.G. Colella. "Cleaning the Air and Improving Health with Hydrogen Fuel-Cell Vehicles." *Science* 308 (2005): 1901-05.

Johnson, R. Roy, Jean-Luc E. Cartron, Louis T. Haight, Russell B. Duncan, and Kenneth J. Kingsley. "Cactus Ferruginous Pygmy-Owl in Arizona, 1872-1971." *Southwestern Naturalist* 48, no. 3 (2003): 389-401.

Johnson, Tim. "The Economics of Grass-Based Dairy." In *Livestock Business Guide, Appropriate Technology Transfer for Rural Areas*. Fayetteville, AR: National Sustainable Agriculture Information Service, 2002.

Jordan, David P. *Transforming Paris: The Life and Labors of Baron Haussmann*. Chicago: University of Chicago Press, 1995.

Kanter, James. "Not So Fast, Nukes: Cost Overruns Plague a New Breed of Reactor." *New York Times*, May 29, 2009, B1.

Kempton, Willett, James S. Boster, and Jennifer A. Hartley. *Environmental Values in American Culture*. Boston: M.I.T. Press, 1996.

Koteen, Laura. "Climate Change, Whitebark Pine, and Grizzly Bears in the Greater Yellowstone Ecosystem." In *Wildlife Responses to Climate Change: North American Case Studies*, edited by Stephen H. Schneider and Terry L. Root, 343-411. Washington D.C.: Island Press, 2001.

Krugger, Paul. *Alternative Energy Resources: The Quest for Sustainable Energy*. Hoboken, NJ: John Wiley & Sons, 2006.

Lasky, Mark. *The Economic Costs of Reducing Emissions of Greenhouse Gases: A Survey of Economic Models*. U.S. Congressional Budget Office, 2003. Available from http://www.cbo.gov/ftpdocs/41xx/doc4198/2003-3.pdf.

Layard, Richard. *Happiness: Lessons from a New Science*. New York: Penguin, 2005.

Leopold, Aldo. *A Sand County Almanac: With Essays on Conservation from Round River*. New York: Ballantine Books, 1970.

Lewis, Judith. "High Noon: As the Climate Warms, Environmentalists Square Off over Big Solar's Claim to the Mojave Desert." *High Country News*, May 4, 2009.

Leytem, A.B., D.L. Bjorneberg, and R.S. Duncan. *Emissions of Ammonia and Methane from Concentrated Dairy Production Facilities in Southern Idaho*. 2009 [cited November 2, 2009]. Available from http://adsa.asas.org/meetings/2009/abstracts/0146.PDF.

Litman, Todd. *Evaluation Rail Transit Criticism*. Victoria Transport Policy Institute, 2009 [cited May 12, 2009]. Available from http://www.vtpi.org/railcrit.pdf.

Lucas, Richard E. "Adaptation and the Set-Point Model of Subjective Well-Being: Does Happiness Change after Major Life Events?" *Current Directions in Psychological Science* 16, no. 2 (2007): 75-79.

McHarg, Ian L. *Design with Nature*. Reading, MA: Addison-Wesley Publishing, 1973.

Metro. *Urban Growth Boundary.* Metro Regional Government, 2009 [cited June 8, 2009]. Available from http://www.oregonmetro.gov/index.cfm/go/by.web/id=277.

Metrolinx. *Ontario to Get Started on New Transit Projects.* Metrolinx, 2009 [cited May 7, 2009]. Available from http://www.metrolinx.com/en/default.aspx.

Miller, Joe. *The Smart Grid--Benefits and Challenges.* U.S. Department of Energy, Office of Electricity Delivery and Energy Reliability, 2008 [cited December 11, 2008]. Available from http://www.oe.energy.gov/DocumentsandMedia/SG_Benefits_Challenges_J_Miller.pdf.

MIT Energy Initiative. *Update of the MIT 2003 Future of Nuclear Power: An Interdisciplinary Study.* MIT, 2009 [cited May 19, 2009]. Available from http://web.mit.edu/nuclearpower/pdf/nuclearpower-update2009.pdf.

Mitchell, Cynthia. "Stabilizing California's Demand: The Real Reasons Behind the State's Energy Savings." *Public Utilities Fortnightly*, March 2009, 50-62.

Morford, Stacy. *Friends of the Earth: Why It's Suicide to Base Our Future on Offsets.* SolveClimate, 2009 [cited January 14, 2010]. Available from http://solveclimate.com/blog/20090910/friends-earth-why-its-suicide-base-our-future-offsets.

Mortenson, Eric. *Court Orders Multnomah County to Pay $1.15 Million to Dorothy English Estate.* The Oregonian, 2009 [cited May 27, 2009]. Available from http://www.oregonlive.com/environment/index.ssf/2009/04/court_reverses_multnomah_count.html.

Mufson, Steven. "In Energy Conservation, Calif. Sees Light." *Washington Post* 2007, A1.

Murphy, Pat. *Plan C: Community Survival Strategies for Peak Oil and Climate Change.* Gabriola Island, BC, Canada: New Society Publishers, 2008.

Naipaul, V.S. *The Enigma of Arrival.* New York: Random House, 1987.

National Resources Defense Council. *Case Study: The Center for Health and Healing, Oregon Health & Science University.* National Resources Defense Council, 2009 [cited May 26, 2009]. Available from http://www.nrdc.org/buildinggreen/casestudies/ohsu.pdf.

National Wildlife Federation. *Red-Cockaded Woodpecker.* National Wildlife Federation, 2005 [cited October 7, 2005]. Available from http://www.nwf.org/wildlife/redcockadedwoodpecker/.

NationMaster.com. *Health Statistics: Obesity (Most Recent) by Country.* NationMaster.com, 2008 [cited November 20, 2008]. Available from http://www.nationmaster.com/graph/hea_obe-health-obesity.

New York City, Mayor's Office of Operations, Office of Long-Term Planning and Sustainability. *Inventory of New York City Greenhouse Gas Emissions.* New York City, 2007 [cited May 7, 2009]. Available from http://www.nyc.gov/html/om/pdf/ccp_report041007.pdf.

Newman, Peter, and Jeffrey R. Kenworthy. *Sustainability and Cities: Overcoming Automobile Dependency*. Washington D.C.: Island Press, 1999.

Niemi, Ernie, and Ed Whitelaw. "Bird of Doom...Or Was It?" *Amicus Journal*, Fall (2000): 19-25.

Norquay, Geoff. "Organization without an Organization: The Obama Networking Revolution." *Policy Options*, October 2008, 58-61.

Nossiter, Adam. "Largely Alone, Pioneers Reclaim New Orleans." *New York Times*, July 2, 2007, A1.

OECD. "OECD Regions at a Glance, 2009." Paris: OECD, 2009.

Oregon Department of Land Conservation and Development. *DLCD Measure 37*. Oregon Department of Land Conservation and Development, 2008 [cited May 27, 2009]. Available from http://www.oregon.gov/LCD/MEASURE37/legal_information.shtml#top.

————. *Dlcd Measure 37: Summary of Claims*. Oregon Department of Land Conservation and Development, 2007 [cited May 27, 2009]. Available from http://www.oregon.gov/LCD/MEASURE37/summaries_of_claims.shtml.

————. *Measure 49 Guide*. Oregon Department of Land Conservation and Development, 2008 [cited May 27, 2009]. Available from http://www.oregon.gov/LCD/MEASURE49/docs/general/m49_guide.pdf.

Oregon State Archives. *Governor Tom McCall's Administration: Biographical Note*. Oregon State Archives, 2009 [cited May 26, 2009]. Available from http://arcweb.sos.state.or.us/governors/McCall/mccallbiography.htm.

Packard, Stephen, and Cornelia F. Mutel, eds. *The Tallgrass Restoration Handbook: For Prairies, Savannas, and Woodlands*. Washington D.C.: Island Press, 1997.

Pantell, Susan. *Tipping the Playing Field: How America's Federal Funding Policy Heavily Favors Roads over Transit*. Light Rail Now, 2009 [cited June 8, 2009]. Available from http://www.lightrailnow.org/features/f_lrt_2009-05a.htm.

Paris Office of Tourism. *Tourism in Paris: 2006*. Paris Office of Tourism, 2007 [cited April 30, 2009]. Available from http://www.parisinfo.com/uploads/bd//chiffres_cles_2007_2.pdf.

Patzek, Tad W. *Thermodynamics of the Corn-Ethanol Biofuel Cycle*. University of California, Berkeley, Department of Civil and Environmental Engineering, 2006 [cited November 21, 2008]. Available from http://petroleum.berkeley.edu/papers/patzek/CRPS416-Patzek-Web.pdf.

Pearce, Douglas G. "Tourist Districts in Paris: Structure and Functions." *Tourism Management* 19, no. 1 (1998): 49-65.

Peterson, Merrill D. *The Portable Thomas Jefferson*. New York: Viking Press, 1975.

Phillipps, Justin, and Eban Goodstein. "Growth Management and Housing Prices: The Case of Portland, Oregon." *Contemporary Economic Policy* 18 (2000): 334-44.

Pima County. "Pima-County Multi-Species Conservation Plan." Tucson, AZ: Pima County, 2006.

Pimentel, D., A. Pleasant, J. Barron, J. Gaudioso, N. Pollock, E. Chae, Y. Kim, A. Lassiter, C. Schiavoni, A. Jackson, M. Lee, and A. Eaton. "U.S. Energy Conservation and Efficiency: Benefits and Costs." *Environment, Development and Sustainability* 6 (2004): 279-305.

Pimentel, David, and Tad W. Patzek. "Ethanol Production Using Corn, Switchgrass, and Wood; Biodiesel Production Using Soybean and Sunflower." *Natural Resources Research* 14, no. 1 (2005): 65-76.

Pimentel, David, and Marcia H. Pimentel. *Food, Energy, and Society*. Third ed. Boco Raton, FL: CRC Press, 2008.

Pinchot Institute for Conservation. "Stewardship Contracting: A Summary of Lessons Learned from the Pilot Experience." Washington D.C.: Pinchot Institute for Conservation, 2006.

Pollan, Michael. *Omnivore's Dilemma: A Natural History of Four Meals*. New York: Penguin Books, 2006.

Pollin, Robert, Garrett-Peltier, James Heintz, and Helen Scharber. "Green Recovery: A Program to Create Good Jobs and Start Building a Low-Carbon Economy." Amherst, MA: Political Economy Research Institute and the Center for American Progress, 2008.

Pollin, Robert, and Jeannette Wicks-Lim. "Job Opportunities for the Green Economy: A State-by-State Picture of Occupations That Gain from Green Investments." Amherst, MA: Political Economy Research Institute, University of Massachusetts Amherst, 2008.

Popkin, Susan J., Margery A. Turner, and Martha Burt. "Rebuilding Affordable Housing in New Orleans: The Challenge of Creating Inclusive Communities." Washington D.C.: The Urban Institute, 2006.

Program of Agricultural Technology Studies. *Economic Indicators of Wisconsin's Dairy Industry*. Program on Agricultural Technology Studies, University of Wisconsin, Madison, 2002 [cited November 25, 2005]. Available from http://www.pats.wisc.edu/daigra10.html.

Pruitt, Lori. "Henslow's Sparrow: Status Assessment." Bloomington, IN: U.S. Fish and Wildlife Service, 1996.

Rabalais, Nancy N., R. Eugene Turner, and Donald Scavia. "Beyond Science into Policy: Gulf of Mexico Hypoxia and the Mississippi River." *BioScience* 52, no. 2 (2002).

Raju, Sudhakar. "Project NPV, Positive Externalities, Social Cost-Benefit Analysis--the Kansas City Light Rail Project." *Journal of Public Transportation* 11, no. 4: 59-88.

Reed, J.M., P.D. Doerr, and J.R. Walters. "Minimum Viable Population Size of the Red-Cockaded Woodpecker." *Journal of Wildlife Management* 52 (1988): 385-91.

Rehdanz, Katrin, and Davide Maddison. "Climate and Happiness." *Ecological Economics* 52, no. 1 (2005): 111-25.

Richardson, Harry W., and Chang-Hee Christine Bae, eds. *Urban Sprawl in Western Europe and the United States*. Burlington, VT: Ashgate, 2004.

Robbins, William G. *Landscapes of Conflict: The Oregon Story, 1940-2000*. Seattle: University of Washington, 2004.

———. *People, Politics, and the Environmental since 1945: Pollution in Paradise*. Oregon Historical Society, 2002 [cited May 26, 2009]. Available from http://www.ohs.org/education/oregonhistory/ narratives/subtopic.cfm?subtopic_ID=173.

Runte, Alfred. *National Parks: The American Experience*. 2nd ed. Lincoln: University of Nebraska Press, 1987.

Saint-Quentin-en-Yvelines. *Observatoire De La Ville: Fiche Population*. Saint-Quentin-en-Yvelines, 2008 [cited November 4, 2009]. Available from http://www.saint-quentin-en-yvelines.fr/fileadmin/ portail/MEDIA/Decouvrir/SQY_en_chiffres/ Thematiques_de_territoire/Demographie/Agglom%C3%A9ration %20-%20demographie.pdf.

Salatin, Joel. *Salad Bar Beef*. Swoope, VA: Polyface, Inc., 1995.

———. *You Can Farm: The Entrepreneur's Guide to Start and Succeed in a Farm Enterprise*. Swoop, VA: Polyface, Inc, 1998.

Sample, David W., and Michael J. Mossman. "Managing Habitat for Grassland Birds: A Guide for Wisconsin." Madison, WI: Wisconsin Department of Natural Resources, 1997.

Sample, V. Alaric, Will Price, Jacob S. Donnay, and Catherine M. Mater. "National Forest Certification Study: An Evaluation of the Applicability of Forest Stewardship Council (FSC) and Sustainable Forest Initiative (SFI) Standards on Five National Forests." Washington D.C.: Pinchot Institute for Conservation, 2007.

Samson, Fred B., and Fritz L. Knopf, eds. *Prairie Conservation: Preserving North America's Most Endangered Ecosystem*. Washington D.C.: Island Press, 1996.

Sartre, Jean-Paul. *Being and Nothingness: A Phenomenological Essay on Ontology*. New York: Washington Square Press, 1992.

———. *Nausea*. Norfolk, CN: New Directions Paperbook, 1964.

Sasser, Bill. "New Orleans Lower Ninth Ward Stires and Rebuilds." *Christian Science Monitor*, November 5, 2008, 1.

Schumpeter, Joseph A. *Capitalism, Socialism, and Democracy*. New York: Harper Torchbooks, 1950.

Schweitzer, Martin, and Joel F. Eisenberg. *Meeting the Challenge: The Prospect of Achieving 30 Percent Energy Savings through the Weatherization Assistance Program*. Oak Ridge National Laboratory, 2002 [cited December 6, 2008]. Available from http:// weatherization.ornl.gov/pdf/Con-479%20May22-FINAL.pdf.

Scott, J. Michael, Frank W. Davis, R. Gavin McGhie, R. Gerald Wright, Craig Groves, and John Estes. "Nature Reserves: Do They Capture the Full Range of America's Biological Diversity?" *Ecological Applications* 11, no. 4 (2001): 997-1007.

Second International Symposium on the Ocean in a High-CO$_2$ World. *Monaco Declaration*. Second International Symposium on the Ocean in a High-CO$_2$ World, 2008 [cited March 30, 2009]. Available from http://www.igbp.net/documents/MonacoDeclaration2009.pdf.

Seligman, Martin E. P. *Authentic Happiness: Using the New Positive Psychology to Realize Your Potential for Lasting Fulfillment*. New York: Free Press, 2002.

Sengupta, Somini. "Sea's Rise in India Buries Islands and a Way of Life." *New York Times*, April 11, 2007, A.1.

Shearmur, Richard, and Christel Alvergne. "Regional Planning Policy and the Location of Employment in the Ile-De-France: Does Policy Matter?" *Urban Affairs Review* 39, no. 1 (2003): 3-31.

Simpson, Andrew. *Cost-Benefit Analysis of Plug-in Hybrid Electric Vehicle Technology*. U.S. Department of Energy, 2006 [cited May 11, 2009]. Available from http://www.nrel.gov/vehiclesandfuels/vsa/pdfs/40485.pdf.

Skog, Kenneth E., and Geraldine A. Nicholson. *Carbon Sequestration in Wood and Paper Products*. USDA Forest Service, 2000 [cited December 1, 2008]. Available from http://www.fpl.fs.fed.us/documnts/pdf2000/skog00b.pdf.

Smith, Rebecca. "Lightening the Load: Solar-Energy Advocates Look for Innovative Ways to Reduce the Upfront Installation Costs." *Wall Street Journal*, October 6, 2008, R7.

Smith, W. Brad, Patrick D. Miles, John S. Vissage, and Scott A. Pugh. "Forest Resources of the United States, 2002." St. Paul: USDA Forest Service, North Central Research Station, 2002.

Spink, Kathryn. *Mother Teresa: A Complete Authorized Biography*. New York: HarperCollins, 1997.

Stavins, Robert N., and Kenneth R. Richards. *The Cost of U.S. Forest-Based Carbon Sequestration*. Pew Center on Global Climate Change, 2005 [cited December 1, 2008]. Available from http://www.pewclimate.org/docUploads/Sequest_Final.pdf.

Steves, Rick, Steve Smith, and Gene Openshaw. *Rick Steves' Paris 2006*. Emeryville, CA: Avalon Travel Publishing, 2005.

Sullivan, Patrick, Daniel Hellerstein, Leroy Hansen, Robert Johansson, Steven Koenig, Ruben Lubowski, William McBride, David McGranahan, Michael Roberts, Stephen Vogel, and Shawn Bucholtz. "The Conservation Reserve Program: Economic Implications for Rural America." In *Agricultural Economic Report Number 834*. Washington D.C.: USDA, Economic Research Service, 2004.

The Nature Conservancy. "Ecoregional Planning in the Northern Tallgrass Prairie Ecoregion." Minneapolis, MN: The Nature Conservancy, Midwest Regional Office, 1998.

Toronto Transit Commission. *Projects and Initiatives.* Toronto Transit Commission, 2009 [cited May 7, 2009]. Available from http://www3.ttc.ca/About_the_TTC/Projects_and_initiatives/index.jsp.

U. S. Library of Congress. *H.R. 2454: American Clean Energy and Security Act of 2009.* The Library of Congress, 200[cited June 17, 2009]. Available from http://thomas.loc.gov/cgi-bin/query/z?c111:H.R.2454:.

U. S. Library of Congress. *S. 1733: The American Power Act.* The Library of Congress, 2010 [cited June 15, 2010]. Available from http://thomas.loc.gov/cgi-bin/query/z?c111:S.1733:.

U.S. Bureau of the Census. *The 2007 Statistical Abstract.* U.S. Bureau of the Census, 2007 [cited January 4, 2007]. Available from http://www.census.gov/compendia/statab/.

———. *The 2009 Statistical Abstract.* U.S. Bureau of the Census, 2009 [cited April 29, 2009]. Available from http://www.census.gov/compendia/statab/.

———. *American Fact Finder.* U.S. Bureau of the Census, 2009 [cited April 27, 2009]. Available from http://factfinder.census.gov/home/saff/main.html?_lang=en.

———. *Historical Census Statistics on the Foreign-Born Population of the United States: 1850-1990.* U.S. Bureau of the Census, 1999 [cited April 8, 2009]. Available from http://www.census.gov/population/www/documentation/twps0029/twps0029.html.

———. *Per Capita Consumption of Meat and Poultry, by Country.* U.S. Bureau of the Census, 2000 [cited November 20, 2008]. Available from http://www.allcountries.org/uscensus/1370_per_capita_consumption_of_meat_and.html.

U.S. Census Bureau. *Population Projections.* U.S. Census Bureau, 2008 [cited December 8, 2008]. Available from http://www.census.gov/population/www/projections/usinterimproj/.

U.S. Central Intelligence Agency. *World Fact Book.* U.S. CIA, 2009 [cited April 39, 2009]. Available from https://www.cia.gov/library/publications/the-world-factbook/geos/fr.html#People.

U.S. Congressional Budge Office. *Estimated Changes in Direct Spending and Revenues under H.R. 5351, the Renewable Energy and Energy Conservation Tax Act of 2008.* U.S. Congressional Budget Office, 2008 [cited December 9, 2008]. Available from http://www.cbo.gov/ftpdocs/90xx/doc9001/hr5351.pdf.

U.S. Congressional Budget Office. *Congressional Budget Office Cost Estimate: H.R. 2454 American Clean Energy and Security Act of 2009.* U.S. Congressional Budget Office, 2009 [cited June 17, 2009]. Available from http://www.cbo.gov/ftpdocs/102xx/doc10262/hr2454.pdf.

U.S. Department of Commerce, Bureau of Economic Analysis. *Gross Domestic Product (GDP)*. Bureau of Economic Analysis, 2009 [cited May 5, 2009]. Available from http://www.bea.gov/national/index.htm#gdp.

U.S. Department of Energy. *20% Wind Energy by 2030: Increasing Wind Energy's Contribution to U.S. Electricity Supply*. U.S. Department of Energy, 2008 [cited December 8, 2008]. Available from http://www1.eere.energy.gov/windandhydro/pdfs/41869.pdf.

————. *Annual Energy Review, 2008*. U.S. Department of Energy, 2009 [cited December 18, 2008]. Available from http://www.eia.doe.gov/aer/pdf/aer.pdf.

————. *Careers in Renewable Energy*. U.S. Department of Energy, 2001 [cited January 9, 2009]. Available from http://www.nrel.gov/docs/fy01osti/28369.pdf.

————. *Solar America Initiative: A Plan for the Integrated Research, Development, and Market Transformation of Solar Energy Technologies*. U.S. Department of Energy, 2007 [cited December 8, 2008]. Available from http://www1.eere.energy.gov/solar/solar_america/pdfs/sai_draft_plan_Feb5_07.pdf.

————. *Solar Energy Technologies Program: Multi-Year Program Plan*. U.S. Department of Energy, 2007 [cited December 8, 2008]. Available from http://www1.eere.energy.gov/solar/pdfs/set_myp_2007-2011_proof_1.pdf.

————. *Weatherization Assistance Program*. U.S. Department of Energy, 2008 [cited December 6, 2008]. Available from http://apps1.eere.energy.gov/weatherization/.

U.S. Department of Energy, and Environmental Protection Agency. *Carbon Dioxide Emissions from the Generation of Electric Power in the United States*. U.S. Department of Energy and the Environmental Protection Agency, 2000 [cited December 5, 2008]. Available from http://www.eia.doe.gov/cneaf/electricity/page/co2_report/co2emiss.pdf.

U.S. Department of Energy, and Litos Strategic Communication. *The Smart Grid: An Introduction*. U.S. Department of Energy, 2004 [cited December 15, 2008]. Available from http://www.oe.energy.gov/DocumentsandMedia/DOE_SG_Book_Single_Pages.pdf.

U.S. Department of Energy, Energy Information Administration. *Annual Energy Outlook, 2010*. U.S. Department of Energy, Energy Information Administration, 2010 [cited June 28, 2009]. Available from http://www.eia.doe.gov/oiaf/aeo/.

————. *Emissions of Greenhouse Gases Report*. U.S. Department of Energy, Energy Information Administration, 2008 [cited June 3, 2009]. Available from http://www.eia.doe.gov/oiaf/1605/ggrpt/index.html.

————. *Units for Measuring Greenhouse Gases*. U.S. Department of Energy, 2003 [cited December 10, 2008]. Available from http://

www.eia.doe.gov/oiaf/1605/archive/gg03rpt/summary/
special_topics.html.

U.S. Department of Energy, Energy Star Program. *Federal Tax Credits for Energy Efficiency.* U.S. Department of Energy, 2008 [cited December 8, 2008]. Available from http://www.energystar.gov/index.cfm?c=products.pr_tax_credits#s3.

U.S. Department of the Interior, Office of the Secretary. *Secretary Kempthorne Announes Decision to Protect Polar Bears under Endangered Species Act.* U.S. Department of the Interior, 2008 [cited January 19, 2009]. Available from http://www.doi.gov/news/08_News_Releases/080514a.html.

U.S. Department of Transportation. *U.S. Department of Transportation Fiscal Year 2009 Budget in Brief.* U.S. Department of Transportation, 2008 [cited December 6, 2008]. Available from http://www.dot.gov/bib2009/htm/FTA.html.

U.S. Department of Transportation, Federal Transit Administration. *Analysis of Capital Costs and Their Effect on Operating Costs.* U.S. Department of Transportation, 2005 [cited December 6, 2008]. Available from http://www.utrc2.org/research/assets/107/utrc-2005-fta1.pdf.

U.S. Department of Transportation, Research and Innovative Technology Administration. *Pocket Guide to Transportation 2007.* U.S. Department of Transportation, 2007 [cited December 6, 2008]. Available from http://www.bts.gov/publications/pocket_guide_to_transportation/2007/.

U.S. Fish and Wildlife Service, Northeast Region. *The Red Knot (Calidris Canutus Rufa).* U.S. Fish and Wildlife Service, Northeast Region, 2008 [cited April 1, 2009]. Available from http://www.fws.gov/northeast/redknot/index.html.

U.S. Geological Survey. *About the Gap Analysis Program.* U.S. Geological Survey, National Biological Information Infrastructure, 2009 [cited May 29, 2009]. Available from http://gapanalysis.nbii.gov/portal/server.pt?open=512&objID=1482&PageID=5113&cached=true&mode=2&userID=2.

———. *A Gap Analysis of California.* U.S. Geological Survey, 1998 [cited May 29, 2009]. Available from http://gapanalysis.nbii.gov/portal/server.pt?open=512&objID=1483&PageID=5125&cached=true&mode=2&userID=2.

U.S. Green Building Council. *Leed.* U.S. Green Building Council, 2009 [cited May 26, 2009]. Available from http://www.usgbc.org/DisplayPage.aspx?CategoryID=19.

Uchitelle, Louis. "Economists Warm to Government Spending but Debate Its Form." *New York Times*, January 7, 2008, 1,8.

UN Economic Commission for Europe. *Bulletin of Housing and Building Statistics.* UN Economic Commission for Europe, 2002 [cited May 6, 2009]. Available from http://www.unece.org/hlm/prgm/hsstat/02pdf/pubH01_02.pdf.

USDA Economic Research Service. *Agricultural Productivity in the United States.* USDA Economic Research Service, 2009 [cited June 8, 2009]. Available from http://www.ers.usda.gov/Data/AgProductivity/.

————. *Feedgrains Database: Yearbook Tables.* USDA Economic Research Service, 2008 [cited November 20, 2008]. Available from http://www.ers.usda.gov/Data/FeedGrains/FeedYearbook.aspx.

USDA Forest Service, Pacific Northwest Research Station. "Understanding the Social and Economic Transitions of Forest Communities." *PNW Science Update* Fall, no. 18 (2008): 1-11.

USDA National Resources Conservation Service. *National Resources Inventory: 2003 Annual NRI.* Natural Resource Conservation Service, 2003 [cited April 27, 2009]. Available from http://www.nrcs.usda.gov/technical/NRI/2003/national_landuse.html.

USDA Natural Resources Conservation Service. "2001 Annual NRI: Urbanization and Development of Rural Land." Washington D.C.: Natural Resources Conservation Service, 2001.

Voisin, Andre. *Grass Productivity.* Washington D.C.: Island Press, 1989.

Walloon Region of Belgium, Department of Housing. *Housing Statistics in the European Union 2002.* Walloon Region of Belgium, Department of Housing, 2002 [cited April 30, 2009]. Available from http://mrw.wallonie.be/dgatlp/dgatlp/Pages/Log/DwnLd/Stats2002/housingStats2002.pdf.

Walser, Jeffrey, and John Anderlik. "Rural Depopulation: What Does It Mean for the Future Economic Health of Rural Areas and the Community Banks That Support Them?" *FDIC Banking Review* 16, no. 3 (2004): 57-95.

Warde, Alan, Shu-Li Cheng, Wendy Olsen, and Dale Southerton. "Changes in the Practice of Eating: A Comparative Analysis of Time-Use." *Acta Sociologica* 50, no. 4 (2007): 363-85.

Warner, Sam B., Jr. *Streetcar Suburbs: The Process of Growth in Boston, 1870-1900.* New York: Atheneum, 1974.

Weiler, Stephan, and David T. Theobold. "Pioneers of Rural Sprawl in the Rocky Mountain West." *Review of Regional Studies* 33 (2003): 264-83.

Wilcove, David S., Michael J. Bean, Robert Bonnie, and Margaret McMillan. "Rebuilding the Ark: Toward a More Effective Endangered Species Act for Private Land." New York: Environmental Defense Fund, 1996.

Winston, Clifford, and Vikram Maheshri. "On the Social Desirability of Urban Rail Transit Systems." *Urban Economics* 62, no. 2 (2007): 362-82.

Wood Products Council Market Research. *Wood Used in New Residential Construction: U.S. And Canada.* NAHB Research Center, 2005 [cited April 27, 2009]. Available from http://www.fpl.fs.fed.us/documnts/pdf2005/fpl_2005_mckeever002.pdf.

World Nuclear Association. *Nuclear Power in France.* World Nuclear Association, 2009 [cited May18, 2009]. Available from http://www.world-nuclear.org/info/inf40.htm.

Yuan, Yuan, and Ivan Eastin. "Forest Certification and Its Influence on the Forest Products Industry in China." In *Working Paper 110*. Seattle: Center for International Trade in Forest Products, University of Washington, 2007.

Zweibel, Ken. *Harnessing Solar Power: The Photovoltaics Challenge.* New York: Plenum Press, 1990.

Index

A

accidification, 167-168
    ocean, 168
Acciona, 138
African famines, 164
agricultural production
    global capacity of, 151
    global organic capacity of, 150-151
American Automobile Association, 11
Audubon Society, 97-98

B

Baird's Sparrow, 106
Bald Eagle, 121
Bangladesh, 164
Bay of Bengal, India, 162-163163
beef cattle
    corn versus grass consumption for, 109
    income from grass-fed, 108-109
    methane emissions from, 112n21
    pasture management and the production of, 108-109, 111, 139
    productivity of grass-fed, 110
Being and Nothingness, 32
Bonaparte, Louis-Napoléon (Napoléon III), 34-35
Boston, Massachusetts, 4-5, 57
Brazil, 76
Brookfield, Wisconsin, 7-8, 16
Brown-Headed Cowbirds, 113
Bureau of Public Roads, 10

C

Cactus Ferruginous Pygmy-Owl, 95-97, 99
Calcutta, Indian, 161
California
    clean energy in, 78-79
    energy conservation in, 78-79
    energy consumption in. 79
    gap analysis for, 100-102
    gold fields, 120
    habitat protection in, 101-102
    habitat protection in compared to the United States, 102
    species diversity in, 100-102
    utility regulation in, 78-79
Camus, Albert, 32

About the Author

Douglas E. Booth lives in Milwaukee, Wisconsin, with his wife, Carol Brill. After teaching for 26 years at Marquette University, he retired in 2002 to spend more time working with the land trust movement and writing. While at Marquette he taught macroeconomics, environmental and natural resource economics, and a variety of other courses, and he coordinated an interdisciplinary undergraduate major and minor in urban and environmental affairs. He is the author of *Land Trusts and Biodiversity, Hooked on Growth: Economic Addictions and the Environment, Searching for Paradise: Economic Development and Environmental Change in the Mountain West, The Environmental Consequences of Growth: Steady-State Economics as an Alternative to Ecological Decline, Valuing Nature: The Decline and Preservation of Old-Growth Forests,* and *Regional Long Waves, Uneven Growth, and the Cooperative Alternative* as well as numerous academic articles. He is also a founding board member of the Driftless Area Land Conservancy, a land trust located in southwestern Wisconsin. In his spare time, he loves to backpack, hike, and botanize. The author can be contacted at cominggoodboom@gmail.com. The web site associated with this book is http://cominggoodboom.blogspot.com/.